THE
HARDINESS
EFFECT

THE
HARDINESS
EFFECT

GROW FROM STRESS
OPTIMISE HEALTH
LIVE LONGER

DR PAUL TAYLOR

WILEY

First published 2026 by John Wiley & Sons Australia, Ltd

© MindBodyBrain Performance Institute Pty Ltd 2026

The right of Paul Taylor to be identified as the author of *The Hardiness Effect* has been asserted in accordance with law.

ISBN: 978-1-394-34613-4

A catalogue record for this book is available from the National Library of Australia

Registered Office
John Wiley & Sons Australia, Ltd. Level 4, 600 Bourke Street, Melbourne, VIC 3000, Australia

For details of our global editorial offices, customer services, and more information about Wiley products visit us at www.wiley.com.

Wiley also publishes its books in a variety of electronic formats and by print-on-demand. Some content that appears in standard print versions of this book may not be available in other formats.

Cover images: © Hendra Su/Getty Images, © M Design/Adobe Stock, © stas111/Adobe Stock, © SkyLine/Adobe Stock, © Mehedi/Adobe Stock
Cover design by Wiley
Internal icons: © Sensvector/Adobe Stock; © Himel/Adobe Stock; © Thanuja/Adobe Stock; © Rhudzhan/Adobe Stock; © Oksana/Adobe Stock; © Iryna Petrenko/Adobe Stock; © flitzrain/Adobe Stock; © inspiring.team/Adobe Stock; © Cansu/Adobe Stock; © Vikivector/Adobe Stock; © Tartila/Adobe Stock; © ssstocker/Adobe Stock; © Macrovector/Adobe Stock; © Creativa Images/Adobe Stock; © xoxolove/Adobe Stock; © maniki/Adobe Stock; © vesvocrea/Adobe Stock; © marina_ua/Adobe Stock; © designua/Adobe Stock; © Jan/Adobe Stock; © GraphicsRF/Adobe Stock; © OKAN/Adobe Stock; © LorenaPh/Adobe Stock; © Mustafa/Adobe Stock; © ケイーゴ·K/Adobe Stock; © Mustafa/Adobe Stock; © KeronnArt/Adobe Stock; © Nadezhda Buravleva/Adobe Stock; © Алёна Игдеева/Adobe Stock; © bella/Adobe Stock; © 川本まる/Adobe Stock; © sakurra/Adobe Stock; © graphicignite/Adobe Stock; © rob3000/Adobe Stock; © Rada Covalenco/Adobe Stock; © yzor.std/Adobe Stock; © Александр Михайлюк/Adobe Stock

Set in 11/16 pt and Baskerville URW by Straive, Chennai, India.

Contents

About the author

Dr Paul Taylor is a Psychophysiologist, keynote speaker, podcast host and the bestselling, multiple-award-winning author of *Death by Comfort*.

Paul is co-director of the Hardiness Lab, which is dedicated to advancing research and real-world application of hardiness-based interventions to help people live better lives. He recently completed his PhD in Applied Psychology, with research focused on enhancing psychological and physiological hardiness and cognitive fitness.

With university qualifications in psychology, exercise physiology, neuroscience and human nutrition, Paul brings a unique, evidence-based perspective to human performance and flourishing. His work blends academia with real-world grit, grounded in his background as a former British Royal Navy Aircrew Officer, trained in anti-submarine warfare, helicopter search-and-rescue and combat survival.

As a corporate speaker and consultant, Paul delivers hardiness and performance training to many global businesses, government agencies and the Australian Military. He hosts the Hardiness Lab

Podcast and created the Hardiness app, which has resources and tools to help people implement the strategies in this book.

Driven by the belief that we can grow from stress and live longer, healthier lives with the right habits, Paul helps individuals and teams unlock the power of psychophysiological hardiness to perform at their best — physically, mentally and emotionally.

When not working, Paul has previously enjoyed competitive boxing, soccer and karate and in 2021, Paul and his son Oscar became Australian Karate Kumite Champions. Now in his 50's, and due to an increasing amount of 'old bastard' niggly injuries, he has reluctantly hung up the soccer boots, boxing gloves and Karate gi and taken up cross-fit, scuba-diving and soccer coaching to stay fit, healthy and engaged in life.

He lives on the Mornington Peninsula in Victoria, Australia, with his wife Carly and two kids, Ceara and Oscar.

Introduction

The choice
of Hercules

The philosophical narrative of Hercules at the crossroads has shaped much of Western thought, encapsulating the eternal struggle between a life of comfort or ease, and a life of virtue. As recounted by the great philosopher Socrates, the tale highlights a defining moment for Hercules (known as Heracles in the ancient Greek parable), a young man poised between two life paths, each represented by a mythological figure.

The choice Hercules is offered at these crossroads epitomises the human struggle with self-discipline and endurance. His story isn't just a myth but a philosophical template that examines the nature of human character and moral fibre, and it sets the scene for this book.

At the crossroads

In the myth, the young Hercules, already known to be one of the God Zeus's mightiest sons, finds himself at a literal and metaphorical fork in the road. Here he encounters two goddesses, each offering him divergent paths that symbolise life's potential trajectories. The first to approach him is Kakia, named Vice but who calls herself Happiness ('Eudaimonia' in ancient Greek). She is enchantingly beautiful, her allure magnified by her promise to Hercules of an easy life filled with luxury and pleasure obtained at the expense of others. She seductively suggests that following her would mean an easy and comfortable life devoid of hardships — a tempting offer that promises immediate gratification and comfort.

The second goddess, Aretê (Virtue), presents a stark contrast. Plain in appearance yet possessing a natural beauty, she offers Hercules a challenging path. She warns of a life that would be arduous and fraught with dangers and trials greater than any man might bear. Aretê outlines a journey where true happiness and fulfilment can only be achieved through continuous effort, moral integrity and the overcoming of great adversities. She emphasises that nothing genuinely worthy or admirable can be attained without significant struggle and perseverance.

Faced with these choices, Hercules chooses the path of Aretê, embracing the promise of a life filled with meaningful challenges over one of superficial ease and comfort, as offered by Kakia. This choice leads to his legendary '12 labours' — tasks so daunting that they would crush any ordinary man. From slaying the multi-headed Hydra to capturing the fierce Cerberus from the depths of Hades itself, Hercules not only faces these trials, but also overcomes them with extraordinary courage and wisdom.

Hercules's journey was marked by immense struggles and suffering, culminating in his tragic death from a poisoned garment that bore the blood of the Hydra. Yet, the moral integrity and greatness of spirit he displayed throughout his trials led Zeus to bestow on him the ultimate honour — that of deification (becoming a god).

Hercules's story was so influential that it reportedly moved Zeno, the founder of Stoicism (a philosophy that I mention throughout this book), to embrace philosophy as a way of life. Zeno saw in Hercules the embodiment of psychological resilience and was inspired by his choice, which mirrored the Stoic virtues of wisdom, courage, justice and temperance (self-mastery). Zeno's philosophical journey, and that of the Stoics who followed, was likened to Hercules's, because they were all heroes of self-discipline and moral rigour. The story of Hercules at the crossroads became a metaphor for the Stoic ideal: the belief that a life well-lived requires confronting and rising above hardships with good character, thereby achieving true excellence and enriching the soul.

Hercules's choice teaches that embracing challenges and living virtuously, though often difficult, is ultimately more rewarding and fulfilling, leading to a life to be proud of. This narrative inspired Zeno's embrace of philosophy and continues to influence those seeking to understand the essence of a life well-lived. Through this ancient myth, we are reminded that true happiness, which the Stoics referred to as 'eudaimonia' (and modern psychologists call 'flourishing'), is not handed to us, but must be earned through a steadfast commitment to living virtuously and embracing challenges. Hercules's choice at the crossroads was seen as being about more than the individual heroics of a demigod; it was a guiding parable for anyone seeking to lead a meaningful life.

This poses the fundamental question: what type of life do you wish to lead?

Embracing our modern-day Hercules

Today, we stand at our own crossroads, but the choice has morphed in ways the ancient Greeks couldn't have imagined. While Hercules chose between virtue and vice, we're choosing between vitality and stagnation, between biological excellence and accelerating decline. The path of Kakia has evolved, no longer promising obvious debauchery but instead seductive comfort—climate-controlled environments, convenient foods and endless entertainment that cocoon us from the very challenges that make us strong. Meanwhile, the modern embodiment of Aretê asks us to embrace not just moral virtue but also physiological wisdom—to reclaim the robust health so many of our ancestors took for granted.

The decisions we make today—whether to succumb to the siren calls of modern-day Kakia or to follow the rigorous trails blazed by Aretê—will determine our own health and vitality, and that of generations to come. This book is a call to action: to reject the deceptive ease of a life of comfort and convenience (which is unlikely to end well) and to instead dive deep into the tumultuous but ultimately rewarding waters of a fully engaged life. Choosing to deliberately cultivate psychological and physiological hardiness is what this book is all about.

By redefining your relationship with discomfort, reconnecting with the inherent wisdom of ancient philosophers and implementing the research provided by modern science, you can reclaim robust physical and mental health and enduring happiness. This book serves as your guide on the journey towards becoming your best self—a hardier person who faces life's challenges with courage, discipline and a steadfast commitment to the higher virtues exemplified by Aretê.

The choice you face is this: do you want to end up on your deathbed, reflecting on your life and thinking, *That was a life of ease and comfort*, or do you want to reflect, *That was a life that was full of challenges, but one that I can be proud of?*

If you want the former, close this book now and gift it to someone else. If you want the latter, read on — and prepare to get uncomfortable and inspired in equal measure.

Contemplating the lure of modern Kakia

Everywhere we look, Kakia's path tempts us. It's in the ultra-processed 'comfort foods' that crowd our supermarket shelves, nutritionally bankrupt but designed to be irresistible. Rather than nourish us, these foods are a significant driver of poor physical and mental health. It's in the endless hours we spend binge-watching streaming services or scrolling through social media. Although entertaining, this piss-poor form of engagement is far removed from the development of meaningful connections that are critical to our mental health. Our sedentary lifestyles, increasingly devoid of the physical exertion that once defined human activity, mirror this trend. Even our approach to health has become reactive rather than proactive — a *sick*care system, rather than a *health*care system. Too often, we wait until diseases and conditions are diagnosed. Doctors then prescribe medications (and sometimes secondary medications to address the side effects of the first), instead of helping to address the root causes, often driven by Kakia-inspired lifestyles of ease, comfort and indulgence.

The impact of Kakia's path on our physical and mental health is truly shocking, and a quick look at four countries that are the poster-children of Kakia's way — Australia, the United States, the United Kingdom and Canada — bring this clearly into focus. These four 'developed' nations are the highest consumers of ultra-processed foods in the world. The United States leads the way, with an estimated 73 per cent of their grocery store food items being ultra-processed, but the others aren't far behind. The health statistics in these countries make for sobering reading — starting with those relating to being overweight and obese:

- A whopping 74 per cent of Americans are overweight or obese, with 42.4 per cent specifically classified as obese in the 2017–18 period, according to the Centers for Disease Control and Prevention (CDC).

- According to the Health Survey for England, 64 per cent of Brits were overweight or obese in 2022, with 29 per cent obesity.

- In 2024, 66 per cent of Australians were overweight or obese, with 32 per cent obesity, based on data from the Australian Institute of Health and Welfare (AIHW).

- In 2023, 65.5 per cent of Canadians were overweight or obese, with 30 per cent obesity, according to Statista.

The upshot? Being overweight or obese is the new normal.

Even more scary is the data for our kids, with research showing overweight or obesity predisposes those kids to a lifetime of health problems, with increased risks of cardiovascular disease, diabetes, mental health issues, cancer and dementia, to name but a few. Here's the breakdown for the percentage of kids overweight or obese in these four countries, according to recent national surveys:

- *Australia:* 26 per cent of 2 to 17 year olds.

- *Canada:* 25.7 per cent of 5 to 17 year olds.

- *United Kingdom:* 37.7 per cent of 10 to 11 year olds.

- *United States:* 35.4 per cent of 2 to 19 year olds.

Even more shockingly, a study published in the *Journal of the American Medical Association* in 2015 reported that 52.3 per cent of Americans had either diagnosed or undiagnosed diabetes in 2012, and we know the trends are getting worse.

All of this is strongly linked to Kakia-inspired lifestyles of comfort food and lack of physical activity. And what are governments doing about it? Overwhelmingly, they're treating the symptoms, not the cause.

In all of these countries, over 95 per cent of healthcare spending is focused on managing chronic conditions, with less than 5 per cent being spent on prevention. And in the United States, the weight-loss drug Saxenda has already been approved by the Food and Drug Administration (FDA) for use in 12 year olds to manage obesity, with safety and effectiveness trials already having been conducted.

It gets worse — Novo Nordisk, the maker of Saxenda, plans to use their Phase III SCALE Kids trial data to expand the Saxenda approvals label to include obese children older than six years! That's right — weight-loss drugs for seven year olds.

We need to be focusing on the causes of these issues, not using a series of ever more complex bandaids that just kick the can down the road.

Kakia's impact on mental health

The mental health picture in our Kakia-dominated countries is equally concerning. In Australia and the United States, approximately one in five adults experienced mental illness in 2020, representing 53 million Americans and over five million Australians. In England, it was one in four — around 14 million people.

More alarmingly, mental health conditions among adolescents in these countries have been steadily worsening, with mental health issues and suicide rates among the youth skyrocketing.

Mental health is a complex component of our overall wellbeing that deserves thoughtful, comprehensive care. For people with severe conditions such as major depression, bipolar disorder or schizophrenia, proper diagnosis and medication can be truly lifesaving interventions. However, our current system often defaults to a primarily pharmaceutical approach that frequently overlooks the deeper roots of mental suffering and the powerful lifestyle interventions that can both prevent and address many mental health challenges. This book advocates for a more balanced and holistic approach that recognises when medical intervention is needed, while also empowering individuals with evidence-based strategies to build robust mental health from the ground up.

The medicalisation of normal experience

Once, if a person felt sad, anxious or completely overwhelmed, a caring doctor might have dug deeper, taking the time to discuss what might be going on the person's life that was influencing these feelings. Through this discussion, the doctor and patient might have been able to acknowledge this as a normal human response to difficult circumstances — something that would pass with time and proper support.

Now, the system too often responds with a quick fix. You might be mentally ill — here's a label and a prescription.

This is the path of Kakia — offering quick relief without effort, and solutions without addressing root causes. And while this option seems appealing — tidy, clinical and perhaps covered by health insurance — the evidence suggests it's failing us on a massive scale.

The *Diagnostic and Statistical Manual of Mental Disorders* (*DSM*), published by the American Psychiatric Association, serves as a guide for diagnosing and classifying mental health disorders. This manual is now in its fifth edition (*DSM-5*), and has seen its definitions of psychiatric conditions quietly broaden with each revision. Psychiatrist Dr Mark Horowitz, a clinical research fellow at University College London, points out that these expanding conditions mean that by the age of 45, a staggering 86 per cent of us meet the criteria for a mental illness.

This raises a profound question: are we collectively suffering an unprecedented mental health epidemic, or is the mental health industry expanding its diagnostic categories to pathologise normal human experience — minting patients like Central Banks mint money?

Emeritus Professor Allen Frances, the psychiatrist who co-authored the *DSM-IV* edition in 1994, expressed concern even then about expanding diagnoses. In a recent interview, he noted, 'There's a kind of societal push to find a medication panacea for many problems that previously would have been conceived of as within the range of the normal difficulties of everyday life.'

Again, this isn't to diminish genuine suffering or deny the benefit of medication within a holistic approach, especially for those with severe mental illness. And the temptations of a Kakia lifestyle are undoubtedly contributing to feelings of loneliness, isolation, anxiety and depression. However, we've increasingly medicalised normal responses to stress, grief and trauma. Despite all the medications and ever-expanding diagnoses, mental health outcomes continue to worsen by several metrics.

The faulty foundation: Chemistry versus experience

The cornerstone of modern psychiatric medication — particularly for depression — has been the 'chemical imbalance' theory, which posits that conditions such as depression result from low serotonin levels. This persuasive narrative has driven billions of dollars in pharmaceutical sales and shaped public understanding for decades.

However, a landmark umbrella review, published in 2023 in the journal *Molecular Psychiatry* by Professor Joanna Moncrieff, Dr Mark Horowitz and colleagues, analysed decades of research and reached a startling conclusion: no reliable evidence indicates depression is caused by low serotonin levels. This finding wasn't based on fringe science but on a comprehensive, peer-reviewed analysis. And while it sparked global debate, the serotonin theory was firmly debunked.

For decades, pharmaceutical company marketing promoted the idea that depression was a 'chemical imbalance' that antidepressants fixed by restoring serotonin. In the United States (one of two countries in the world to permit direct drug advertising to consumers), the image of sad cartoon characters perking up after taking the antidepressant Zoloft, for example, was brilliant, simple and reassuring — and, it turns out, scientifically unsupported. Chemicals are a part of this process, but it is not as simple as one chemical being too low.

What does the research consistently show? The profound impact of life experiences, particularly trauma and chronic stress, on mental health. As an example of this, Professor John Read, a psychologist at the University of East London, has conducted detailed research on adverse childhood experiences (ACEs) and their ongoing effects. His research demonstrates how early trauma can rewire brain function and predict mental health conditions such as psychosis, depression and suicidal tendencies. Yet, remarkably, the vast majority of mental health services often don't even ask about trauma when treating someone with psychiatric symptoms. I recently interviewed Professor Read for my podcast, and he noted that surveys show fewer than 25 per cent of psychiatric patients are ever asked about childhood trauma.

Previously mentioned psychiatrist Dr Horowitz also emphasises the importance of life experience. I also spoke with Dr Horowitz and, when examining what truly predicts depression, he pointed out,

If you take away the genes, take away the biology, and you just look at exposure to stressful life events – divorce, job loss, chronic illness – you can quite accurately predict who will be depressed within a year.

Again, chemical and hormonal imbalances do have a part to play, especially in conditions such as postnatal depression and depression during perimenopause. However, simply counting the number of stressful life events someone experiences can prove to be a better predictor of depression than any genetic marker or chemical theory.

The silenced side effects

Perhaps most concerning in the rise of medication to treat mental illness is how limited our understanding of the side effects of this medication remains. And this ignorance is not because the side effects don't exist, but because they've never been properly documented. As Professor Read explained in our interview, clinical trials typically ask about just a handful of predefined symptoms. He then told me, 'If you don't ask, they don't exist.'

This means many commonly reported adverse effects — including emotional blunting, sexual dysfunction, cognitive impairment and even suicidal thoughts — simply may not appear in the data submitted to regulators. The result? Doctors and patients make decisions without complete information.

In a 2018 study co-authored by Professor Read involving over 1400 people taking antidepressants across 38 countries, the findings on their side effects were sobering. These findings included:

- 61 per cent experienced ten or more side effects
- 71 per cent reported emotional numbness
- 70 per cent reported feeling foggy or detached
- 66 per cent felt 'not like themselves'
- 60 per cent experienced a reduction in positive feelings
- 59 per cent experienced withdrawal symptoms
- 50 per cent reported suicidal thoughts from the medication itself
- 40 per cent felt addicted to the drugs.

Professor Read found strikingly similar results in another study of over 1800 New Zealanders, 62 per cent of whom also experienced sexual difficulties. Perhaps the most shocking finding was that fewer than 5 per cent of the survey participants were told about any of these risks by their doctor. This represents a profound failure of informed consent — something that would surely trigger outrage in any other medical specialty.

A path forward: Reclaiming mental health

Encouragingly, the tide is beginning to turn. In 2024, the Royal Australian College of General Practitioners endorsed *The Maudsley*

Deprescribing Guidelines for use in antidepressant deprescribing—that is, stopping or reducing the medication. These UK guidelines, co-authored by Dr Horowitz and Dr David Taylor (co-author of *The Maudsley Prescribing Guidelines*), estimate that a whopping 30 to 50 per cent of patients on selective serotonin reuptake inhibitors (SSRIs) do not have evidence-based reasons for being on these drugs, and that they may work for as little as 15 per cent of patients.

Think about this. That's millions of Americans, Australians and Brits who are potentially on drugs they shouldn't be on, and which are often addictive. These drugs are destroying their sex lives, making them emotionally numb and making around half have suicidal thoughts—which tend to spike when they try to get off them. These people are suffering horribly while the pharmaceutical companies rake in profits.

This certainly isn't about stigmatising anyone taking antidepressants. These medications can and do help some people, and can be lifesaving for those with severe mental illness. But we must confront the elephant in the mental health room—we've over-medicalised human emotion, underestimated our capacity for growth, and under-delivered on addressing root causes. Instead, we've too often opted for bandaids that don't work, and can do more damage.

Remember—if you're currently taking these medications and perhaps questioning your treatment plan, this isn't about shame. It's about rightful anger at a system that has perhaps failed to provide you with complete information or explore alternative approaches. It's about demanding better mental health care that addresses you as a whole person, not just your symptoms. (For more on alternative prescriptions for improving mental health, see appendix A.)

Embracing the modern path of Aretê

The path forward—the modern path of Aretê—recognises that mental health isn't just about brain chemistry and physical health is more than the absence of disease. This path acknowledges the profound impact of stress, trauma, lifestyle and environment on your physical and psychological wellbeing. Psychological and physiological hardiness—the subject of this book—offers a comprehensive approach to optimising physical and mental health by restoring your evolutionary biology, and your capacity for resilience, connection, meaning and vitality—capacities that have been undermined by modern life and the seductive comforts of Kakia's way.

This approach doesn't reject medication when truly needed, but does place equal emphasis on addressing the fundamental biological, psychological, environmental and social factors that shape your physical and mental health. This book is about building a foundation of hardiness strong enough to weather life's inevitable storms—not by avoiding challenges, but by developing the capacity to face them with courage, clarity and purpose.

So what does it actually mean to be hardy?

Psychological hardiness is the courage to grow from stress. It helps you to see change and adversity not as a threat, but as a challenge. It's the mindset that helps you respond with clarity instead of panic, and purpose instead of paralysis. It gives you the tools to bounce forward from setbacks, and face difficulty with courage and meaning.

Physiological hardiness, equally important, is the body's ability to resist, recover from and adapt to physical stressors. It means having the energy, resilience and internal systems—cardiovascular, immune, metabolic, musculoskeletal, neural—all tuned for life in a demanding world. It's the result of how you eat, move, sleep, expose yourself to light, heat and cold, and reconnect with nature.

Together, these two domains form *The Hardiness Effect*—a powerful, evidence-based framework for a better life. A life that's not only longer, but also richer; not just healthier, but also more meaningful.

And here's the real reason this matters.

Hardiness doesn't promise you a life without pain or setbacks. What it offers instead is a life worth being proud of. It offers a life with fewer regrets, where you don't crumble under pressure, but instead meet it with poise and purpose. It offers a life where you walk through the storms with a spine made of steel and a heart full of intent. That's what Aretê's path looks like in the 21st century.

And this isn't just about the global health statistics, the scientific studies or even the inspiring parables. This book is for you—for the part of you that's tired of being tired, that's overwhelmed by stress, dulled by routine or stuck in habits that leave you feeling less than your best. It's for the part of you that knows something more is possible—a version of yourself you haven't fully lived yet, or crave to get back to.

This book is your guide to getting there.

Your journey to psychological and physiological hardiness

This book is divided into two complementary parts, each designed to make you more resilient, capable and alive.

Part I focuses on psychological hardiness, teaching you how to build an unshakeable mindset that transforms adversity into strength. You'll discover:

◆ how to develop the four pillars of psychological hardiness that have been proven across military, corporate and academic settings

◆ why reframing challenges as opportunities changes your biology at the cellular level

◆ the ancient Stoic practices that modern neuroscience now validates

◆ how to focus your attention on what's important, controlling what you can while releasing what you cannot

◆ the difference between meaningless activity and deep life engagement

◆ why connection with others isn't just nice — it's a biological imperative for health and longevity.

Part II is all about physiological hardiness, showing you how to optimise your biology for resilience and vitality. You'll learn:

◆ how the science of hormesis —intermittent, moderate stress— can make your physiology stronger and more adaptable

◆ why exercise is the closest thing we have to a fountain of youth, and how your muscles function as endocrine organs

◆ how to use nutrition principles to target the fundamental mechanisms of ageing

◆ how light and darkness work as powerful medicines for every system in your body

- recovery protocols that build strength rather than just prevent breakdown

- why 'rewilding' your biology isn't about going backwards — it's about reclaiming your genetic heritage.

This is the path of Aretê in modern form. It will challenge you. But it will also help you to fulfil your potential.

By the end of this journey, you won't just understand hardiness, but will also be equipped to embody it. You'll have practical tools to face whatever life throws at you, not by avoiding stress, but by becoming the kind of person who grows stronger through it. This isn't about becoming superhuman; it's about becoming fully human in an age that's forgotten what that means.

The question isn't whether you'll face hardship; it's who you'll become because of it.

So ask yourself again — what kind of life do you want to look back on? If you want a life of ease and comfort, this book might not be for you. But if you want a life that's difficult in the best possible way — a life of growth, grit, connection and purpose — then turn the page.

The road ahead may not be easy. But it leads somewhere worth going.

Let's begin.

PART I
Psychological hardiness

1

The mindset that makes or breaks you

Resilience is an outcome—it doesn't tell us how to get there. Hardiness does.

Dr Paul Bartone

Let's get something straight from the start: life can be amazing, but it isn't meant to be easy. Yet we've done a remarkable job of convincing ourselves that it should be. Our modern culture has become obsessed with comfort, convenience and quick fixes. If even a hint of challenge emerges—mentally, physically, emotionally—we often rush to eliminate it.

But here's the uncomfortable truth: comfort doesn't prepare you for the inevitable challenges of life. Hardiness does.

Understanding the importance of hardiness

Hardiness is more than just being tough or resilient. It's a specific psychological construct representing a pattern of attitudes and skills that provides the courage and strategies to turn unexpected change and stressful circumstances from potential disasters into growth opportunities. First identified by researchers Salvatore Maddi and Suzanne Kobasa through a groundbreaking 12-year study at Illinois Bell Telephone during massive industry disruption (and outlined in their 1984 book *The Hardy Executive: Health Under Stress*), hardiness has emerged as the key factor that distinguishes those who thrive under extreme stress from those who succumb to it.

While two-thirds of employees in Maddi and Kobasa's study experienced significant health and performance deterioration during their workplace disruption, one-third not only maintained their health and performance but also flourished. What made the difference? These resilient individuals demonstrated three interrelated attitudes that together constitute hardiness:

- *Challenge:* The view that change is normal and a challenge that presents opportunities for growth and learning, and the willingness to lean into challenges rather than shy away from them.

- *Control:* The belief that you can influence outcomes and your overall destiny through your efforts, rather than feeling powerless in the face of external forces.

- *Commitment:* A tendency to involve yourself deeply in whatever you're doing with a genuine sense of purpose, rather than feeling detached or alienated from your life and work.

In this chapter, I outline how the 3Cs of hardiness work together as a buffer against stress, helping you transform potential crises into opportunities for personal growth, improved performance and better health. You'll discover how, in the decades since the initial hardiness study, hundreds of studies have confirmed that hardiness is a powerful predictor of both physical and mental health. You'll learn how it also influences performance under pressure, and overall life satisfaction across diverse populations.

I also explain why I have decided to add a fourth 'C', connection, into the mix due to the sheer amount of compelling research behind its benefits —but more on that later.

The Stoics: Hardiness pioneers

Long before clinical psychology gave us terms such as 'resilience' and 'hardiness', the Stoics were living and breathing these principles. They didn't just write about adversity—they ran headfirst into it, wrestled it to the ground and asked for another round.

If a Hall of Fame existed for the 3 Cs—challenge, control and commitment—the Stoics would be on the podium with laurel wreaths and dusty sandals.

Challenge orientation: Seeing adversity as opportunity

The Stoics believed that adversity wasn't something to be avoided; instead, it was the forge where character was made. They didn't just expect challenges; they welcomed them.

Take the great Stoic philosopher Epictetus. Born into slavery, crippled early in life and later exiled from Rome, he didn't complain about his misfortune. Instead, he taught his students that difficulties are things that show a person who they are.

Or consider Cato the Younger. Famous for his moral integrity (and his stubbornness), Cato deliberately wore simple clothing, walked barefoot in Rome's chaotic streets and even subjected himself to public mockery—all as training to endure hardship without losing his dignity.

The Stoics understood that challenge wasn't punishment. It was an opportunity. For them, a good life wasn't about avoiding hardship, but about leaning into it with Aretê (virtue and character) and growing stronger through it.

Control orientation: Mastering what you can, letting go of what you can't

The Stoics gave us one of the most powerful psychological tools ever: the dichotomy of control. What is up to us? What is not? Knowing the difference is the first rule of sanity.

Marcus Aurelius, Roman Emperor and reluctant philosopher-warrior, put it simply: 'You have power over your mind, not outside events. Realise this, and you will find strength.'

The Stoics understood what modern hardiness research confirms: focusing on what you can control while accepting what you cannot is the foundation of psychological resilience.

Commitment: Living according to core values, no matter what

Commitment is the glue that holds the Stoic philosophy together. It's the fierce loyalty to live according to one's highest values, even when life gets brutal—and even when nobody is watching.

Seneca, who navigated the treacherous court of the Roman Emperor Nero before ultimately being ordered by him to commit suicide, wrote: 'It is not that we have a short time to live, but that we waste a lot of it.'

For the Stoics, commitment wasn't passive. It was fierce, deliberate and urgent. It was measured not in big promises but in small, consistent actions, especially when those actions were painful, tedious or invisible.

The Stockdale paradox: Hardiness tested in the crucible of war

No discussion of hardiness would be complete without examining the extraordinary case of Vice Admiral James Stockdale, whose experience as a prisoner of war in Vietnam represents perhaps the most profound real-world test of hardiness principles in modern times.

Stockdale was shot down over North Vietnam on 9 September 1965. He spent the next seven and a half years in Hôa Lò Prison (sardonically nicknamed the 'Hanoi Hilton' by American POWs), including a mind-boggling four years in solitary confinement and two years in leg irons. He was also tortured 15 times.

What makes Stockdale's story remarkable is not just that he survived, but also how he survived — by consciously applying the principles of Stoic philosophy he had studied before his capture. Stockdale had learned about the Stoics from a philosophy lecturer during his time at university, where the American Navy had sent him to study a master's degree in international relations to prepare him for senior roles. Stockdale was so impressed by the teachings of the Stoics that he brought a copy of the book *The Enchiridion*, by Epictetus, to war with him.

'I'm leaving the world of technology and entering the world of Epictetus', Stockdale whispered to himself as he parachuted into enemy territory after his aircraft had been shot down early in the war. This wasn't just a poetic thought; it was a profound psychological shift that would prove crucial to his survival.

In the prison, Stockdale put the principles of hardiness into action:

◆ *Challenge:* He viewed his imprisonment not just as suffering to endure, but also as a test of character with meaning and purpose. He saw himself as responsible for maintaining the honour of his fellow prisoners and upholding the military code of conduct.

◆ *Control:* He focused relentlessly on what he could control — his own responses, his leadership of other prisoners, his internal discipline — while accepting what he couldn't control, such as his captivity and the torture.

◆ *Commitment:* He remained deeply engaged with his role as the senior officer among the prisoners, establishing a chain of command, creating the mission 'To return with honour', and developing a code of conduct that helped many prisoners maintain their integrity under extreme duress.

Stockdale later articulated what became known as the 'Stockdale Paradox', which embodies the essence of hardiness:

You must never confuse faith that you will prevail in the end — which you can never afford to lose — with the discipline to confront the most brutal facts of your current reality, whatever they might be.

This cognitive balancing act of maintaining unwavering faith while facing hard truths is precisely what hardiness research reveals about resilient individuals: they simultaneously accept the reality of their situation while maintaining the belief that they can eventually overcome it.

Hardiness in military psychology

The torch of hardiness research within military contexts was carried forward significantly by Paul Bartone, a military psychologist and retired U.S. Army Colonel who has conducted dozens of studies on hardiness over the past three decades, and been a mentor for me in the area of hardiness.

Bartone's research has consistently found that psychological hardiness is a key predictor of success in military training and operations. In one notable study, he found that U.S. Army Special Forces candidates with higher hardiness scores were significantly more likely to successfully complete the rigorous selection process. Those who scored lower in hardiness at the start of the course were much more likely to fail. Similar findings have been reported in other military and law enforcement contexts. For example, a 2013 study of Norwegian Armed Forces candidates confirmed that hardiness was a strong predictor of success in a border patrol selection course, and particularly the commitment and challenge components. And in a 2019 study of a law enforcement special operations selection course, hardiness was shown to be a predictor of success.

Bartone's research also revealed that hardiness serves as a protective factor against post-traumatic stress disorder (PTSD). In studies involving soldiers deployed to combat zones, those who scored high in hardiness were significantly less likely to develop

PTSD symptoms after combat exposure, even when facing life-threatening situations.

Perhaps most striking is Bartone's research from 2021 (co-authored with psychologist Stephen Bowles, also retired from the U.S. Army) focused on severely wounded American servicemen who had lost limbs in combat. They found that hardiness significantly predicted post-traumatic growth (PTG) and wellbeing among these individuals and their spouses. Despite facing arguably one of life's most devastating challenges, those high in hardiness were able to find meaning in their experiences and even identify positive changes in their lives, such as stronger family connections and new perspectives on what truly matters.

This is not an isolated finding unique to this group. A study by Salvatore Maddi and colleagues in 2023 found that individuals with high hardiness were more likely to develop PTG after experiencing stress or trauma, suggesting that the hardy personality not only consistently protects against stress and trauma, but also promotes growth and development in the aftermath.

Hardiness in business and organisational settings

Hardiness has also been extensively studied in relation to how it mitigates the effects of stress in business. Researchers Vickie and Clinton Lambert and Hiroaki Yamase explored the relationship between hardiness and workplace stress, finding that individuals high in hardiness were better equipped to handle stress, because they were less likely to suffer from burnout than those lower in hardiness. Importantly, they also demonstrated through their research that hardiness can be learned.

Hardiness has also been linked to leadership effectiveness and organisational resilience. Leaders who exhibit high levels of hardiness are better able to navigate challenges, inspire their teams and maintain composure under pressure. Research has emphasised that fostering hardiness in the workplace could lead to more resilient organisations, capable of thriving in the face of adversity.

As an example of this, a recent systematic review conducted by Dr Sherrica Senewiratne and colleagues in April 2025 looked at all of the workplace studies on hardiness conducted over the last few decades, and the results are conclusive. The team highlighted hardiness as a key determinant of individuals' capacity to cognitively appraise and adapt to stressors. Being high in hardiness fostered a range of both psychological and performance-related resilience outcomes across multiple workplace sectors, as shown in table 1.1.

Table 1.1: Effect of being high in hardiness across different workplace contexts

Workplace context	Area of improvement
Performance outcomes	• Enhanced leader performance • Improved perseverance during stressful activities • Greater work effort and service engagement • Decreased burnout and improved retention
Work behaviours	• Increased organisational citizenship behaviours • Better adaptation to new cultural environments • Greater moral courage and small-unit cohesion • Improved competence and coping self-efficacy • Enhanced leadership effectiveness and adaptability • Reduced workplace injury and turnover intention
Work attitudes	• Improved job satisfaction and embeddedness • Enhanced organisational commitment • Reduced employee cynicism and presenteeism • Greater dedication and vigour

(continued)

Table 1.1: Effect of being high in hardiness across different workplace contexts *(cont'd)*

Workplace context	Area of improvement
Health and wellbeing	• Reduced anxiety, depression and psychological distress • Decreased burnout and emotional exhaustion • Lower risk of eating disorders and alcohol abuse • Improved general and spiritual health • Enhanced basic need satisfaction and happiness • Better sleep quality and shift work tolerance

It's a bloody impressive list, right? And this is why I call hardiness 'resilience 2.0'—and why it's such an important factor in the workplace.

Hardiness in academic settings: From playground to classroom

While I've so far explored hardiness in military and organisational contexts, its benefits for children and young students in academic settings deserve special attention. After all, school can be its own special kind of battleground, complete with tests that feel like ambushes, playground politics that would make Machiavelli blush and the sheer terror of being called on when you weren't paying attention. (We've all been there, haven't we?)

Academic hardiness is essentially the same core construct—commitment, control and challenge—applied to educational settings. It represents a student's ability to persevere through academic pressures while maintaining enthusiasm for learning. And the research is compelling: students with higher levels of hardiness demonstrate significant advantages across several domains.

First and foremost, hardy students simply perform better academically. Research shows a positive correlation between hardiness and academic achievement in university students, with psychological hardiness directly predicting academic success and indirectly predicting it through academic engagement. Hardy students are more likely to persevere through difficult coursework, manage their time effectively and maintain a positive attitude toward their studies — all contributing to higher grades and overall performance.

But the benefits extend far beyond grades. Students with higher hardiness levels show increased academic engagement — that magical state of being enthusiastic, dedicated and absorbed in learning activities rather than staring blankly at the clock waiting for the bell to ring. In the 2024 article 'Sense of belonging, academic self-efficacy and hardiness: Their impacts on student engagement in distance learning courses', Suping Yi and colleagues outline their findings that academic hardiness positively and significantly impacts cognitive, emotional and behavioural engagement, particularly in distance learning environments — something that became critically important during the pandemic when children suddenly found themselves trying to learn maths while the family dog barked at the postie in the background.

Perhaps most significantly for young learners, hardiness serves as a powerful buffer against academic burnout. We've all seen that glazed-over look when a child has simply had enough of times tables and spelling lists. Research has found that hardiness is negatively associated with academic burnout, with hardy students less likely to experience the burnout components of cynicism, emotional exhaustion and reduced personal accomplishment. In other words, these students maintain their spark for learning even when facing challenges.

Hardiness also equips young students with effective coping mechanisms. Research reveals strong inverse correlations between hardiness and maladaptive schemes such as vulnerability and distrust. Hardy students are less likely to rely on avoidant strategies (like a tummy ache appearing out of the blue on exam days) and more likely to engage in problem-focused coping, such as seeking support or developing effective study habits.

The good news is that hardiness isn't simply an innate trait—it can be developed and enhanced by adults and kids alike with the strategies provided in subsequent chapters.

By fostering hardiness in children and young students, we're not just helping them achieve better grades—we're also equipping them with a psychological toolkit that will serve them throughout life's inevitable challenges. Because let's face it, if they can handle the pressure of a spelling bee or a trigonometry exam, they're building the capacity to handle whatever life throws at them later on.

The physical benefits of hardiness

The benefits of hardiness extend well beyond psychological resilience to also include significant physical health advantages. Further studies from Paul Bartone (from 2008 and 2016) demonstrate that hardiness predicts better cardiovascular health in individuals, as indicated by higher levels of high-density lipoprotein (HDL) cholesterol and lower body mass index (BMI). These studies suggested that hardiness may influence cholesterol metabolism, thereby reducing the risk of cardiovascular diseases.

Further evidence comes from studies examining immune response. Research has found that individuals with high levels of hardiness had stronger immune responses, as measured by a range of biomarkers.

This suggests that hardiness may help mitigate the physiological impacts of stress and enhance immune function while reducing vulnerability to illness.

Additionally, research on physical fitness and hardiness in military personnel has shown that those with higher hardiness levels not only perform better in physical tasks but also recover more quickly from stress-related physical challenges. This relationship highlights the intertwined nature of psychological and physical resilience, where hardiness serves as a critical factor in maintaining both mental and physical health — and I explore this mind–body hardiness connection in more detail in part II of the book.

Clearly, psychological hardiness plays a crucial role in fostering resilience, enhancing performance and promoting health in various high-stress environments. Whether in the military, law enforcement, healthcare, business or educational settings, hardiness provides individuals with the tools to manage stress, overcome challenges and thrive under pressure. The extensive body of research on hardiness underscores the importance of understanding and cultivating hardiness if you want to deal with the inevitable shit-sandwiches from the universe!

A fourth dimension: Connection

While the original hardiness model focuses on the 3Cs (commitment, control and challenge), I've added a fourth crucial component based on overwhelming research: connection. This captures the quality of our relationships with others and our sense of belonging within a community.

This component recognises that human resilience is not solely an individual trait but is also deeply embedded in our social connections. The research is clear: social support is one of the most potent buffers against trauma and stress. In fact, the Vietnam veteran studies showed that social support was a further variable that predicted resilience in the face of extreme stress.

These four components of hardiness interact with each other, and the whole becomes greater than the sum of the parts. Whether you're facing everyday pressures or life-altering challenges, hardiness will help you emerge stronger, wiser and more fulfilled. This is not about avoiding discomfort — it's about embracing the right kinds of stress and learning how to transform pressure into progress.

Putting it all together: Bouncing forward with hardiness

The journey through hardiness research reveals a powerful truth: resilience isn't just about bouncing back — it's also about bouncing forward. From the ancient Stoics to modern military personnel, from corporate boardrooms to classroom settings, the evidence is overwhelming: hardiness represents one of the most significant predictors of success, health and wellbeing under pressure.

The four components of hardiness — challenge, control, commitment and connection — work synergistically to transform how we experience and respond to stress. Rather than seeing difficulties as threats to be avoided, hardy individuals view them as opportunities for growth. They focus their energy on what they can influence while accepting what lies beyond their control. They remain deeply engaged with their values and purpose, even when the path gets rocky. And they cultivate meaningful relationships that provide both support and accountability.

What makes hardiness particularly compelling is its breadth of application. Whether you're a student facing academic pressures, a leader navigating organisational change, a parent juggling multiple responsibilities or simply someone wanting to live more fully, hardiness provides a robust framework for thriving rather than merely surviving.

Perhaps most encouraging is that hardiness isn't a fixed trait you either have or don't have. It's a set of learnable skills and attitudes that can be developed and strengthened over time. The Stoics understood this centuries ago, and modern research has validated their insights with rigorous scientific evidence. In the chapters that follow, we'll dive deep into each component of hardiness, exploring practical strategies for developing these crucial capabilities.

2
Embrace the challenge

A gem cannot be polished without friction, nor a man perfected without trials.

Seneca

I mention in the previous chapter that although life can be amazing, it is also quite often hard. By this, I don't just mean 'sometimes hard' in that Instagram 'look at me in an ice bath' way. I mean consistently hard. From the moment we're born — screaming and confused — we are launched into a world that is constantly shifting under our feet. The First Noble Truth in Buddhism states that life inherently involves dukkha — suffering — encompassing various forms and levels of pain, dissatisfaction and impermanence. Life's hard. It's messy. It hurts. But here's the twist: that discomfort is your invitation to lean in and grow, rather than numb out or hide. Dukkha isn't a bug in the system. It's the bloody point.

The Stoic philosophers also believed that life is hard and spent much of their time contemplating how to deal with adversity through Areté, or good character. The quote at the start of this chapter sums this up nicely — Stoics believed that hardships and challenges were necessary to shape us, but they also believed that our attitude in the face of adversity was equally important. Seneca reminds us that 'it's not what you endure that matters, but how you endure it'.

Fast-forward to the modern world, and the brilliant psychiatrist Dr Phil Stutz outlines in *The Tools* (co-authored with psychotherapist Barry Michels) that, as humans, we are all guaranteed to experience three things — pain, uncertainty and the constant need for hard work.

The big question isn't whether life will throw curveballs. It's how we choose to react when it does.

Understanding a challenge orientation — and why it matters

Challenge orientation is one of the four vital pillars of psychological hardiness, alongside control (covered in the next chapter), commitment (chapter 4) and connection (chapter 5). At its core, challenge orientation is the ability to view stressful events as opportunities for growth rather than threats to be feared or avoided. It's about seeing changes and challenges as natural parts of life that can build strength and wisdom when approached with the right mindset.

Think about a time when you faced a significant challenge — perhaps a demanding work project, a difficult relationship conversation or even something physically taxing such as running a marathon. Did you approach it as something to endure, perhaps avoid if possible, or as an opportunity to test your limits and grow? Your answer reveals a lot about your challenge orientation.

Research pioneered by Salvatore Maddi and Suzanne Kobasa in the 1970s and 1980s found that this mindset was a critical difference between people who thrived under pressure and those who crumbled. Their groundbreaking study of executives at Illinois Bell Telephone during massive corporate upheaval (mentioned in the previous chapter) showed that those with high challenge orientation maintained their health, happiness and performance, while others suffered significant declines in wellbeing. Challenge orientation wasn't just helpful — it was protective against the harmful effects of stress.

Importantly, the way we perceive and respond to challenges doesn't just affect our mental state — it also transforms our physiology. When we view a demanding situation as a threat, our bodies respond with a harmful stress pattern that constricts blood vessels, impairs cognitive function and, over time, contributes to chronic inflammation and illness. But when we reframe that same situation as a challenge to overcome, our cardiovascular system responds differently — more similar to how it does during exercise rather than panic — improving blood flow to the brain and enhancing performance.

This isn't just about high achievers facing extraordinary circumstances. The benefits of challenge orientation apply to everyday life, including the parent dealing with a teenager's mood swings, the professional facing technological changes in their industry, the student tackling a difficult course or anyone navigating the constant stream of changes that define modern life.

By the end of this chapter, you'll understand the science behind challenge orientation and how to develop this crucial aspect of psychological hardiness. You'll learn how your perception of stress fundamentally changes how your body responds to it. Most importantly, you'll gain tools to transform your relationship with stress and challenge — not by eliminating them (which is impossible), but by learning to work with them. The goal isn't to become immune to stress, but to become stronger because of it.

Welcome to the challenge orientation component of psychological hardiness. This is where we stop whinging about why stuff's happening to us and start asking what it's doing for us. First, though, let's have a closer look at that stress response.

The physiological underpinnings of the stress response

Before we dive headlong into challenge orientation, understanding the physiological mechanisms that underpin the stress response is worthwhile. To do this, we need to familiarise ourselves with the pioneering research of Hans Selye, an endocrinologist who was the first to discover evidence for both the dangers of and the potential benefits of stress.

Like so many scientific breakthroughs, Selye's research began with a mistake. While searching for female sex hormones in rats, Selye noticed that his rats kept getting sick in remarkably consistent ways after being exposed to various stressors, such as surgeries, extreme temperatures or excessive exercise. He eventually realised it wasn't the specific stressor that mattered, but rather the body's generalised response to what he termed 'stress' — borrowing the term from physics and engineering.

Years of subsequent research led Selye to describe what he called the 'stress cascade', a physiological chain reaction that creates a state of alarm in response to perceived threats. This cascade begins in your brain, and specifically in two almond-shaped clusters of nuclei within your temporal lobes called the amygdala. (They come as a pair, one in each hemisphere in your temporal lobe.) One of the roles of the amygdala is to continuously scan your environment for potential dangers. When a threat is detected (which can be physical or psychological, real or imaginary), the amygdala signals the hypothalamus — the command centre that controls your energy balance and many other bodily functions. The hypothalamus then initiates a two-wave response system that fundamentally changes how your body operates.

Your body under stress

The first wave of the two-wave stress response is through what's known as the sympathetic–adrenal–medullary (SAM) axis, commonly summed up as the 'fight-or-flight' response — or, more correctly, the 'fight-flight-or-freeze' response. Your sympathetic nervous system dials up and stimulates the adrenal glands to pump out adrenaline (epinephrine, if you're in the United States) and noradrenaline (or norepinephrine). This system is very fast-acting and these hormones create immediate, dramatic effects throughout your body, including the following:

♦ Your heart beats faster while blood vessels to your extremities constrict to prevent potential blood loss.

♦ Your pupils dilate to take in more information.

♦ Your breathing becomes quick and shallow to maximise oxygen intake.

♦ Your liver releases glucose for immediate energy.

♦ Your digestion temporarily shuts down to divert energy to your muscles.

♦ Your immune system is suppressed, as is your reproductive system, because ovulating or creating sperm is pointless when you're being chased by a lion — it's a waste of precious energy!

Meanwhile, your attention narrows to focus exclusively on the perceived threat. If the threat passes quickly, the adrenaline and noradrenaline response subsides, and you return to normal, or what's known as homeostasis. Importantly, the half-life of these chemicals (that is, the time it takes to reduce by half) is around a minute, so you can achieve homeostasis quite quickly.

However, if the threat persists — or if you just keep perceiving the threat as persistent due to anxiety or over-thinking — a second stress response wave kicks in through your hypothalamus–pituitary– adrenal cortex (HPA) axis, resulting in the release of the major stress hormone cortisol. This stress hormone keeps your brain and body on high alert over the longer term. Unfortunately, this sustained state of arousal is where the damage begins. The racing pulse and constricted blood vessels that form part of the stress response strain your cardiovascular system. The continued cortisol fluctuations suppress beneficial anabolic hormones needed for tissue repair. The response also triggers chronic inflammation, which damages arterial walls and joint tissues. Your hypervigilant mind becomes less creative and flexible because it's stuck in threat-detection mode. Because the half-life of cortisol is over an hour, your body takes a long time to recover homeostasis, even when the stressor has passed.

Selye was so influential in stress research that he was nominated for the Nobel Prize in Medicine numerous times. His work led to the concept that modern stressors — including work, commuting, financial crises, hectic social commitments, and even moody teenagers, annoying mothers-in-law and a drop in social media likes — could put us in a chronic state of arousal that increases vulnerability to what Selye called 'diseases of civilisation'.

But here's where it gets interesting. More recent research has revealed that Selye's model was missing a crucial piece: our expectations about stress dramatically affect how our bodies respond to it.

Stress and the power of expectations

While Selye discovered the biological mechanisms of stress, modern research has revealed something he couldn't have foreseen—that our expectations about stress can fundamentally alter these very mechanisms. And this is where psychological framing comes in.

One of the most compelling demonstrations of the power of psychological framing comes from a now-famous study conducted at Harvard University. Researchers studied a group of female hotel room attendants—women who spent their days doing physically demanding work cleaning hotel rooms. Despite their active jobs, many of these workers didn't perceive themselves as getting much exercise.

The researchers divided the attendants into two groups. They told one group that their daily work was an excellent form of exercise that satisfied the Surgeon General's recommendations for an active lifestyle. They showed them exactly how their work activities, including pushing vacuum cleaners and changing sheets, were burning calories and building strength. The control group received no such information.

Four weeks later, without any changes to their actual work routines, behaviour or lifestyles, the informed group showed remarkable physical improvements. Their weight, blood pressure, body fat, waist-to-hip ratio and BMI had all decreased significantly compared to the control group. Their bodies had responded to the mere knowledge that their work constituted good exercise.

This was more than a placebo effect. It was a profound demonstration of how our expectations shape our physical reality. The hotel workers' bodies responded differently to the same physical activity simply because they now recognised it as beneficial exercise rather than just work.

Similarly, our expectations about stress can transform our physiological responses. In a German survey published in 2016, researchers at the Max Planck Institute for Human Development found that people who find meaning in unpleasant emotions—recognising that feelings such as nervousness, anger or disappointment can be useful and appropriate—tend to be much happier than those who prefer to eliminate these emotions.

The researchers asked participants to rate various emotions on dimensions including unpleasantness, appropriateness, utility and meaningfulness. Those who saw value in negative emotions showed significantly better physical and mental health outcomes. In fact, the ability to find meaning in unpleasant emotions virtually eliminated the typical association between distress and poor health. Even when experiencing frequent distress, these individuals recovered more quickly and showed better muscle strength (a general indicator of fitness) than those who viewed negative emotions as merely harmful.

This suggests that our mindset about stress and negative emotions can be as important as — or perhaps even more important than — the actual frequency of stressful experiences in our lives.

The challenge versus threat mindset

Your ability to choose how you respond to potential stressors is far more malleable than you perhaps realise, and has the capacity to powerfully influence both your performance under pressure and your physiological responses. Over the long-term, this can have an impact on your overall health and wellbeing. In a groundbreaking series of studies, Jeremy Jamieson, chair of the psychology department at the University of Rochester, demonstrated that the way we perceive our bodily responses to stress dramatically affects our performance and wellbeing.

Jamieson's interest in studying our response to stress stemmed from his observations as a student athlete. He noticed how some teammates would get 'amped up' and excited before a game but would feel nervous and fall apart before an exam. Both situations were high-pressure, so why was the arousal helpful in sports but harmful in academics?

Reinterpreting the body's stress signals

Jamieson's insight was that the different responses came down to how they interpreted their body's signals. Before sports competition, the racing heart and quickened breathing were seen by the students as energising; however, in the exam hall, these same sensations were interpreted as warning signs of potential failure. These expectations then influenced their performance and became self-fulfilling prophecies.

To test this idea, Jamieson conducted an experiment with students preparing for the Graduate Record Examination (GRE) in the United States, a very high-pressure exam required for most applications to postgraduate study programs. He arranged for all participants in the study to take a practice exam in the lab. Before taking this practice exam, however, half the participants were given a simple message that took less than a minute to read:

> *People think that feeling anxious while taking a standardised test will make them do poorly on the test. However, recent research suggests that arousal doesn't hurt performance on these tests and can even help performance ... If you find yourself feeling anxious, simply remind yourself that your arousal could be helping.*

The other half — the control group — weren't given any message.

The results were astonishing. This minimal instruction not only improved students' scores on the mock exam but also led to better performance on the real GRE months later. The differences were particularly notable in math, where anxiety typically has the most debilitating effects. In this area, the intervention group scored around 10 per cent better than the control group—a difference that could easily determine university admission outcomes, and potentially the trajectory of someone's life.

With a little bit of what is known as 'psychological priming', Jamieson had shifted students' mindsets from dreading their anxiety to harnessing it as fuel—with immediate and lasting performance benefits.

Follow-up studies that Jamieson conducted showed even more remarkable results. Another set of subjects were put through the Trier Social Stress Test, a standardised battery of stressful situations that consistently stresses the crap out of people. Half of the participants received similar psychological priming to the first experiment, and were told that physiological arousal signs (racing heart, quickened breathing) were actually the body's natural, helpful response to challenge. Again, the control group received no such priming.

While the control group showed the classic stress reaction—racing heart with constricted blood vessels priming for injury—the reappraisal group showed a healthier stress reaction pattern. Their cardiovascular systems responded differently—while their hearts still worked harder, their blood vessels dilated, allowing blood to flood throughout the body, similar to what happens during exercise. This energised their bodies without straining their cardiovascular system and allowed more blood to reach their brains, enhancing cognitive performance.

The implication is clear: it's not the stress itself that determines the outcome, but how you interpret it. When you view your racing heart as a positive, energising response, rather than a liability, your body can respond accordingly. The stress response becomes an ally rather than an enemy.

Recasting threats as challenges

Building on this research, the Biopsychosocial Model of Challenge and Threat has now been well established. This model highlights that when you view a potentially stressful event as a challenge — something within your capabilities and an opportunity for growth — you engage with it more positively, reducing the body's stress response and enabling proactive coping strategies. Conversely, when you perceive it as a threat, you can become overwhelmed by potential negative outcomes, which can paralyse you into inaction or induce despair.

According to research from Professor Mark Seery from the University of Buffalo, who has spent decades studying stress and our response to it, when you view something as a challenge rather than a threat, not only do you activate the more adaptive fight-or-flight SAM axis of the human stress response (introduced earlier in this chapter), but your brain also releases chemicals such as noradrenaline, which enhances your focus and performance, your immune system functions optimally and you recover quickly once the stressor is gone.

Professor Seery has shown that viewing the same potential stressor as a threat activates the HPA axis (also introduced earlier), which results in the release of cortisol. A short burst of cortisol acts in concert with the SAM axis, as they work together like a SWAT team to confront the threat. Remember, however, that the half-life of cortisol is more than an hour, whereas the half-life of adrenaline and noradrenaline is only around a minute.

As shown in the figure 2.1 (overleaf), this means that viewing adversity as a challenge brings your body back to homeostasis quickly, whereas viewing it as a threat puts you in a stressed state for way longer. Research has clearly shown that chronically elevated cortisol makes you fat and sick, and destroys your brain function and mental health, so how you frame adversity really counts!

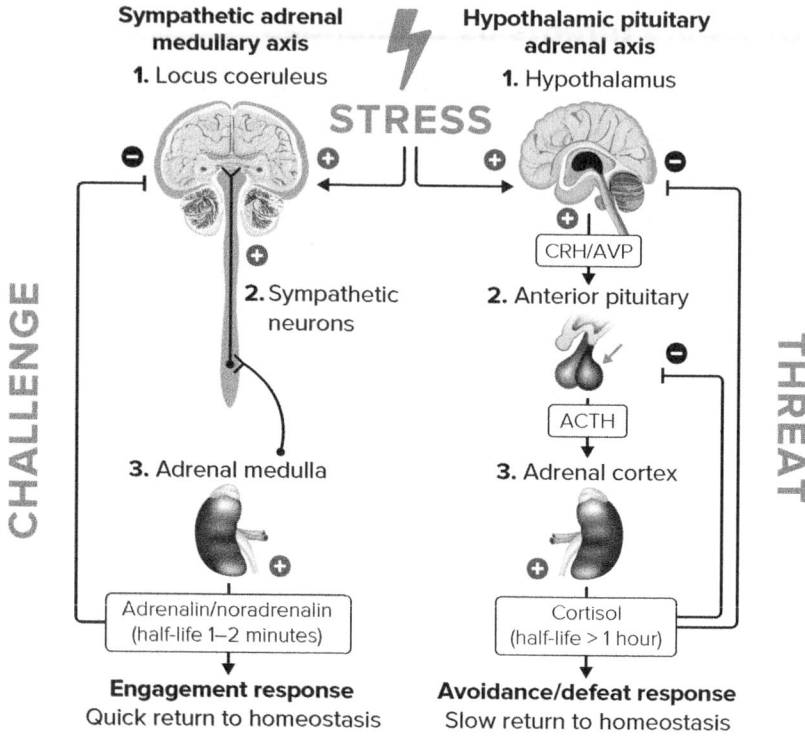

Figure 2.1: Viewing adversity as a challenge versus a threat
Adapted from: © Carlton, Morgan & Voisey, Joanne & Parker, Tony &
Punyadeera, Chamindie & Cuttle, Leila. (2021). 'A review of potential biomarkers
for assessing physical and psychological trauma in paediatric burns.'

Long-term studies suggest these benefits extend far beyond immediate performance gains. A year-long survey of German doctors and teachers (with the findings published in the 2015 article 'Will you thrive under pressure or burn out? Linking anxiety motivation and emotional exhaustion') highlighted that those who view anxiety as a source of energy are much less likely to suffer emotional exhaustion than those who see it as a threat.

Perhaps most striking is the potential impact on long-term physical health. An eight-year longitudinal study of more than 28 000 people (outlined in 'Does the perception that stress affects health matter? The association with health and mortality') found that high stress levels were indeed associated with a 43 per cent increase in mortality — but only among people who believed stress was harmful to their health. Those experiencing high stress who didn't see it as harmful were even less likely to die than those reporting very little stress at all. These results held up even after the researchers controlled for confounding factors (that could potentially influence the results), such as income, education, physical activity and smoking. The researchers calculated that the belief that stress is harmful contributes to approximately 20 000 premature deaths annually in the United States alone — a sobering testament to the power of our expectations.

Focusing your attention

To explore this further, let's understand a very important principle — your brain commits cells to what you pay attention to. Your attention is the conductor of the brain and your overall experience on this planet, and the level of control that you have over your attention has a huge bearing on your life.

Fortunately for me, over the last decade or so, I have been paying a lot of attention to Stoic philosophy, because it resonates deeply with me. I've also been pursuing a PhD in psychology, and designing and testing resilience and hardiness strategies with the Australian Defence Force and various corporate organisations. Sometimes life works in mysterious ways, presenting us with opportunities to put our learning into practice.

Walking the talk

A few months ago, I had a chat to a cardiologist friend of mine who I play soccer with. I mentioned that, given that I was now in my 50s and like to be proactive about my health (a trait of most people high in hardiness control), I wanted to have a full check-up of my heart. In our discussion, he used the analogy of my heart as a house, and suggested that we run some tests to check my 'electrics', 'plumbing' and 'rooms', as he put it. The four rooms of the heart are the two chambers on top and two ventricles underneath, and just as your house has plumbing, your heart has arteries. The electricity is what creates the contractions of the heart.

My friend organised several tests, including an exercise stress test, a cardiac MRI and a CT angiogram, because he had detected a small heart murmur with his stethoscope. When I went for the debrief after completing these tests, my cardiologist confirmed that I was as fit as a fiddle; however, a surprising discovery had emerged. I had a congenital heart defect (meaning I was born with the issue), in the form of a bicuspid aortic valve rather than a tricuspid valve. This meant that my aortic valve had only two leaflets, rather than the normal three. Over time, the valve could stop closing properly, leading to regurgitation, where some blood leaks back into the left ventricle after it has been pumped out through the aortic valve.

Although I was currently symptom-free, my friend explained I did already have significant regurgitation, which would slowly get worse over time. He explained that, although I didn't need to act immediately, this condition would eventually catch up with me and, if left untreated, could lead to an aortic aneurysm or heart failure as the ventricle becomes overworked and stretched to the point of no return. A very small chance also existed that my aorta would stretch and burst, meaning that I would be 'brown bread', as we say in Belfast. Not good!

We had a quick chat about my options, which were to 'watch and wait' and act when the regurgitation got significantly worse, or do something about it now. Either way, I didn't have to rush my decision. The treatment would involve open-heart surgery, not without its risks and requiring extended recovery. My cardiologist told me to have a think about it and we could reconvene later. I told him I didn't need to think any longer — I wanted to get on the front foot. My military training had taught me that it's best to go into battle on your terms, when you are strong and ideally your enemy is not. Waiting would only let my 'enemy' get stronger, and age was not on my side. (Fortunately, I had the resources available to be able to make this decision.)

A worthy opponent

As I walked out of the initial consult, having received the news, I got into my car and was immediately struck by the words of the Stoic philosopher Seneca:

> *I judge you unfortunate because you have never lived through misfortune. You have passed through life without an opponent – no one can ever know what you are capable of, not even you.*

In that moment, I chose to view my upcoming open-heart surgery as a worthy opponent — one that would test and develop my resilience, strength, endurance and mindset. This is the essence of the challenge orientation of hardiness — seeing potential threats as opportunities for growth and learning rather than as dangers to be avoided.

As I was driving home, lots of stuff was going through my head and I suddenly remembered a conversation with my mate Reg, who was an ex-Australian SAS Commanding Officer. We had been talking about his deployment to the first Iraq war in Kuwait, where he was among the first to enter the conflict. I remembered asking him about how it felt and he spoke of an understandable feeling of nerves — he was going to war, after all. However, he told me that the overwhelming feeling was a perverse sense of excitement, because this was what he had trained for his entire professional life — and this was a chance to put that training to the test.

Inspired by Reg's thinking, I decided to adopt this attitude (because you get to choose your attitude). I told myself, 'This is what I've trained for.' All those gruelling pre-season soccer training sessions of hill sprints at university that often induced vomiting, the extra voluntary log runs at 6 am in basic military training with a few other unhinged mates, the ten challenging days of military combat survival and resistance-to-interrogation training with stressor after stressor imposed on us, a three-week expedition deep into the Amazon jungle with my Italian mate Giovanni, training and competing in boxing and karate in my 40s, the countless cold showers and ice baths and, of course, all of the reading of Stoic philosophy and research on hardiness — it was all to train me to face my worthy opponent.

On the drive back home, I then recalled one of my favourite quotes from the Stoic philosopher Epictetus (also included at the start of chapter 6):

> *We must undergo a hard winter training and not rush into things for which we have not prepared.*

It's time to giddy up, I thought, *and put in some extra training to meet this worthy opponent on my terms.* I provide more detail on this in the next chapter but, as a summary, I decided to adapt my exercise regime to focus on strengthening my heart and body in preparation for the physical demands of the operation and to optimise my recovery. Additionally, I decided to reduce my alcohol consumption to a minimum, tweak my supplements and look for other '1 to 5 percenters'. This was not just about surviving the surgery; it was about thriving through it and beyond. This worthy opponent was a positive reinforcer, validating that all the hard work I had invested in exercise and mindset training over my life had been worth it—this was the moment I had trained for.

Flatlining on stress

Researchers have recently discovered a further twist in the challenge–threat response. Most people associate stress with over-activation—heart racing, palms sweating, thoughts spinning like a fidget spinner on Red Bull. However, another, sneakier, stress response is just as dangerous: blunted reactivity.

According to recent research by Dr Adrian Hase and colleagues published in 2020, when someone enters a challenge they perceive as too overwhelming—or if they've been burned or failed one too many times in the past—their system doesn't go into overdrive. It shuts down, physiologically and motivationally.

This state, called blunted cardiovascular reactivity (CVR), shows up as a flatline response to stress. The heart rate doesn't rise as it should. Blood vessels don't open up to ramp up performance. The person doesn't engage. They check out. Not because they're weak, but because, deep down — either consciously or subconsciously — they've already decided they'll fail.

This is the motivational disengagement end of the spectrum in the Biopsychosocial Model of Challenge and Threat. This response isn't about laziness; instead, it's a protective mechanism, often developed after repeated threat experiences that are overwhelming (think early-life adversity, trauma, toxic work environments, being in a controlling relationship or repeatedly failing to lose weight). This response is your brain saying, 'Let's not even try. That way, we can't lose.'

But here's the rub: this disengagement isn't harmless. It's been linked to low resilience, poor performance, depression, obesity, burnout and more. Over time, the avoidance of challenge becomes the biggest threat of all.

The solution? Gradual, intentional re-engagement through a hardiness orientation. Focus on small wins and manageable discomfort as you train the system — physiologically and psychologically — to lean into stress again, one step at a time.

So, if you've ever felt like you 'just don't have the energy' to deal with challenges anymore, don't just push harder. Rebuild your engagement. Start where you are. And remember: hardiness isn't about pretending you're fine. It's about choosing to show up, even when your system says hide. (I provide more tips on building your challenge muscle at the end of this chapter.)

Motivational disengagement isn't just psychological theory — it's hardwired into our biology. Nobel Prize–winning chemist Ilya Prigogine's theory of 'bifurcation points' explains that when a system (like a human or an ecosystem) is under chronic stress, it eventually reaches a point where it either adapts and becomes more complex and resilient — or it collapses. The key takeaway is that stress and challenges don't have to break you — they can force you to evolve into something better. Much of your response is determined by how you choose to view the stressor and how you choose to react. And much of how you choose to react is driven by what you pay attention to over your life.

In the words of Epictetus, 'It's not what happens to you, but how you react to it that matters.'

Acceptance versus reappraisal: Different paths to regulation

Recent research in emotion regulation offers fascinating insights into different strategies for handling stressful situations. The work of Philippe Goldin and colleagues (outlined in the article 'Acceptance versus reappraisal: Behavioral, autonomic, and neural effects') has compared two distinct approaches: cognitive reappraisal and acceptance.

Cognitive reappraisal involves actively changing how you think about a stressful situation, and reframing the meaning to reduce its emotional impact. For example, you could view a job interview not as a judgement of your worth but as an opportunity to find a mutual fit.

Acceptance, by contrast, involves adopting a decentred observer perspective, where you notice your thoughts, emotions and bodily sensations without judgement or attempts to change them. This approach is about recognising these experiences as transient mental events rather than facts that define you.

In neuroimaging studies, these approaches show distinct brain activation patterns. Reappraisal activates brain networks involved in cognitive control and language processing, while reducing activity in the amygdala (the brain's alarm system). Acceptance activates regions involved in attention regulation but shows less impact on amygdala activity.

Interestingly, reappraisal appears to be more effective at immediately reducing negative emotions, but may require more cognitive resources. Acceptance, while sometimes less immediately powerful in changing emotions, requires less effort and may provide broader psychological flexibility over time.

These findings suggest that both strategies have their place in your emotional regulation toolkit. Reappraisal might be best when you need to perform under pressure immediately, while acceptance might be more sustainable for chronic stressors or situations where changing your perspective isn't realistic or helpful. These two responses also work in with the two faces of the challenge orientation, covered in the next section.

The two faces of challenge

The challenge orientation of hardiness has two distinct but interrelated aspects:

1. the ability to view adversity as an opportunity for growth rather than a threat

2. the capacity to embrace change as a natural part of life rather than something to be feared or resisted.

So far in this chapter, I've discussed the challenge versus threat aspect of adversity. Let's now shift our focus to dealing with change.

Perhaps you've heard of the Zen koan about two trees: the sturdy oak and the flexible willow. As fierce winds blow, the oak, proud and unyielding, tries to resist. But as the storm intensifies, its rigid branches snap under the pressure. Meanwhile, the willow bends gracefully, moving with the wind, swaying to survive. When the storm passes, the oak is damaged, but the willow stands tall. This metaphor beautifully illustrates that flexibility, not brute strength, is often the key to weathering life's inevitable changes and challenges.

Nature's lesson: Change is life

Here's something that might blow your mind: you're not the same person you were when you started reading this chapter.

At a cellular level, your body is in a constant state of flux through a process called apoptosis, or programmed cell death. But before our cells die, they give birth to daughter cells, passing on their essential functions. This means we only continue to live because we are constantly changing.

Think about that for a moment: change isn't just something that happens to us—it's the very essence of being alive. Your body replaces:

◆ your skin cells every two to four weeks

◆ your stomach lining every two to nine days

◆ your liver cells every 150 to 500 days

◆ most of your brain cells over your lifetime.

We are quite literally renewed through constant change. Yet despite this biological reality, many of us resist change in our lives, seeing it as a threat rather than the natural order of things.

Ancient wisdom, modern science and psychological flexibility

The *I Ching*, or *Book of Changes*, teaches that change is the only constant in the universe. This ancient Chinese text doesn't present change as something to be feared or resisted, but as the natural flow of life itself. When we align ourselves with this flow rather than fighting against it, we reduce our suffering and increase our effectiveness.

Charles Darwin's insights about adaptation support this view. A famous summary of his theory (often misattributed to Darwin himself) was offered by Leon Megginson in 1963:

> *According to Darwin's Origin of Species, it is not the most intellectual of the species that survives; it is not the strongest that survives; but the*

species that survives is the one that is able best to adapt and adjust to the changing environment in which it finds itself.

In other words, adaption is not just about biological evolution — it's a fundamental truth about thriving in any environment.

This leads us to psychological flexibility, which is a fancy way of saying we need to be mentally nimble in the face of life's uncertainties. Research on hardiness shows that people who adopt a challenge orientation see change as an opportunity for them to grow, develop or learn new skills, rather than something to resist or be avoided. That mindset then makes the change more manageable, and they adapt much better and suffer less stress than non-hardy people who resist and avoid change.

Acceptance and commitment therapy (ACT) guides us on how to do this successfully. ACT encourages us to accept the things we can't change while committing to actions that align with our values. Instead of getting stuck in the mental tug-of-war of resisting or avoiding stress and change, ACT teaches us to embrace discomfort, much like the willow accepts the wind. It's a mental jiu-jitsu that helps you flow with life rather than being knocked down by it.

Similarly, Morita therapy from Japan emphasises acceptance of life as it is. Instead of trying to change or suppress emotions such as anxiety, Morita therapy tells us to accept those emotions and focus on taking action. The beauty of this approach is in its simplicity: stop fighting reality, stop resisting change and get on with your life, doing what matters most to you and acting in accordance with your values.

Your brain on challenge and change

Here's where it gets really interesting: your brain actually needs both challenge and change to stay healthy. Neuroscience research has shown that new experiences, change and learning create new neural pathways. This ability to constantly rewire and adapt, known as neuroplasticity, helps protect against neurodegenerative diseases such as Alzheimer's disease and keeps your mind sharp as you age.

When you learn a new skill, travel to new places, meet new people, try new experiences, solve novel problems or even brush your teeth with your other hand, you're not just having fun or expanding your horizons — you're literally building a more resilient brain. On the flip side, doing the same job for 30 years, hanging out with the same people, going on holidays to the same place, parking your car in the same spot at work, and lots of routine hurtles your brain towards dementia through lack of stimulation.

So what can you do about it? The key is to embrace adversity and change as opportunities for you to grow and develop.

Building your challenge muscle

Developing a challenge orientation isn't about positive thinking or denying reality. It's about building your capacity to engage with change and adversity in a productive manner. Think of both change and challenge as invitations to enter what I call the 'growth zone' — that space just beyond your comfort zone where learning and development occur. It's like exercise for your adaptability muscles. Just as physical training requires progressive overload, your capacity to handle both change and challenge grows through regular exposure to new situations and difficulties.

Here's how to start building your challenge muscle:

◆ *Reframe stress as enhancement:* When you feel your heart racing before a presentation or competition, remind yourself that your body is preparing for peak performance, not falling apart. Tell yourself that you're excited, not anxious (it's the exact same chemicals in your body, but how you perceive them makes the difference). This physiological arousal is your friend, not your enemy.

◆ *Seek progressive challenge:* Just as you wouldn't try to deadlift 200 kilograms without training, build your challenge orientation progressively. Start with small challenges and gradually increase the difficulty. Each success builds your confidence for bigger challenges and facilitates a challenge orientation, rather than a threat orientation. If you fail, regress a step and start again.

◆ *Practise intentional discomfort:* Regular exposure to manageable challenges builds your resilience. Voluntary hardships such as cold showers, hard workouts and learning new skills prepare you for life's involuntary ones.

◆ *Study your successes:* After successfully navigating a challenge, analyse what worked. What strategies did you use? How did you maintain your focus? What character strengths did you express? This builds your toolkit for future challenges.

◆ *Start small with change:* Make small, intentional changes to your routine, such as:

- Take a different route to work.
- Try new foods.
- Learn a new skill.
- Adopt a new hobby.

- Change up your exercise routine.

- Go out of your way to meet new people.

- Go to a completely different place for your holidays than normal.

◆ *Practise mindful adaptation:* When change occurs, pause and ask:

- What opportunities does this present?

- What can I learn from this?

- How might this help me grow?

- What new possibilities are opening up?

- What might the silver lining be six months from now?

Practical application

Let's return to my personal story about my upcoming heart surgery. Instead of viewing it as a threat, I'm applying the challenge orientation in several ways:

◆ *Physical preparation:* Adapting my exercise regime to strengthen my heart and body in preparation for the physical demands of the operation and to optimise my recovery. I'm treating my worthy opponent with the respect that it deserves and am rising to the challenge.

◆ *Mental preparation:* Using visualisation and mindset work to prepare for the challenge, much like an athlete preparing for competition.

◆ *Strategic planning:* Making plans for my recovery and using this as an opportunity to test my resilience strategies. I'm boosting my iron and vitamin B12 levels (most heart surgery patients end up with anaemia, which impacts on their recovery), and have a red light panel I'll be using every day to boost my mitochondrial function and speed up the wound healing of the rather large cut in my chest. (See chapter 8 for more on nutrition, and chapter 9 for more on the benefits of red light.)

◆ *Finding meaning:* Using this experience as a way to deepen my understanding of resilience and share these insights with others.

Putting it all together: Facing adversity and embracing change

As I prepare for my heart surgery (which happens to be in three days from writing this chapter. *Spoiler alert:* If you're reading this book, I made it!), I'm reminded that both aspects of the challenge orientation—facing adversity and embracing change—are really about the same thing: choosing growth over comfort, possibility over fear, and engagement over avoidance.

Remember—you are changing right now, whether you choose to or not. The only question is whether you'll resist that change or use it as fuel for growth. The path of Aretê isn't about avoiding challenges or resisting change—it's about embracing both as the natural teachers they are. When you develop this mindset, you don't just survive life's inevitable changes and challenges—you thrive because of them.

The challenge orientation of hardiness is all about maintaining a fundamental openness to life's dynamic nature. It's about combining:

- the ability to view adversity as opportunity
- the capacity to embrace change as natural
- the understanding that growth requires both.

When you do so, you develop a powerful psychological advantage that serves you in all areas of life.

3

Focus on what you can control

You have power over your mind — not outside events.
Realise this, and you will find strength.

Marcus Aurelius

Life is filled with curveballs. We can't predict when adversity will strike, but we can control how we respond. Some people navigate through life's challenges with resilience, adapting and overcoming. One key to this adaptability is hardiness control orientation — the belief that you have the power to control or influence your environment, outcomes and destiny. This belief provides a sense of control over life's unpredictable nature, fostering both mental and physical wellbeing. An integral part of this hardiness is attentional control — how and where you direct your mental focus.

In this chapter, I explore how locus of control, attentional control and attentional focus on the controllable aspects of life contribute to a more resilient mindset. I also examine how misdirected attention — focusing on things outside of our control — fuels anxiety and depression. Drawing from psychological research, including a recent study on how often our worries do not materialise, I highlight how cognitive reorientation can increase our sense of control and reduce mental distress.

What are you focused on?

First, let's consider different theories on control and focus, and the benefits they highlight, starting with the locus of control.

Internal versus external locus of control

Julian Rotter's concept of locus of control (developed in the 1950s) remains fundamental in understanding how individuals perceive their ability to control their lives. A person's locus of control exists on a spectrum, ranging from internal to external:

◆ *Internal locus of control:* Individuals who operate from an internal locus of control believe they heavily influence their environment and their destiny through their actions. They see themselves as the primary agent of change and, therefore, feel empowered to take action. Research consistently shows that people with an internal locus of control experience less stress, better physical health, lower rates of mental health issues and greater satisfaction in life. Their confidence in controlling their environment leads to lower levels of the stress hormone cortisol and promotes behaviours that enhance wellbeing, such as regular exercise and a healthy diet.

◆ *External locus of control:* Those with an external locus of control see external forces — such as fate, luck or the behaviour of others — as the primary determinants of events in their lives. An external locus of control correlates with higher stress levels, lower resilience, and poorer physical and mental health outcomes. This is largely because an external locus of control fosters feelings of helplessness, which can lead to learned helplessness, a state that perpetuates passivity and inaction in the face of challenges.

Consider the different responses to the COVID-19 pandemic. Some people felt utterly helpless, focusing on what governments weren't doing or how unfair the situation was. This kind of response is classic external locus of control. Others asked, 'What can I control here?' This kind of response helped these people, my family included, focus on using the time to get fitter, build immune systems through exercise and nutrition, maintain social connections via video calls and develop new skills. The same circumstances saw radically different outcomes based on where people placed their locus of control.

Stoic philosophy and the zones of control

Back in ancient Greek and Roman times, the Stoic philosophers also discussed the importance of focusing on what we can control. In *The Enchiridion*, Epictetus offers timeless advice on how to navigate life's uncertainties:

Some things are within our power, while others are not. Within our power are opinion, motivation, desire, aversion, and, in a word, whatever is of our own doing. Not within our power are our body, our property, reputation, office, and, in a word, whatever is not of our own doing.

Here's the Stoic mic drop: control what you can (known as zone 1), let go of what you can't (zone 2). It sounds simple, but it's one of the most powerful mental shifts you'll ever make. Most people waste their energy raging at traffic, politics, other people's behaviour and even the weather — as if outrage is a strategy. It's not. Focus on what's in your hands. That's where your power lives.

This Stoic principle parallels modern psychological understanding of control. By focusing on what we can influence—our attention, responses and actions—we can enhance our sense of agency. Attempting to control what is beyond our influence—such as the behaviour of others or events in the distant future—leads to frustration, anxiety and despair.

Focusing on acceptance and commitment

Modern psychology has brought this ancient wisdom into sharper focus through acceptance and commitment therapy (ACT—introduced in chapter 2). Within this theory, psychologist Russ Harris (bestselling author of *The Happiness Trap*) introduces the idea of the 'choice point'. This is the exact moment when you decide whether to move towards the person you want to be, or away from that person.

This idea echoes the ideas of Holocaust survivor Viktor Frankl, who endured the horrors of Auschwitz and who said:

> *Everything can be taken from a man but one thing; the last of human freedoms—to choose one's attitude in any given set of circumstances, to choose one's own way.*

For Frankl, our ability to choose how we react to any circumstance, no matter how brutal, was the last of human freedoms.

This choice is our crossroads, the one I mention at the start of the book. We each face these crossroads—not once in a lifetime, but many times a day. These are the moments, often subtle and fleeting, when we stand between two paths: the easy drift toward Kakia, or the intentional climb toward Aretê. Kakia seduces us with comfort, avoidance and gratification. Aretê asks for courage, effort and alignment with who we *truly* want to be. The crossroads is where choice lives. It's not in grand speeches or epic battles — it's when you get home exhausted and decide whether to collapse with a drink or do some exercise. It's when the alarm goes off, and you choose between snoozing and rising with purpose. The more aware you become of the crossroads, the more power you reclaim. Table 3.1 provides some further examples of the crossroads.

When you stand at the crossroads, the key is to pause and think about what sort of person you want to be, and what values are important to you. Then consider what action will lead you down the right path right now — and commit to that action. These decisions *accumulate*, shaping your character, your health, and ultimately, your destiny.

Table 3.1: The crosswords: Choosing daily between Kakia and Aretê

Situation	Path of Kakia	Path of Aretê
You come home from work stressed	Pour a drink and scroll your phone while streaming	Do some exercise to de-stress and reinvigorate yourself
Your alarm goes off	Press snooze, several times	Get up and contemplate how you want to show up today
You're waiting for a coffee	Scroll social media mindlessly	Practise breathwork or talk to a stranger
You make a mistake at work	Blame, deny or hide it	Own it, learn and grow
Your colleague is being a dickhead	Fantasise about sabotaging their project	Take the moral high ground
Your child is behaving like a pint-sized psycho	Snap, shout and google 'boarding schools near me'	Take a deep breath and talk to them calmly
You go for lunch after a hard morning at work	Eat the most appetising thing in the food court, followed by a doughnut	Choose something nutritious to replenish your energy

The key takeaway from both Stoic philosophy and modern psychology is that clarity in distinguishing what we can control is essential for mental health and resilience. Those who habitually focus on the controllable aspects of life, rather than the uncontrollable aspects, are less likely to feel overwhelmed by adversity and more likely to adopt a proactive stance in solving problems.

Understanding internal versus external locus of control and the Stoics zones of control provides the framework, but knowing where to direct your attention provides the practical tool. Japanese psychology offers a powerful metaphor for this: the flashlight of attention.

Your flashlight of attention

In Japanese psychology, attention is often likened to a flashlight. Wherever you shine this flashlight is where your focus — and energy — goes. The problem arises when people shine this flashlight inwards for too long, focusing obsessively on their thoughts and emotions, and particularly those related to things outside of their control. Another common tendency is to focus the flashlight of attention on other people's behaviour, the past or the future — all areas that are inherently uncontrollable. Worrying about these factors leads to a mental loop where solutions seem out of reach. Fixating on past events you cannot change, for example, can lead to feelings of guilt, regret and depression. Similarly, focusing excessively on the future, trying to predict and prevent every possible negative outcome, fuels anxiety.

Consider mental health. In simplistic terms, depression is exacerbated by lamenting on the past, while anxiety is exacerbated by concerns about the future. In both cases, the past or future are brought into the present moment, and the flashlight of attention is shone inside our heads, struggling with our thoughts and emotions. Japanese psychology (and Stoicism) encourages you to instead focus the flashlight of your attention onto your actions, and do what needs to be done, despite the negative thoughts and emotions.

A powerful example of how this plays out is provided in a 2020 study by Lucas LaFreniere and Michelle Newman. In this study, participants with generalised anxiety disorder (GAD) were asked to track their worries over time through a journal. When they then looked back on those journal entries, they found that 91.4 per cent of their worries never came true. Even more striking, 30 per cent of the worries that did come true turned out better than expected. The implications of this study are profound: the vast majority of the mental energy we invest in worrying (with the flashlight shone inside our head) is wasted, because the vast majority of the time the feared outcomes either don't happen or aren't as bad as we anticipate.

This research underscores the importance, whenever possible, of re-directing the flashlight of attention from uncontrollable, anxiety-inducing thoughts to more practical, solution-oriented thinking. Rather than ruminating on potential future disasters or dwelling on past mistakes, we should aim to shine our attention on the present moment and on actions we can take now.

Your attention heat-map

I was chatting recently with former AFL player Dylan Buckley on his podcast *Dyl and Friends* about how professional athletes use GPS data to track movement during games. The result is a visual heat map of where they've spent time on the field—bright red areas indicate heavy activity, while blue areas indicate less activity. We were discussing this in terms of the places we have visited in the world, and how the diversity of our geographical heat maps massively contributes to our life experiences and view of the world. Some people's heat maps are concentrated in very small geographical areas, because they haven't travelled much, and some people's maps have great diversity, which broadens their view of the world.

That evening, it hit me that we all have an attentional heat map — not for where we've moved, but where our *mind* has been. Imagine mapping your attention over the past 24 hours. Where did your mental spotlight spend the most time? Was it consumed by emails, social media, news, worry or regret? How much of it was aligned with what you truly value — your health, your relationships and your personal growth?

Now zoom out. What would your attentional heat map look like across a week? A month? A year? If you visualised it, would you see time and energy focused in meaningful places, or would your map reveal a scattershot of distraction and mental noise?

This matters. Just like a footballer's heat map reveals their game plan, your attentional heat map reveals your *life plan*. It shapes your beliefs, moods, relationships and even your mental health. Anxious people tend to have heat maps dominated by future-based worry. Depressed individuals' heat maps are often focused inward on the past. People with good mental health generally distribute their attentional heat map more intentionally — toward connection, action, creativity and presence.

And what about your kids? Especially if you have teens, asking what their attentional heat map looks like is definitely worthwhile. Is it largely dominated by social media and comparison-driven platforms? If so, it could be increasing their risk of mental health issues — which are surging in young people, and especially teenage girls.

Your attention is not neutral. It is shaping your brain, your emotions and your experience of the world.

Attention in the world of high performance

I recently co-authored (with many others) a research paper with the rather wordy title 'Building a transdisciplinary expert consensus on the cognitive drivers of performance under pressure: An international multi-panel Delphi study'. The study focused on identifying the cognitive elements of performance in high-pressure situations, such as in the military, first responders, upper echelons of business and competitive sport. The study included 68 experts from the military, elite sport, high-stakes business and performance neuroscience, of which I was one. Our task was to identify the cognitive drivers under pressure and rate them in order of importance. Across those four high-performance fields, the experts unanimously ranked attentional control as the most critical trainable skill for thriving under pressure. More than processing speed, more than working memory, more than effort — attentional control was identified as the number one driver of performance under pressure.

Attention was deemed to be so important because it is the brain's gatekeeper. It dictates what we notice, how we feel and, ultimately, how we behave. If your attention is hijacked by external noise — such as notifications, headlines and other distractions — you lose the ability to act with intention.

To master your life, you must master your attention.

Mastering your attention

So, let's tie this all together:

♦ Julian Rotter outlined the internal versus the external locus of control.

♦ The Stoics gave us zone 1 (what we can control) and zone 2 (what we can't).

- Frankl reminded us that even in Auschwitz, the mind could still be free to choose how we react to our circumstances.

- ACT shows us that in every moment, we hit a choice point that determines who we are becoming.

- Both Japanese psychology and peak performance neuroscience tell us that mastering our attention is key to mastering our lives.

- Your attentional heat map can sum up your focus, and your life.

Practical exercises for shifting the flashlight of attention

Before moving on to other aspects of the hardiness control orientation, here are some quick tips to shift the flashlight of your attention:

- *Zones of control exercise:* On a piece of paper, draw two circles. In circle 1, write down everything you can control about a problem. In circle 2, list what is outside of your control. Focus your energy solely on circle 1 — what you can control — and let go of circle 2.

- *Attentional flashlight practice:* Imagine your attention as a flashlight. Throughout the day, periodically pause and ask yourself: Where is my flashlight shining? Is it focused on something productive and within my control, or is it caught in rumination or worry about uncontrollable events?

- *Social media detox:* Take a break from social media for a day or, God forbid, a week. Use this time to observe how much better you feel when you're not comparing yourself to others. Replace your social media time with activities that enrich your life, such as exercise, reading or spending time with loved ones.

♦ *The news headlines challenge:* Set a timer for five minutes. Read today's news headlines on your preferred website (don't click through to articles). List each headline in two columns: zone 1, 'Can I directly influence this?', and zone 2, 'Outside my control'. Notice how the zone 2 column is likely full while the zone 1 control column is nearly empty. This isn't about avoiding important issues — it's about recognising where your energy is most productively spent. Focus on local actions you can take rather than global problems you can't solve.

♦ *Mindful breathing:* Spend five to ten minutes each day practising mindful breathing. This exercise helps redirect attention from racing thoughts and worries to the present moment, grounding you in what you can control — your breath and your immediate surroundings. (I look more at the benefits of mindful breathing, including nasal breathing, in chapter 10.)

♦ *Attentional audit exercise:* Grab a blank page and write out a list of categories for how you spend your time, including work or purposeful activity, social media, TV or streaming, ruminating or worrying in your own head, exercise/movement, meaningful connections, and hobbies or meaningful activities. Now estimate how much time you spent on each category in the last 24 hours. Finally, sketch this as a heat map, using circles of red or orange for activities of high attention, and blue or green circles for low-attention activities. Make sure the size of the circles reflects the time spent. Are you happy with your heat map? If you have a partner and/or kids, this activity is worthwhile doing it together, and then using your heat maps as discussion prompts for what makes a meaningful life.

Figure 3.1 shows an example of what a heatmap from a mentally healthy person could look like as opposed to someone who is suffering from depression or anxiety.

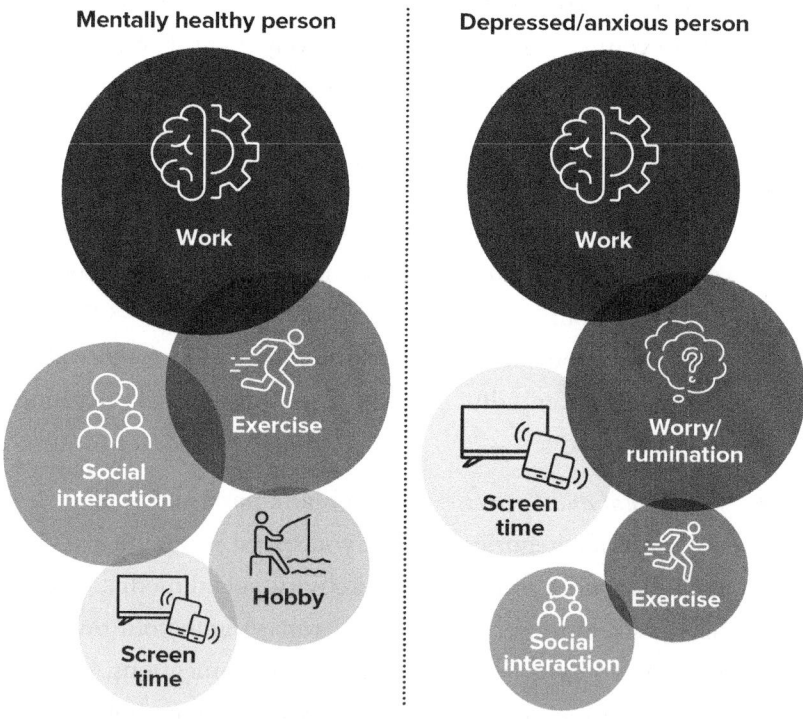

Figure 3.1: Mentally healthy heatmap vs depressed/ anxious heatmap

Applying control orientation

Let's bring this idea of control into focus with a personal example of mine.

When I was told I needed open-heart surgery, I was handed a real-life challenge. This was no metaphorical test. This was about a general anaesthetic, having my chest sawn open and a full-on six-hour operation that required my heart and lungs to be by-passed. But as mentioned in the previous chapter, rather than worrying about it, I reframed it as a challenge. I decided my surgery was a worthy opponent, and something to train for. I was able to do this, not because I'm mentally tough, but because I had paid attention to the right things.

Controlling my attitude: From threat to challenge

I made a conscious decision not to see my upcoming heart operation as a looming threat, but rather as an opportunity — a serious opponent in the ring. I've had boxing and karate fights before, and I viewed this in the same vein. Sure, I wasn't fighting another person this time — I was dancing with a scalpel — but the mindset was the same.

Physiologically, this matters. As discussed in chapter 2, when we perceive something as a challenge, we activate the SAM axis, which gives us a surge of adrenaline and readiness. View it as a threat, and the HPA axis fires up instead — bringing cortisol, immune suppression and a fog of anxiety. Choosing to see surgery as a challenge helped me stay focused and energised and, crucially, kept my stress chemistry from turning me into a nervous wreck.

Controlling my actions: Training for the bus

My surgeon warned me that open-heart surgery is like being hit by a bus. So I figured, if I'm going to be hit by a bus, I'd better damn well prepare for it.

I adjusted my training program to be surgery-specific. This included Norwegian 4×4s to improve cardiovascular fitness and strength of my heart, zone 2 endurance work to build metabolic flexibility, and strength training to build muscular robustness. (I provide more details on these exercise protocols in chapter 7.) I also dialled in my diet, improved my sleep and treated my lifestyle like I was preparing for a title fight.

Controlling recovery: Post-surgical peak performance

Now that I've thankfully come through the other side (as I write this I'm six days post-surgery and just home from hospital), I've maintained the same mindset. I've taken charge of my recovery, using red and near-infrared light therapy (more on that in chapter 9) and supplementing daily with collagen to stimulate tissue repair. I've also started with some gentle exercise and am creating a plan to slowly but steadily ramp up my physical training again.

I'm not waiting for my body to heal. I'm helping it, as much as my current circumstances allow. I am fortunate to have the time and resources to help with this, but that's what control orientation is all about: acting where you can, and not wasting energy where you can't.

The science of self-control: Marshmallows, lifelong success, and the Stoic mind

Let's rewind to the 1970s, to a study so iconic it's practically a rite of passage in psych textbooks: the marshmallow experiment. In this well-known study, Walter Mischel offered preschoolers a choice — one marshmallow now, or two (or a pretzel, if they preferred) if they could wait a few minutes. Some devoured the treat in seconds; others squirmed, sang, covered their eyes or stared at the wall to resist temptation for the required 15 minutes.

What made this study legendary wasn't just the cute antics. Years later, Mischel's PhD students followed up on the original participants. The kids who delayed gratification and didn't eat the marshmallow — those little marshmallow Jedi — grew up to become more academically successful, socially competent and physically healthier. Their SAT scores were higher. They had fewer issues with substance abuse. In other words, in these studies, self-control in childhood was a better predictor of life outcomes than IQ.

The marshmallow experiments from the 1970s have been criticised for not containing a large and diverse enough sample size. So let's fast-forward to the Dunedin Multidisciplinary Health & Development Study (or simply the Dunedin Study) — one of the most ambitious longitudinal studies ever conducted. This 40-year epic followed over 1000 individuals from birth in 1972 New Zealand through to adulthood. The findings? Self-control was the single best predictor of success across the board — health, wealth, parenting skills and law-abiding behaviour — regardless of IQ or socioeconomic background.

And what did they find about those who had lower self-control as kids? They were more likely to smoke, become teenage parents, drop out of school, struggle financially, and have poorer physical and mental health. Self-control wasn't just a 'nice to have' — it was the golden thread running through a successful life.

All of this aligns beautifully with the Stoic philosophy and the hardiness research covered so far in this book. The Stoics would have nodded knowingly, because mastering yourself has always been the ultimate form of strength.

What's now clear from the research is that self-control is an umbrella construct that bridges concepts and measurements from different disciplines, such as self-regulation, impulsivity, conscientiousness, executive function, self-regulation, delay of gratification, inattention, hyperactivity and willpower. Neuroscientists have shown that self-control is an executive function that occurs in the brain's frontal cortex and, critically, acts like a muscle. Just like a muscle, you need to 'use it or lose it' with your self-control, and it can be developed.

Even more exciting, developing your self-control isn't just about willpower or white-knuckling your way through temptation. Modern research shows it's also about strategy. Studies show people with high self-control aren't constantly battling urges. Instead, they've formed habits that remove the friction. They avoid temptations, automate decisions and anchor their actions in goals.

According to the work of psychologist Angela Duckworth and others, beneficial habits mediate the link between self-control and success. In other words, it's not about suppressing every doughnut craving, but about building a routine that makes healthy eating automatic.

Building your self-control muscle

If you're still picturing self-control as some stiff-upper-lip, white-knuckle exercise in denying yourself joy, relax. The science tells a different story. People with high self-control don't rely on grit. They rely on systems. They've engineered their environments, routines and thought patterns so they don't need to constantly battle themselves.

Let's break down four of the best-researched self-control strategies, with practical examples for real life — that is, the sweaty, tempting, modern chaos we actually live in.

Situation selection: Win before the battle begins

Want to eat better? Don't stock your pantry like it's a vending machine. This strategy is about designing your environment to minimise temptation before it even hits you. For example:

- Don't want to eat biscuits? Don't buy biscuits. Simple, brutal, effective.

- Want to exercise more? Sign up for a class that charges you if you don't show up.

- Need better sleep? Charge your phone in another room. No doomscrolling allowed.

- Have a work deadline? Turn off your damned phone and email and do some deep work, rather than procrastinating and getting distracted.

Stoic translation: Don't test your willpower against a cookie at 10 pm. Control the battlefield.

Attentional deployment: Point your flashlight wisely

This is about redirecting your focus away from the unhelpful and toward the helpful. For example:

- Craving junk food? Distract yourself with a five-minute walk or a glass of water. Cravings are like waves — they rise and fall.

- Struggling to start a workout? Put on your gym gear and just stretch for five minutes. Attention begets action.

- Feeling overwhelmed? Instead of staring at your endless to-do list, start a two-minute breathing exercise. It changes your physiological state faster than you think.

Stoic translation: Attention is your mental currency — spend it wisely.

Cognitive reappraisal: Rethink the story you're telling yourself

This is about changing the meaning of the temptation or challenge. It's mental judo: using your opponent's energy against them. Ways to change the narrative include the following:

- 'Skipping the gym today won't matter' becomes 'Every session is a positive action for my future self'.

- 'I deserve this chocolate after the day I've had' becomes 'This chocolate isn't going to undo my boss's email — it's going to undo my goals'.

- 'I'm too stressed to meditate' becomes 'Which is exactly why I need to'.

Stoic translation: You can't always control what happens, but you can control the frame you give it.

Inhibitory control: The last line of defence

When all else fails, it's time to pull the emergency brake. This is pure willpower and, yes, that's finite. However, it's there for when you really need it. Try these last-ditch tactics:

◆ Throw the remaining bag of crisps in the bin (yes, even if they are 'guilt-free' kale chips).

◆ Walk away from a stressful conversation before you say something that belongs in a therapy session.

◆ Choose to close that streaming service and sleep, even when your brain says 'just one more episode'.

Stoic translation: Sometimes you just have to say no. Even when your inner toddler is screaming yes.

Putting it all together: Control over your thoughts, actions and responses

At the heart of psychological hardiness is a sense of control — the belief that you can influence your life through your thoughts, actions and responses. But this control is about more than manipulating external events; it's also about managing where you direct your attention and using proven strategies to direct your actions towards the path of Aretê. By choosing to shine the flashlight of your attention on what you can control, you can help free yourself from the trap of anxiety and depression, which can stem from worrying about uncontrollable aspects of life. Then, you can get into action mode and perform behaviours that take you towards the person you want to be, rather than away from that person.

(continued)

As LaFreniere and Newman's study on untrue worries revealed, most of what we fear never comes to pass. Redirecting attention toward actionable steps, gratitude and what you can control builds hardiness, promotes wellbeing and fosters a healthier, happier life. By combining modern psychological insights with timeless Stoic wisdom, you can cultivate a mindset that is not only resilient but also deeply rooted in the power of focused attention.

So let's say your goal is to improve your health through regular morning workouts. Here's how you'd use all four self-control muscle building strategies from this chapter to take yourself down the path of Aretê towards a better you:

- *Situation selection:* Choose a gym on your commute. Set out your clothes the night before.

- *Attentional deployment:* Focus on how good you'll feel afterwards, not how early you need to get up.

- *Cognitive reappraisal:* Reframe the session as a gift to your future self, rather than a chore.

- *Inhibitory control:* When the alarm goes off, don't negotiate—just get up. Blend this with a situation selection technique by putting your alarm clock on the other side of the room so you have to get out of bed to turn it off. And now you're up!

Apply this same framework to nutrition, stress, recovery, screen time or any habit you want to build (or break). With enough practice, these strategies become automatic—and that's when self-control stops being an effort and starts being your default.

4
Fully commit to life

Life is never made unbearable by circumstances,
but only by lack of meaning and purpose

Viktor Frankl

When I ask people what they value in life, many respond with platitudes about family, career, or health and fitness — yet their daily habits tell a different story. Much of their time is consumed by mindless scrolling, binge-watching and media consumption that leaves them passive spectators in their own lives. If I were to chart their week by hour, I'd likely see more time spent on streaming services and social media than on activities aligned with those supposed commitments.

This isn't a simple case of hypocrisy — it's a symptom of a deeper disconnection that's driven by our dopamine-fuelled world of instant gratification. The commitment component of hardiness isn't about what you *say* matters to you; it's about how fully engaged you are in your life, how deeply you connect with a sense of purpose and how actively you invest in your own wellbeing. These three elements — engaged presence, meaningful purpose and self-stewardship — form the foundation of a commitment orientation that builds psychological strength and resilience.

In this chapter, I explore why commitment matters so profoundly for hardiness and how it differs from simple determination. I also offer practical ways to cultivate commitment even when life feels overwhelming, drawing wisdom from Stoic philosophers, Holocaust survivors and modern psychologists to help you develop a commitment orientation that withstands life's inevitable challenges and ultimately leads you to a life of flourishing.

But first, we need to confront a troubling reality about modern life that makes commitment increasingly difficult to maintain.

The passive consumer problem

When the hell did the purpose of life become about being entertained?

I'm genuinely curious about this. Somewhere along the way, we've sleepwalked into a bizarre arrangement where too many of us spend the majority of our free time within the confines of four walls, faces illuminated by glowing rectangles, consuming content created by others. According to DataReportal, the average Australian or American now spends between six and seven hours a day staring at screens — that's more time than many people spend sleeping.

This isn't just a harmless pastime; it's a fundamental shift in how humans engage with existence. We've transformed from active participants in life to passive consumers of it. Rather than creating memories, we're watching other people's highlight reels. Instead of having conversations, we're scrolling through comment sections. In place of skills developed through practice, we have algorithms suggesting the next video.

I enjoy a good Netflix series as much as anyone and I'm not for one minute suggesting we all become ascetic monks who renounce modern conveniences. But something is profoundly unsettling about the sheer volume of life now spent as spectators rather than participants. Entertainment has its place, but when it becomes the primary orientation of our existence, something vital is lost.

The word 'entertainment' comes (via France) from the Latin *inter* (among) and tenére (to hold). To entertain means 'to hold among' — to occupy someone's attention temporarily. It was never meant to be a life purpose. It was designed to be a brief respite from the real business of living.

And what is that real business? It's creating, connecting, contributing, experiencing, learning, achieving and growing — all the active verbs that make a life worth living when we reach its end. These actions require commitment, which brings me to a fundamental truth about hardiness: passive consumers break easily under pressure, while committed participants develop the strength to endure.

Psychological anchoring: Resetting your expectations

Let's run a thought experiment.

Imagine you live in medieval England. No antibiotics. No central heating. No hot showers. No electricity. No shops. You just have mud, cold, the constant struggle for survival and the concern that the Vikings (or some other invaders) may come at any moment.

Now imagine coming from that era and waking up in your modern life — electricity, clean running water, food on demand, climate control, cars and public transport, TV, computers and mobile phones, as well as safety and security. No doubt you'd see your life as an outrageous paradise.

But to you, now, it's just Monday. The wi-fi's lagging. The coffee's not hot enough. The damned public transport is late and you have a day full of meetings and catching up on work that you're behind on.

This is psychological anchoring. We evaluate our life and calibrate our expectations based on our experiences. If you don't anchor deliberately, the baseline drifts toward entitlement.

The extraordinary gift we take for granted

Scientists estimate your odds of being born, as you, at approximately one in 400 trillion — a number so vast it's essentially incomprehensible. This is due to the interplay of all the variables that needed to combine to arrive at you. So the real miracle goes deeper: every single one of your ancestors, stretching back through millions of years, had to survive long enough to reproduce. One prehistoric ancestor failing to outrun a predator, one medieval forebear succumbing to plague, one great-grandparent not surviving war — any single break in that impossibly long chain, and you wouldn't exist.

This isn't motivational fluff. It's mathematical reality: you've already won the most improbable lottery imaginable. Yet we too often treat our existence as mundane, owed to us, barely worth noticing as we scroll through our phones in climate-controlled comfort.

This is why I have 'Memento Mori' tattooed on my arm. Roughly translating from the Latin as 'Remember, you will die', this is an ancient Stoic reminder that death is inevitable. Marcus Aurelius, the Roman emperor and Stoic philosopher, reminded himself of it frequently in his personal diary to keep him humble and focused on what matters. I glance at my tattoo daily, not as a morbid obsession, but as a reminder of how incredibly lucky I am to be alive at all—and it's a game-changer.

The solution to passive consumption isn't simply doing more—it's fundamentally shifting how you perceive and engage with existence. This transformation begins with three psychological states that, when combined, create a powerful catalyst for genuine engagement.

The alchemy of gratitude, awe and curiosity

How do we shift from passive consumption to active commitment? I believe the transformation begins with three psychological states that, when combined, create a powerful catalyst for engagement: gratitude, awe and curiosity.

Gratitude: The foundation

In 1995, as I was travelling through India, a chance encounter with a man afflicted by both leprosy and elephantiasis—hand outstretched for money—stopped me in my tracks. As I gave him some coins, something in my brain clicked: *Remember this moment. Every time you feel sorry for yourself, remember this man. What has he ever done to deserve his suffering when you are perfectly healthy?*

That encounter gave me the gift of perspective—and gratitude. For 30 years since, I've practised daily gratitude not as a spiritual exercise but as a recognition of statistical absurdity—that I exist at all in perfect health while others suffer through no fault of their own.

I truly believe that focusing on gratitude is a very powerful way to shift the flashlight of attention from what we lack or fear to what we have. In turn, this changes our mindset.

In today's world, where we are exposed to thousands of advertising messages each week, we are constantly reminded of what we do not have — whether it's material possessions, status or experiences. This focus on deficiency creates a sense of scarcity, driving feelings of dissatisfaction and low mood. Social media compounds this effect by encouraging us to compare ourselves to others' curated highlights, leading to upwards social comparison and feelings of inadequacy.

Gratitude offers a powerful counterbalance to these negative influences. Research has shown that regularly practising gratitude has a range of benefits, including increased happiness, reduced depression and anxiety, improved relationships, and even better physical health. A 2003 study by psychologists Robert Emmons and Michael McCullough, for example, found that individuals who kept a gratitude journal reported higher levels of wellbeing, better sleep and lower levels of stress.

By choosing to focus on what you already have, rather than on what you lack, you can shift your attention away from scarcity and toward abundance. This simple shift in focus can dramatically improve your outlook on life, reduce anxiety and increase resilience in the face of adversity.

Gratitude isn't just a warm fuzzy feeling — it's also a perspective shift that can change how you interact with reality. When you truly grasp the incalculable odds against your very existence, gratitude becomes the only rational response to being alive.

Awe: The expander

While gratitude grounds us in appreciation, awe expands our perspective. Awe is that sense of vastness that makes you feel small yet connected to something larger. It's what happens when you gaze at star-filled skies, stand at the edge of the Grand Canyon, or contemplate the unfathomable complexity of a single living cell.

Research by Dacher Keltner at the University of California, Berkeley, shows that experiencing awe has remarkable effects on our psychology. In *Awe: The New Science of Everyday Wonder and How It Can Transform Your Life*, Keltner details how awe makes us more generous, more humble, more creative and more satisfied with life. It literally expands our perception of time, with people who experience awe reporting feeling less rushed and more available to others.

When you combine awe with gratitude, psychological magic starts to happen.

Sometimes I turn on a tap and think, *Jeez, running water—how cool is that shit?* Have you ever really thought about all that needs to happen just for you to have fresh, clean running water? The infrastructure, the purification processes, the people monitoring water quality, the engineering marvels of indoor plumbing—all of this working seamlessly so you can hydrate yourself without trekking to a river or well.

Other times, I'll flip a light switch and think, *Faark—how ridiculously awesome is electricity?* This invisible force, harnessed through human ingenuity, powering devices that would seem like magic to anyone living just a couple of hundred years ago.

Then you have innumerable happenings all around you in nature that can be truly awe-inspiring if you just slow down and notice.

These aren't trivial observations. They're moments of reconnection with the extraordinary nature of ordinary life. When practised regularly, this kind of gratitude and awe creates a foundational shift in your relationship with existence — from entitled consumer to grateful participant.

You can begin to see your life not as a series of tasks, problems and acquisitions, but as an extraordinary opportunity to participate in something vast and meaningful. Your perspective shifts from 'I have to' to 'I get to'.

Curiosity: The activator

The third ingredient in this transformative cocktail is curiosity — the inclination to explore, investigate and learn. While gratitude anchors us in appreciation and awe expands our perspective, curiosity propels us into active engagement with the world.

Curious people ask questions. They wonder how things work. They seek deeper understanding. They're interested in other people's experiences and perspectives. They try new things just for shits and giggles.

In a world designed to hold your attention through passive entertainment, curiosity is a radical act. It transforms you from a consumer of content to an asker of questions, from spectator to explorer.

When these three states — gratitude, awe and curiosity — combine, they create a psychological environment where commitment naturally flourishes. You can't help but engage more fully with a life you're profoundly grateful for, perpetually amazed by and endlessly curious about.

Three guides to a life of meaning and purpose

So what does a committed life with meaning and purpose actually look like? Rather than offering my own prescription, I'd like to introduce you to three profound thinkers whose insights on meaning and purpose have stood the test of time, and who have massively influenced my approach to life: a Stoic philosopher, a Holocaust survivor and a modern researcher on human flourishing.

Seneca: Commitment to being useful

The ancient Roman Stoic philosopher Seneca articulated a vision of a purposeful life centred on usefulness to others. Here's his take from his collection of essays known as *Dialogues*:

> *The duty of a man is to be useful to his fellow men; if possible, to be useful to many of them; failing this, to be useful to a few; failing this, to be useful to his neighbours, and, failing them, to himself: for when he helps others, he advances the general interests of mankind. Just as he who makes himself a worse man does harm not only to himself but to all those to whom he might have done good if he had made himself a better one, so he who deserves well of himself does good to others by the very fact that he is preparing what will be of service to them.*

For Seneca, life wasn't about personal achievement or accumulation. It was about usefulness to the human community. Notice the pragmatic flexibility in his guidance. If you can't be useful to many, be useful to a few. If not even that, then be useful to your immediate neighbours or at least to yourself. In all cases, however, act with the understanding that self-improvement isn't just for you; it also prepares you to be of service to others.

This perspective on purpose in life is fundamentally social. It recognises that humans exist in networks of relationships and that meaning emerges from contributing to the wellbeing of those networks. It's not about grand gestures or world-changing missions (though these aren't excluded); it's about consistent usefulness within your little corner of the universe.

Viktor Frankl: Commitment to meaning-making

Viktor Frankl offers a different but complementary perspective on meaning and purpose. As a psychiatrist who survived the horrors of Auschwitz and three other Nazi concentration camps, Frankl had a unique vantage point on what sustains human resilience under extreme conditions.

In his profoundly moving book *Man's Search for Meaning* — which had a transformative effect on me when I first read it as a 17 year old — Frankl observed that prisoners who maintained a sense of meaning were more likely to survive the camps. His experience led him to develop logotherapy, an approach centred on the human search for meaning.

Frankl concluded that life has no inherent meaning other than what we give it. No 'purpose fairy' arrives to assign significance to our existence. Instead, Frankl believed that meaning is something we must actively create through three primary avenues:

1. what we give to the world (creative work, contributions)

2. what we take from the world (experiences, relationships, beauty)

3. the attitude we take toward unavoidable suffering.

For Frankl, meaning and purpose wasn't about attaching yourself to a particular outcome or goal, but about accepting responsibility for finding meaning in whatever circumstances you face. Even in the brutal conditions of the concentration camps, Frankl discovered that those who maintained a commitment to meaning — whether through helping fellow prisoners, preserving their professional knowledge or simply witnessing the human experience — fared better than those who lost this sense of purpose.

Corey Keyes: Commitment to flourishing

Our third guide to meaningful commitment is contemporary sociologist and researcher Corey Keyes, whose work on the mental health continuum offers a scientific framework for understanding what contributes to human flourishing.

Keyes has extensively studied what he calls 'flourishing', a state of optimal mental health characterised by both feeling good and functioning well. (So this excludes states gained from drinking lots of alcohol or snorting lots of cocaine, for example — you might feel amazing in the moment, but you're highly unlikely to be functioning well!) According to Keyes's research, flourishing individuals exhibit high levels of emotional, psychological and social wellbeing.

What's particularly striking about Keyes's work is his finding that mental health isn't simply the absence of mental illness. You can be free of diagnosable disorders yet still be 'languishing' — going through the motions of life without engagement, purpose or satisfaction (and just that feeling of 'blah'). Conversely, you can face significant challenges, including a diagnosable mental health condition, yet still be 'flourishing' if certain psychological and social needs are met.

Keyes identifies several dimensions that contribute to flourishing, including:

♦ *Purpose in life:* Having goals and a sense of direction.

♦ *Personal growth:* Continued development and openness to new experiences.

♦ *Autonomy:* Self-determination and ability to resist social pressures.

♦ *Environmental mastery:* Managing life's complexities effectively.

♦ *Positive relationships:* Having warm, trusting connections with others.

♦ *Self-acceptance:* Maintaining a positive attitude toward oneself, including past life.

From Keyes' perspective, commitment involves actively cultivating these dimensions rather than passively accepting whatever psychological state happens to emerge from your circumstances.

Synthesising a commitment orientation

When we integrate the wisdom of Seneca, Frankl and Keyes, a comprehensive picture of a committed life of meaning and purpose emerges:

♦ *Commitment is social:* It involves being useful to others and contributing to the human community.

♦ *Commitment is creative:* It requires actively creating meaning and purpose rather than expecting to find it from the 'purpose fairy'.

♦ *Commitment is developmental:* It focuses on growth and flourishing rather than mere maintenance or survival.

This multidimensional view of commitment helps explain why it contributes so powerfully to hardiness. When you're committed in this fuller sense — socially engaged, actively creating meaning and oriented toward development — you have deeper resources to draw upon when facing adversity. You're not just resilient in spite of difficulties, but also able to incorporate those difficulties into a larger narrative of purpose and growth.

Commitment to self: The foundation for service

While commitment to something beyond yourself is essential for meaning, you must also be committed to your own health and wellbeing if you are to be effective. This isn't selfishness; it's pragmatism. A healthier, stronger, more balanced you will be more effective in whatever you're committed to, and be a better all-round human being.

Think of this as the 'oxygen mask principle': on airplanes, you're instructed to secure your own mask before helping others. This isn't because your life is more valuable; it's because you can't help anyone if you've passed out from lack of oxygen.

Similarly, neglecting your physical and mental health ultimately diminishes your capacity to be useful, to create meaning and to flourish. Self-care isn't separate from commitment, but is an essential component of it.

In part II of this book, I explore physiological hardiness in depth, examining evidence-based approaches to optimising your physical health as a foundation for psychological resilience. For now, remember that genuine commitment includes a commitment to your own wellbeing — not as an end in itself, but as the foundation for everything else you care about.

Building your commitment muscle

Like other aspects of hardiness, commitment isn't a fixed trait. Instead, it's a capacity that can be developed through deliberate practice. In this section, I outline some evidence-based exercises to strengthen your commitment orientation.

The gratitude-awe-curiosity practice

Start building the three transformative states of gratitude, awe and curiosity into your daily experience with the following:

◆ *Daily gratitude:* Each morning, identify three specific things you're grateful for. Go beyond obvious blessings to notice the things that normally go unappreciated, such as running water or electricity.

◆ *Awe hunting:* Once a day, deliberately seek out an experience of awe. This might involve spending five minutes immersed in nature, going camping in a place with low ambient light and looking at stars, watching a nature video, listening to powerful music, watching an ant colony or simply paying closer attention to the remarkable complexity of ordinary things.

◆ *Curiosity questions:* At the end of each day, write down three questions about things you encountered through the day but don't fully understand. They could be about how something works, why someone behaved a certain way or what might happen if you tried something different.

The usefulness inventory

For one week, go to work (or about your daily business) with an intention to be useful to others. Keep a daily log of ways you've been useful, from small kindnesses to significant contributions. At the end of the week, review your inventory and ask yourself:

- Which acts of usefulness felt most meaningful to me?
- What skills or qualities enabled me to be useful in these ways?
- What constraints or obstacles limited my usefulness?
- How might I expand my usefulness in areas that felt most meaningful?

This exercise helps you identify your natural channels of contribution and the conditions that support or hinder them.

The meaning framework

Spend time reflecting on each of Frankl's three pathways to meaning, answering these questions:

- *Creation:* What can you create or contribute that has value to others? How might you expand this contribution?
- *Experience:* What aspects of life do you most fully appreciate or enjoy? How can you more frequently or deeply engage with these experiences?
- *Attitude:* What unavoidable difficulties are you facing? What attitude toward these challenges would infuse them with meaning? Can you lean into the shit-sandwich from the universe, and use it as an opportunity to practise a virtue or sharpen your character, as the Stoics encourage us to? Or, even better, embrace it as your worthy opponent?!

Values exercise

You may already be clear on your values. If not, a list of values is provided in table 4.1 (overleaf), which you can add to if you like.

Select ten or so values that resonate with you or that you admire deeply in others. Next, whittle that list down to five core values that really resonate with you. Here are some things to think about when you select your top five values:

◆ Ideally, they will act as a compass, guiding you when you need to make decisions.

◆ They should be able to be linked to behaviours or actions that you can do.

◆ Ideally, these are the things you'd like to be remembered for when your number's up.

Table 4.1: Which values resonate with you?

Acceptance	Equanimity	Kindness
Accountability	Fairness	Leadership
Adventure	Fitness	Love
Altruism	Flexibility	Mindfulness
Assertiveness	Forgiveness	Optimism
Authenticity	Friendliness	Patience
Commitment	Fun	Respect
Compassion	Generosity	Responsibility
Connection	Gratitude	Safety
Contribution	Growth	Skilfulness
Courage	Health	Supportiveness
Creativity	Honesty	Trust
Curiosity	Humour	Vulnerability
Engagement	Independence	Wisdom

That was the easy part — the tricky bit is living true to your values, so here's the important bit. Ideally, write your values on your bathroom mirror so that you see them every day. When you wake up in the morning (before you look at your goddamned phone), do what the Stoic philosopher and Roman Emperor Marcus Aurelius used to do: think about your day ahead, and who you want to be. What values do you want to express? Select one or two from your list of five, and think about how you might live in accordance with them. That evening, when you go to bed, reflect on your day. What were your plans, and how did you go? If you went well, nice work. If you forgot or behaved like a dickhead, resolve to do better tomorrow.

Here's the beauty of writing your values on your bathroom mirror: if you forget to do this exercise when you first wake up, when you go into the bathroom, you'll be triggered to do it. And in the evening, you'll be triggered to reflect. You can also do this exercise when brushing your teeth or even sitting on the loo — instead of looking at your phone!

Here's another exercise linked to values and tied into behaviours I have found to be useful. Imagine you are 80 years old and looking back on your life to this point (that is, up to today). Complete these three sentences:

◆ 'I spent too much time worrying about ... '

◆ 'I did not spend enough time doing things such as ... '

◆ 'If I could go back in time, what I'd do differently is ... '

This question can really help you get clear on the tweaks you should make in order to live a meaningful life. The key is making the tweaks now so you don't end up with regrets later. Yes, the tweaks will be hard. However, regrets at the end of your life will be harder — so choose your hard!

The tombstone statement

The previous exercise will help prepare you for the ultimate commitment exercise — writing your own 'tombstone statement'. This should be a concise expression (ideally 10 words or fewer) of how you want to be remembered and the impact you hope to have had on your little corner of the universe.

A tombstone statement isn't a career goal or achievement target. It's an articulation of your core purpose and the difference you want your existence to make. I first created my tombstone statement back in my days flying helicopters in the British Armed Forces, after a very unfortunate situation when eight colleagues (including two very good friends) got killed in a helicopter crash out in the Gulf. I'll not go into detail, but I was at a crossroads at the time — I had signed up for an eight-year contract (short career commission) that was coming to an end and was offered the chance to extend to a full career commission. The circumstances of that incident helped make my decision, because I didn't want someone else to be in control of my destiny.

At the time, I was flying as a Search and Rescue crew member in Scotland as well as completing a part-time master's degree in nutrition at Glasgow University. I already had a master's degree in exercise science and, given my secondary role was Sports and Fitness Officer, I took it upon myself to write a wellbeing newsletter for the Squadron. One day an older Chief Petty Officer stopped me and thanked me for writing the newsletter, telling me it was most helpful for him and his family, and his kids even read it. As I walked away, I had a lightbulb moment about my future career. I went home and wrote my tombstone statement: 'Military man turned educator, helping people become better versions of themselves.'

Your tombstone statement can be about work or your personal life or, ideally, a combination of both. The key is to keep it short and to orient it around how you can be of service. Here are some further examples:

- ◆ 'She helped others discover their own strength.'

- ◆ 'He found beauty in broken places and shared it.'

- ◆ 'She built bridges where others saw only divides.'

- ◆ 'He was a committed father, loyal friend and useful employee.'

Your tombstone statement ideally serves as a commitment compass, helping you evaluate whether your daily choices are aligned with your deeper purpose. When faced with decisions, you can ask: 'Which option brings me closer to embodying my tombstone statement?'

This isn't about perfection or rigidity, and your statement may evolve over time as your understanding deepens. The point is to have a consciously chosen direction rather than drifting with whatever currents happen to be strongest in the moment.

Purpose isn't just a nice-to-have. It's your rocket fuel. When you know your 'why', the 'how' might suck, but you'll be much more likely to do it anyway. Purpose keeps you in the fight when your body says stop and your brain says quit. Without it? You're just drifting — easy to knock over, hard to motivate. Want to live fully? Get a reason bigger than yourself.

Putting it all together: The courage to matter

At its core, commitment requires the courage to believe that what you do matters—that your choices, contributions and attitudes make a meaningful difference in the world. This isn't always easy in an age of global challenges and algorithmic distraction that can make individual efforts seem insignificant.

But remember those one-in-400-trillion odds of your existence. You've already beaten astronomical probabilities just by being here. Your life isn't an accident or an afterthought, but a remarkable opportunity to write your place in the human story.

The passive consumption of entertainment and media offers a temporary escape from the weight of this responsibility, but it can never provide the deep satisfaction that comes from full engagement. True hardiness emerges from commitment to saying 'yes' to life with all its complexities and challenges.

As you move through the remaining chapters, remember that commitment is an important foundation for everything else. Without a fundamental 'yes' to life, the other components have nothing to build upon.

So let your gratitude for existing fuel your commitment to engaging fully. Let your sense of awe expand your vision of what's possible. Let your curiosity drive you toward deeper understanding and more meaningful participation.

You've won the cosmic lottery. Start fucking acting like it.

5

Create meaningful connections

For friendship is nothing else than an accord in all things, human and divine, conjoined with mutual goodwill and affection, and I am inclined to think that, with the exception of wisdom, no better thing has been given to man by the immortal gods.

Cicero

How we approach health optimisation reveals something interesting. Many of us will meticulously track our steps, carbs and sleep cycles, but when it comes to social connection — which research shows is equally vital — we tend to treat it as an afterthought, something that just happens naturally in the background of our busy lives.

Here's the shocking truth: your social relationships might be more predictive of how long you'll live than your cholesterol levels, smoking status or whether you hit the gym regularly. The research is clear, consistent and, frankly, a bit alarming for those of us who occasionally prefer Netflix and solitude over another dinner party.

The evidence is simply too compelling to ignore. So, while the original hardiness model developed by Salvatore Maddi and Suzanne Kobasa (introduced in chapter 1) focused on the three Cs — challenge, control and commitment — I've added connection as the fourth C. This isn't just about having someone to call when you get a flat tire (though that's nice too). It's about a fundamental human need that, when unfulfilled, can actually make you physically sick.

In this chapter, I explore why our brains and bodies are so deeply influenced by our social connections, how loneliness can be as damaging as smoking 15 cigarettes a day (yes, really), and why even the toughest among us crumble without human contact. You'll discover how American POWs in Vietnam used a simple tap code to maintain their sanity and will to live. And, finally, you'll discover a range of practical, evidence-based ways to strengthen your social connections — even if you're an introvert who shudders at the phrase 'networking event'.

Let's dive in.

The survival value of connection: Hardwired for togetherness

Humans are, to put it bluntly, weird animals. We lack the impressive physical attributes of many other species — no razor-sharp claws, no venomous bites and no ability to outrun most predators. What we do have is an extraordinarily social brain that has allowed us to cooperate in ways no other species can match. This social capability isn't just a nice add-on; it's central to how we survived and thrived as a species.

Our ancestors didn't make it through the harsh realities of prehistoric life by being lone wolves. They survived by forming tight-knit groups where they could share resources, divide labour, watch each other's backs and pass down knowledge. Those who were better at maintaining social bonds had a survival advantage, and over thousands of generations, this shaped our biology in profound ways.

Today, we carry those ancient adaptations in our modern bodies. Our brains dedicate enormous resources to social cognition, including reading facial expressions, understanding others' intentions and navigating complex social hierarchies. We get an actual neurochemical reward (primarily oxytocin, dopamine and endorphins) when we connect positively with others. This isn't an accident or a quirk; it's evolution. Even the most independent among us typically maintain some form of meaningful social connection, and those who truly don't often pay a steep price in terms of both mental and physical health.

The biology of belonging

When we feel socially connected, our bodies operate differently than when we feel isolated. Research has shown that connected individuals typically show:

- lower levels of circulating stress hormones such as cortisol
- better immune system functioning
- lower inflammation markers
- more efficient cardiovascular functioning
- better sleep quality.

These aren't just comfortable coincidences; they're biological responses that evolved because social connection helped keep us alive. Our bodies react to social isolation as a threat because, throughout our evolutionary history, being separated from the group often meant serious danger.

This is why solitary confinement is considered among the most severe forms of punishment. The human mind literally starts to unravel without social contact. As former prisoner of war and senator John McCain once said about his time in isolation, 'It crushes your spirit and weakens your resistance more effectively than any other form of mistreatment.' McCain endured brutal physical torture, yet identified isolation as the most devastating punishment.

The dark side of disconnection: The loneliness epidemic

Before we go further, let's clarify something important: being alone isn't the same as being lonely. Solitude can be restorative and valuable when it's chosen. Loneliness, on the other hand, is the distressing feeling that occurs when your social connections don't meet your needs. You can feel lonely in a crowded room if you don't feel meaningfully connected to anyone there.

Unfortunately, loneliness appears to be on the rise in many developed nations. A 2018 survey by Cigna found that nearly half of Americans report sometimes or always feeling alone or left out, with younger generations (gen Z and millennials) reporting higher levels of loneliness than older people — contrary to the stereotype of the isolated senior citizen.

This trend predates the COVID-19 pandemic, which only amplified the issue. The reasons are complex; however, changing family structures, increased geographic mobility, the rise of digital communication replacing in-person interaction, longer work hours and community disintegration all play a role.

The research on how this social isolation affects health is both extensive and sobering—so much so that former US Surgeon General Vivek Murthy called loneliness a growing health epidemic. This isn't hyperbole. The health consequences are substantial enough that the United Kingdom actually appointed a 'minister for loneliness' in 2018 to address the issue as a public health crisis.

Let's look at some key findings:

◆ A 2010 meta-analysis by Julianne Holt-Lunstad and colleagues of 148 studies with over 300 000 participants found that having strong social relationships was associated with a 50 per cent increased likelihood of survival compared to those with weak social connections. This effect is comparable to quitting smoking and larger than the impact of addressing obesity or physical inactivity.

◆ A further review from Holt-Lunstad in 2015 found social isolation increases the risk of premature death from all causes by 29 per cent, and loneliness increases it by 26 per cent.

◆ Numerous studies report that lonely people show poorer immune function, increased inflammation and higher blood pressure.

◆ Social isolation is associated with about a 30 per cent increased risk of stroke and coronary heart disease.

◆ Loneliness is linked to a 40 per cent increased risk of developing dementia.

Researcher John Cacioppo points out that loneliness isn't a minor discomfort. It's a serious threat to health and wellbeing. Indeed, the

2010 analysis from Holt-Lunstad highlights that the health impact of chronic loneliness is roughly equivalent to smoking 15 cigarettes per day. Yet while most of us wouldn't dream of lighting up a cigarette, we might think nothing of going days with minimal human contact.

Understanding how loneliness gets under our skin

So how exactly does social isolation translate into physical illness? Numerous pathways have been identified through extensive studies, including those by Cacioppo, Cole, Hawkley and others. These pathways include the following:

◆ *Stress response system activation:* Feeling socially isolated activates our body's stress response systems, including the hypothalamic–pituitary–adrenal (HPA) axis (introduced in chapter 2) and the sympathetic nervous system. This leads to increased levels of cortisol and catecholamines (adrenaline and noradrenaline) — chemicals that are useful in short bursts but harmful when chronically elevated.

◆ *Immune dysfunction:* Prolonged loneliness alters gene expression in immune cells. Research by Steven Cole and colleagues from 2007 found that chronically lonely individuals show increased expression of genes involved in inflammation and decreased expression of genes involved in antiviral responses. This 'conserved transcriptional response to adversity' (CTRA) leaves people more vulnerable to various diseases.

◆ *Sleep disruption:* Lonely individuals often experience poorer sleep quality, with more micro-awakenings during the night. This impaired sleep further compromises immune function and metabolic processes.

◆ *Behavioural pathways:* Social isolation can lead to unhealthy behaviours as coping mechanisms, including reduced physical activity, poorer diet, increased alcohol consumption and medication non-adherence.

◆ *Cognitive changes:* Chronic loneliness creates hypervigilance for social threats, which can lead to negative interpretations of social interactions. This creates a self-reinforcing cycle, where lonely people become more likely to act in ways that push others away.

What's particularly concerning is that these processes can create a downward spiral. The physiological and psychological effects of loneliness can make social interaction more difficult and less rewarding, leading to further isolation.

The neuroscience of social connection: Your social brain

Our brains devote remarkable resources to processing social information. When neuroscientists examine brain activity, they find that a specific network of brain regions — often called the 'social brain' — activates when we engage in social cognition. These areas include the medial prefrontal cortex, temporoparietal junction, superior temporal sulcus and amygdala.

These neural systems help us recognise faces, interpret expressions, understand others' intentions, experience empathy and navigate complex social relationships. Our brains dedicating so much neural real estate to these functions underscores just how important social connection has been to human survival.

The overlap of physical and social pain

One of the most fascinating discoveries in social neuroscience is that social pain (such as rejection or isolation) activates many of the same brain regions as physical pain. In a groundbreaking study from 2003, Naomi Eisenberger and colleagues found that when people experienced social exclusion during a computer game, they showed increased activity in the dorsal anterior cingulate cortex and anterior insula — the same regions that process the distress of physical pain.

This neural overlap explains why we use physical pain language to describe social hurts ('My heart is broken', 'That was a slap in the face'). This use of language is not just poetic metaphor, but also reflects a shared neurobiological experience. This also helps explain why social isolation can feel so viscerally unpleasant — our brains process it as a genuine threat to our wellbeing, not unlike physical danger.

Neurochemistry of connection

Several neurochemicals play important roles in how we experience social connection:

- ◆ *Oxytocin:* Often called the 'love hormone' or 'cuddle chemical', oxytocin is released during positive social interactions, particularly touch, and promotes bonding and trust. It reduces anxiety and stress responses, partly explaining why hugs can be so calming.

- ◆ *Endorphins:* These natural opioid-like chemicals are released during social laughter and synchronised activities (such as singing together or team sports), creating feelings of pleasure and wellbeing.

- *Dopamine:* This reward neurotransmitter is released during positive social interactions, making us seek out further connection. Interestingly, it's the same system targeted by many addictive substances, suggesting that social connection is inherently rewarding in a similar way.

- *Serotonin:* This mood-regulating neurotransmitter is influenced by social status and belonging. Lower serotonin levels are associated with depression, which can both result from and contribute to social isolation.

Understanding this neurochemistry helps explain why positive social connections feel so good — they literally trigger the brain's reward systems in ways that promote further connection. It's a virtuous cycle built into our biology.

Connection in extremis: The tap code

Perhaps nowhere is the critical importance of human connection more evident than in the stories of prisoners of war (POWs), particularly American POWs held in North Vietnam's infamous Hỏa Lò Prison (the 'Hanoi Hilton' mentioned in chapter 1).

Cut off from the outside world, subjected to torture, malnourished and kept in isolation, these men faced conditions designed to break them psychologically. Their captors knew that humans deprived of social contact become more vulnerable to manipulation and lose their will to resist. But the prisoners developed an ingenious system that allowed them to maintain this most basic of human needs — connection with others.

The 'tap code' was a simple but effective communication method based on a 5×5 grid of letters (excluding K, which was represented by C). By tapping sequences that indicated coordinates on this grid, prisoners could spell out messages to each other through the walls of their cells.

The first set of taps indicated the row (one to five), and the second set indicated the column (also one to five). For example, the letter 'c' would be communicated as one tap, followed by a pause, and then three taps (row one, column three).

This rudimentary communication system became a lifeline. Through it, prisoners shared news, military information, encouragement, jokes and personal stories. They also maintained their sense of community and military structure, with senior officers issuing orders and establishing a code of conduct. They even taught each other poetry, literature and foreign languages through the walls.

As POW and future senator Jeremiah Denton explained:

> *The tap code was an extremely important factor in our ability to resist ... Through it, we established a chain of command, passed news, taught courses on all subjects from mathematics to religion, shared experiences, maintained discipline, and attempted to maintain morale.*

Admiral James Stockdale, the most senior naval officer in captivity (discussed in chapter 1), later wrote that 'the most important thing for survival is communication with someone, even if it's only a wave or a wink, a tap on the wall, or to have a guy put his thumb up. It makes all the difference.'

John McCain, mentioned earlier in this chapter, credited the tap code and the connection it provided with helping him survive, saying, 'I was finding that prayer helped. And I was finding that keeping in touch with my fellow prisoners by tapping on the wall helped.'

The tap code story illustrates a profound truth: human beings will go to extraordinary lengths to maintain social connection, even in the most dehumanising circumstances. Connection isn't a luxury; it's a necessity for psychological survival. Real relationships are your stress buffer, your emotional Kevlar vest. When life kicks your ass, your people will help you get back up — not your follower count, not your likes, your people. They help you see straight when your world tilts sideways. Want to build real resilience? Start by building real relationships.

Beyond survival: The benefits of strong relationships

While avoiding loneliness is important for health, the benefits of social connection extend far beyond improving healthy functioning or avoiding negative outcomes. People with strong social ties experience numerous positive effects to their overall wellbeing:

◆ greater resilience in the face of stress and adversity

◆ higher levels of happiness and life satisfaction

◆ better cognitive functioning as they age

◆ lower rates of anxiety and depression

◆ faster recovery from illness and surgery

◆ greater sense of meaning and purpose in life.

A particularly powerful longitudinal study, the Harvard Study of Adult Development, has followed participants for over 85 years, studying their health trajectories along with their broader lives. Its fourth director, psychiatrist Robert Waldinger, summarised their findings in 2016 simply: 'The clearest message that we get from this 75-year study is this: Good relationships keep us happier and healthier. Period.'

Quality versus quantity: What matters most?

When it comes to social connection, quality generally trumps quantity. Having hundreds of acquaintances or thousands of social media followers doesn't provide the same benefits as having a few close, trusting relationships.

Indeed, in today's digital age, social media has become a significant source of distraction and comparison. While platforms such as Instagram, TikTok and Facebook offer connections, they also promote constant comparison. People often find themselves measuring their lives against the highly curated and often unrealistic portrayals of others. This phenomenon, known as 'upwards social comparison', has been shown to increase feelings of inadequacy, particularly among teenagers and young adults, where it can drive mental health issues.

As an example of this, research by the psychologist Jean Twenge found that increased social media use among teenagers is correlated with higher rates of depression and anxiety. Teenagers who spend more time on their screens are more likely to experience feelings of loneliness and sadness, primarily due to the constant comparison with peers. The research highlights the negative effects of social media on mental health, as individuals focus on external validation and societal expectations rather than their internal locus of control.

In opposition to this, research by anthropologist and psychologist Robin Dunbar suggests that humans can maintain stable social relationships with about 150 people (often called 'Dunbar's number'), but our closest circle—those we can truly count on in times of need—typically consists of only three to five people.

What matters most in these core relationships appears to be:

- *Perceived support:* Believing that help is available if needed.

- *Intimacy:* Being able to share important thoughts and feelings.

- *Reciprocity:* Mutual give and take in the relationship.

- *Consistency:* Regular, reliable contact over time.

This isn't to say that broader social networks aren't valuable. Different types of relationships serve different functions. Close friends and family provide emotional support and intimacy, while more distant connections often provide information, novel perspectives and opportunities. Both are important for a well-rounded social life.

Building your connection muscle

Now you understand why connection matters so profoundly, let's focus on practical, evidence-based strategies to strengthen your social relationships. Like any other aspect of hardiness, connection is a skill that can be developed with intentional practice.

Assessing your current connection status

The statistics outlined through this chapter aren't just abstract research—they're also a wake-up call for your daily life. So, before making changes, start with a quick self-assessment:

- In the last 24 hours, how many meaningful face-to-face conversations did you have?

- When did you last feel truly 'seen and heard' by another person?

- Are your primary social interactions happening through screens or are they face to face?

Now take some time to reflect more deeply on your current social landscape:

- *Quantity:* How many people do you interact with regularly? Do you have enough social contact, or do you often feel isolated?

- *Quality:* How satisfied are you with your relationships? Do you have people you can confide in? Do you feel understood and supported?

- *Diversity:* Does your social network include different types of relationships (family, friends, colleagues, community members) and people with varied backgrounds and perspectives?

- *Balance:* Is there reciprocity in your relationships, or do you find yourself always giving or always receiving?

A universal 'right' answer to these questions doesn't exist, because optimal social connection looks different for everyone. Introverts may thrive with fewer, deeper relationships, while extroverts may need a broader network. The key is whether your social connections meet your personal needs.

Evidence-based strategies for building connection

Now let's get into some practical strategies for boosting connection, starting with face-to-face interaction.

PRIORITISE FACE-TO-FACE INTERACTION

While digital communication can supplement relationships, research shows it doesn't provide the same neurobiological benefits as in-person interaction. A 2017 study from Susan Holtzman and colleagues, for example, found that face-to-face social interaction was significantly associated with wellbeing, while social media use was not.

Here are some practical steps to increase your in-person interactions:

◆ Schedule regular in-person meetups with friends or family.

◆ Join local clubs, classes or volunteer groups.

◆ Consider communal living arrangements or coworking spaces.

◆ Make eye contact and put away phones during in-person interactions.

DEVELOP ACTIVE LISTENING SKILLS

Quality connections require genuine understanding, which comes from good listening. As an example of this, a 2006 study by Shelly Gable and others found that how partners understand and respond to each other's good news significantly affects relationship quality and stability.

Consider the following ways to boost your listening and understanding:

◆ Practise 'active constructive responding' by showing authentic interest when others share good news.

◆ Use the 70/30 rule: listen 70 per cent of the time, speak 30 per cent.

◆ Ask open-ended questions that invite elaboration—for example, replace 'How was your day?' with 'What was the best part of your day?'

◆ Validate others' emotions, even when you don't share their perspective.

◆ Summarise what you've heard to ensure understanding.

PRACTISE VULNERABILITY

Research by social scientist Brené Brown has shown that vulnerability— sharing our authentic thoughts, feelings and struggles—is essential for developing close connections. While it may feel risky, appropriate self-disclosure typically deepens relationships.

Try these practical steps:

◆ Start small with minor disclosures and gradually build trust.

◆ Share both struggles and successes.

◆ Ask for help when you need it (people generally like being helpful).

◆ Express appreciation and affection openly.

MANAGE CONFLICT CONSTRUCTIVELY

All relationships involve conflict at times. Research from psychologists John and Julie Gottman shows that it's not the presence of conflict but how it's handled that determines relationship health.

Consider the following strategies:

◆ Focus on specific behaviours rather than character criticisms.

◆ Use 'I' statements to express your feelings.

- Look for areas of agreement even during disagreements.

- Take breaks when emotions run high, but commit to returning to the conversation.

- Express appreciation for the other person even during disagreements.

CREATE RITUALS OF CONNECTION

Regular routines that promote connection help ensure relationships don't get lost in the busyness of life. Research by Carol Bruess and Judy Pearson found that shared rituals significantly contribute to relationship satisfaction and stability.

Try these practical steps:

- Establish regular check-ins with important people (such as weekly calls and monthly dinners).

- Create traditions around holidays or special events.

- Develop inside jokes or special ways of communicating.

- Share regular activities (for example, walking, cooking or game nights).

CULTIVATE EMPATHY

The ability to understand others' perspectives is crucial for meaningful connection. Studies show that empathy can be deliberately developed through practice.

Here's how:

- Read literary fiction, which has been shown to increase empathy.

- Practise perspective-taking in everyday situations.

- Ask curious questions about others' experiences.

- Pay attention to non-verbal cues in conversations, such as facial expressions and body language.

LEVERAGE TECHNOLOGY WISELY

While not a substitute for in-person interaction, technology can help maintain connections when used intentionally. Research from 2011 by Keith Hampton and colleagues found that internet users had more diverse social networks and more in-person contact than non-users.

Here's how to use social networking wisely:

- Use video calls rather than just text or voice when connecting remotely.

- Share meaningful content rather than just passively scrolling.

- Use technology to plan in-person gatherings.

- Be mindful of how different platforms affect your mood and adjust accordingly.

INVEST IN COMMUNITY

Belonging to communities beyond individual relationships provides important social benefits. Studies show that involvement in community groups is associated with greater wellbeing and reduced depression.

Consider the following ways to get involved in your community:

- Join or create a neighbourhood group.

- Participate in faith communities if spirituality is important to you.

- Volunteer for causes you care about.

- Attend local events and festivals.

Special considerations for different situations

Perhaps you're an introvert or have been through a major life transition and don't feel much like connecting with other people. Here are some extra tips for you.

FOR INTROVERTS

If social interaction depletes your energy, focus on quality over quantity:

- Schedule social time followed by recovery time.

- Choose smaller gatherings over large parties.

- Develop one-on-one relationships.

- Select activities with built-in conversation topics (such as subject-specific classes or organised sports).

AFTER MAJOR LIFE TRANSITIONS

Relocations, job changes, divorces and other transitions can disrupt social networks. Here's how to build them back up:

- Maintain important existing relationships through scheduled contact.

- Say yes to invitations, even when it feels easier to decline.

- Join groups related to your interests in new locations.

- Be patient — it takes time to build real friendships.

Putting it all together: Connection as the fourth C of hardiness

The body of research on social connection is clear and compelling: humans need meaningful social bonds to thrive, not just psychologically but also physically. This is why I've added connection as the fourth C to the traditional hardiness model. Like the other Cs—commitment, control and challenge—connection represents a core psychological resource that helps you weather life's difficulties and emerge stronger.

As with the other hardiness components, connection isn't just a personality trait you either have or don't have. It's a set of skills and attitudes that can be deliberately developed. Even those who feel awkward in social situations or who have experienced relationship disappointments can learn to build healthier, more satisfying connections.

In many ways, connection amplifies the other hardiness factors. Your commitments often involve other people and gain meaning through shared purpose. Having supportive relationships increases your sense of control in difficult situations. And facing challenges alongside others can make those challenges feel more manageable and even growth-promoting.

As we navigate an increasingly complex and often isolating modern world, consciously cultivating connection may be more important than ever. The effort required to build and maintain meaningful relationships is substantial, but so are the rewards—including greater resilience, better health, longer life and, most importantly, the profound satisfaction that comes from being truly known and valued by others.

Remember: we are fundamentally social creatures. Disconnection can make you sick — physically, mentally and emotionally. Want to be truly hardy? Build strong bonds. They're your invisible armour. Your brain, body and mind function best when you're connected to others. This isn't a weakness or a luxury, but is instead the core of your humanity and a powerful source of strength in difficult times. By developing your connection muscle, you're not just improving your health; you're also embracing what makes you human.

PART II
Physiological hardiness

6

Forge the body that's hard to break

We must undergo a hard winter training and not rush into things for which we have not prepared.

Epictetus

We've established that psychological hardiness is critical for navigating life. But mindset alone won't carry you through when your body folds under pressure. If you want to be truly resilient in the modern world, you need more than a great mindset and willpower. You need cells that adapt under fire, a body that bends without breaking, and an internal engine that doesn't melt at the first sign of stress.

Enter physiological hardiness.

This isn't about six-packs or personal-record (PR) deadlifts. It's about building biological systems that respond to stress by getting stronger. Instead of avoiding strain, you can use it as the fuel for adaptation. And at the core of this transformation is a concept

111

more elegant—and more essential—than any supplement stack or wearable.

That concept is hormesis.

What the hell is hormesis?

Hormesis is nature's original self-improvement plan. It's the principle that low doses of stress stimulate growth, adaptation and resilience, while high doses cause damage—and no stress at all leads to stagnation and decline.

Picture a curve that looks like a J or an inverted U, as shown in the figure 6.1. At the bottom left of the curve, you're experiencing no stress, but also no benefit. Flatline. As you climb the curve, you hit the sweet spot, with just enough stress to signal your system to upgrade. But go too far, and the curve drops off. Overdo the ice baths, fasting or ultra-endurance, in other words, and you fall off the cliff. It's not 'more is better', but 'smart is better'.

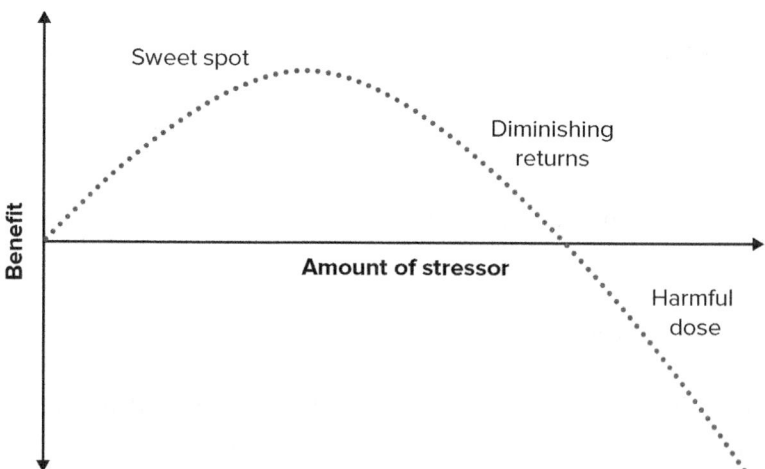

Figure 6.1: The sweet spot of stress and the point of diminishing returns

Hormesis is how your body turns adversity into adaptation.

The origin story: Calabrese, fungi and scientific redemption

While the idea of hormesis has ancient roots, dating back to Paracelsus, a physician and alchemist in the 16th century, it was largely ignored by modern science until the 1970s, when toxicologist Edward Calabrese stumbled across it in the most unlikely place: fungus.

As a young PhD student, Calabrese was studying how tree extracts affected fungal growth. Instead of the expected kill curve, he found something strange: low doses of toxins made the fungi grow faster. Confused but intrigued, he dug through dusty literature and found that others — such as toxicologist Hugo Schulz in the 1880s — had observed the same thing.

Fast-forward to the 1990s, and Calabrese is publishing paper after paper showing this same biphasic response across species and substances. He became the world's foremost champion of hormesis, battling the dominant linear no-threshold (LNT) model of toxicology that insisted any dose of a toxin is bad. Calabrese said, not quite. The dose makes the adaptation.

And then came a defining story from Michigan State University. A graduate student's research had shown transgenerational hormesis in insects, where tiny stressors not only made the insects hardier, but their offspring too. But the student's PhD was rejected. Calabrese stepped in, fought to validate the work, and helped revive one of the most extraordinary findings in resilience biology: hormesis can be inherited.

It's not just your cells that get stronger. It might be your lineage.

Hormesis isn't a hack—it's evolution's signature move

From the moment life emerged, it's been shaped by pressure. Hunger, cold, heat, movement, scarcity and risk weren't bugs in the system. They were the system. Every organism that survived long enough to pass on its genes had to get better at adapting to its environment.

Today, that same stress-adaptation loop exists in everything from yeast to humans. Fruit flies live longer when given tiny doses of radiation. Worms show better memory and mobility after mild oxidative exposure. Plants generate protective antioxidants—polyphenols—when stressed, which in turn trigger hormesis in us when we eat them.

Even our beloved lab mice, when put through moderate fasting or exercise, develop superior metabolic control, stronger mitochondria, and reduced rates of cancer and neurodegeneration.

This isn't fringe biology. It's foundational.

Inside the body: How hormesis builds resilience

Your body has evolved to be tested. Run, lift, sweat, carry—this isn't punishment but programming. Train your body, and you unlock a machine built for hardship. Skip the work, and that machine rusts. Physical resilience isn't about physical looks—it's about being hard to kill. Fit enough to survive. Tough enough to thrive. Hormetic stress does more than toughen you up at the macro level. It also rewires your cells to respond better to threats—down to the mitochondria, DNA repair and gene expression. Let's walk through the mechanisms.

The cell danger response: Threat mode

Every cell has a panic button. When it detects danger—be it a toxin, pathogen or inflammation—it shifts into the cell danger response (CDR). Normal operations stop. Production of adenosine triphosphate (ATP; essentially the energy currency of the body) drops. The cell walls harden. Immune signals go out. It's DEFCON 1 in the cytoplasm.

Over the short-term, this is a vital process. However, if the threat never resolves, the system gets stuck in alert mode. You get chronic fatigue, brain fog, metabolic slowdown and systemic inflammation.

Hormetic stress resets this loop. It mimics a threat just enough to activate the CDR, and then clears it. That 'challenge and release' trains your body to respond and recover.

Mitochondrial hormesis (mitohormesis): Powerhouse training

Mitochondria are often reduced to being known as the 'cellular power plants' because they produce most of the cell's energy. That's cute, but incomplete. They're also stress sensors and adaptation coordinators.

When you fast, sprint or shiver in a cold plunge, your mitochondria temporarily produce more reactive oxygen species (ROS). High ROS = damage. But low ROS = signal. And these signals tell your cells to:

♦ build more mitochondria (mitogenesis)

♦ boost fat metabolism

♦ improve energy efficiency

♦ increase antioxidant defences.

This is mitohormesis, where a controlled pressure results in stronger, more efficient energy systems. It's metabolic weightlifting.

Autophagy: Spring cleaning your cells

Autophagy (literally 'self-eating') is your body's built-in recycling program. This process breaks down damaged organelles, misfolded proteins and cellular debris, preventing mutations, neurodegeneration and metabolic chaos.

Autophagy is also triggered by hormetic stress — including fasting, training and temperature extremes — and allows for deeper recovery and repair.

Without autophagy being triggered, your cells slowly become dysfunctional. Trigger it regularly, and you protect cellular health. Overdo it, and you trigger apoptosis (cell death).

The antioxidant elite: SOD, catalase, glutathione

When stress hits, your body calls in the biochemical cavalry. Among them are the following:

◆ *Superoxide dismutase (SOD):* Converts superoxide (a damaging ROS) into hydrogen peroxide — a far less volatile threat.

◆ *Catalase:* Breaks that peroxide down into water and oxygen, safely.

◆ *Glutathione peroxidase:* Uses glutathione (the master antioxidant) to mop up remaining oxidative residue.

Hormetic stress has been shown to upregulate all three, making your cells more agile in handling metabolic fire. Instead of being overwhelmed, they neutralise threats with the finesse of an elite bomb squad.

Transcription factor triage:

The factors known as Nrf2, HIF-1, AMPK and mTOR are the master switches of adaptation—molecular conductors that orchestrate growth, recovery and defence. Here's what all those letters and numbers mean:

- *Nrf2:* The antioxidant general. Activates hundreds of genes responsible for detoxification and cellular repair.

- *HIF-1α:* Responds to hypoxia (low oxygen), and enhances mitochondrial function, angiogenesis and metabolic flexibility. This factor is triggered by breathwork, altitude and movement.

- *AMPK:* Senses cellular energy, and turns on fat-burning, insulin regulation and autophagy.

- *mTOR:* Governs growth and regeneration. This factor is suppressed during stress, and then activated for rebuilding once the storm passes.

Research shows hormesis carefully toggles these systems, creating waves of breakdown and rebuild that keep your biology plastic and adaptable.

Rebooting the brain: Hormesis and cognitive longevity

The brain benefits enormously from hormesis. Recent studies suggest that low-dose ionising radiation (yes, small CT scans) may improve outcomes in patients with Alzheimer's and Parkinson's. This mild stress has been shown to trigger DNA repair, antioxidant defences and inflammation resolution in the brain—giving it the signal to clean house and restore function.

One study from 2021 led by Jerry Cuttler saw significant cognitive and emotional improvement in Alzheimer's patients after just a few low-dose exposures to radiation. This runs completely counter to the LNT model, which says all radiation is harmful. Hormesis, again, says, it depends on the dose.

Remote ischemic conditioning: The squeeze that saves lives

Another fascinating hormetic protocol is remote ischemic conditioning (RIC), where you briefly restrict blood flow to a limb using a pressure cuff. This isn't some fringe biohacking gimmick. RIC has been shown to:

- reduce damage from heart attacks and strokes
- improve transplant outcomes
- boost athletic endurance and recovery.

By creating a small, local stressor, RIC sends systemic signals that prepare the entire body for future trauma. It's a signal-to-noise upgrade for your internal defences.

Hormesis and ageing

Telomeres are the caps on the ends of chromosomes. Every time your cells divide, those caps get shorter. Telomere shortening has been linked to age-related diseases and reduced lifespan. (See the next chapter for more on telomeres.) Ageing isn't just about telomeres ticking down, however; it's also about accumulating damage, losing plasticity and getting stuck in inflammation mode. Hormesis offers a reset button for these processes.

Studies show that regular exposure to hormetic stress:

- suppresses pro-inflammatory genes

- activates DNA repair and longevity genes

- improves epigenetic plasticity (your body's ability to adapt gene expression).

In short: hormesis keeps your system young, adaptable and repair-ready — not inflamed, rigid and tired.

Intermittent living: The 'study of origin'

Dutch researcher Leo Pruimboom took all this theory and turned it into action. In 2016, he and his team created what they termed the 'study of origin', the focus of which was a fundamental question: what happens if you give modern humans a short, controlled hit of ancestral discomfort?

Participants spent ten days doing the opposite of modern life. Instead, the study included:

- intermittent fasting with wild food

- exposure to heat and cold (saunas and plunges)

- movement, breath holds and barefoot hiking

- circadian rhythm reset and digital detox.

The results? Inflammatory markers dropped. Heart rate variability (HRV) went up. Glucose control improved. Mood, energy and sleep skyrocketed.

In just ten days, people started to rewire themselves toward resilience. It was a biological reset — and a reminder that your body remembers its evolution.

Putting it all together: Build the body that doesn't break

Hormesis is not a trend or a biohack. Instead, it's the original language of resilience. Your biology expects pressure, challenge, heat, hunger and effort. Without it, your adaptive systems atrophy. With it, they thrive.

Hormetic practices include:

- intermittent fasting
- exercise
- cold and heat exposure
- hypoxic breathwork
- nutrient-dense, bitter and colourful foods
- certain supplements.

As shown in figure 6.2, by integrating these practices, you awaken systems that make you harder to kill, and better at living.

Physiological hardiness is about preparation rather than performance. It provides the ability to face stress, and not just survive it, but adapt to it, thrive in it and come out stronger.

Modern life won't give you hormesis by accident. You have to choose it, and go toward the discomfort. You need to train your system, like your ancestors did, against a backdrop of intermittent stress and adaptation.

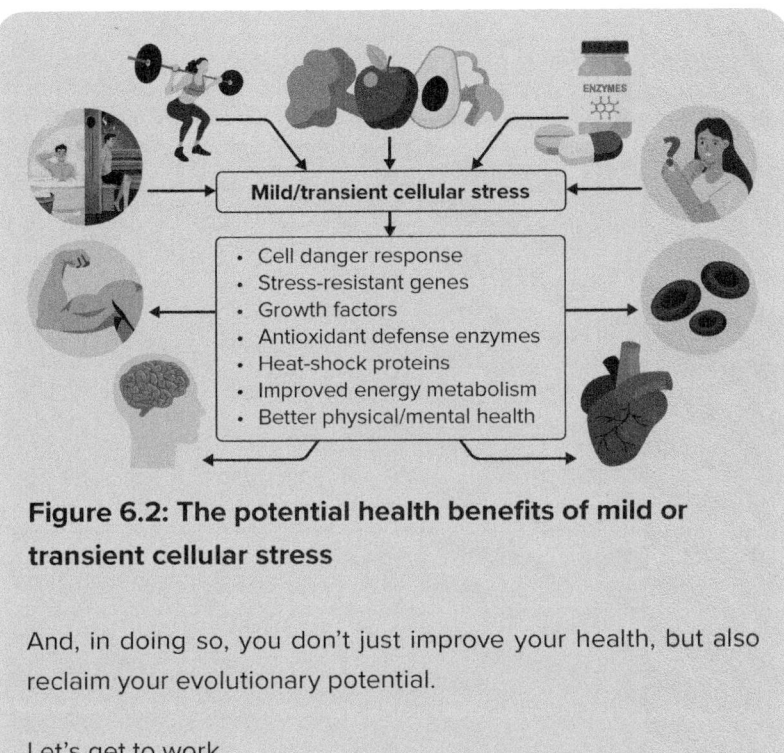

Figure 6.2: The potential health benefits of mild or transient cellular stress

And, in doing so, you don't just improve your health, but also reclaim your evolutionary potential.

Let's get to work.

7
Take your daily medicine

It is a disgrace to grow old through sheer carelessness before seeing what manner of man you may become by developing your bodily strength and beauty to their highest limit.

Socrates

This is a big, important chapter and I'm going to introduce it by talking about a study that is close to my heart (pun intended), given that I just had open heart surgery. The study is called the 'The Dallas Bed Rest and Training Study', but a better name for it would be 'How Doing Nothing Nearly Kills You'.

An astounding study on exercise, health and ageing

In 1966, five young, healthy men did something quite radical. They volunteered to do absolutely nothing. For three weeks, they lay flat on their backs in a research facility in Dallas—no walking, no standing, no sneaky laps to the fridge. Just pure, uninterrupted bed rest. It sounds like a dream holiday to some, but the consequences were more nightmare than nirvana. The Dallas Bed Rest and Training Study was designed to explore what happens to the heart and cardiovascular system when physical activity is completely removed from the equation. What it revealed changed the way we understand exercise, health and ageing—and not in a gentle, 'maybe try moving more' kind of way, but more in a sledgehammer-to-the-face kind of way.

After just three weeks of doing nothing, these otherwise healthy 20 year olds experienced a 27 per cent drop in their VO_2 max—a measure of how much oxygen your body can use during intense exercise and the gold-standard marker of cardiovascular fitness. To put that into perspective, that's like ageing your heart by a whopping 30 years in just 21 days! Their cardiac output plummeted by 26 per cent, and their stroke volume (the amount of blood pumped with each heartbeat) fell by 31 per cent.

Even at submaximal efforts—think cycling gently or climbing stairs—their hearts had to work significantly harder. Heart rate, blood pressure and myocardial oxygen demand were all up. Their cardiovascular system had essentially gone from a Formula One racing car to a knackered second-hand hatchback in 21 days.

Now, here's the beautiful twist in the tale. After the bedrest phase, the men embarked on eight weeks of structured endurance training.

The result? Their VO_2 max increased by 45 per cent, stroke volume surged by 48 per cent, and cardiac output returned to — and even surpassed — baseline. In other words, the damage done by three weeks of being sedentary was reversible, but only through serious graft.

The study was a bombshell. It debunked the then-popular medical approach of prescribing prolonged bed rest following conditions such as heart attacks. Within years, cardiac rehab became a thing. The lesson? The heart hates inactivity — and it thrives on being pushed.

30 years later: The heart remembers

Fast-forward 30 years and the same five men, now in their 50s, were rounded up again (presumably with fewer six-packs and more back complaints) by Dr Benjamin Levine and colleagues from the Division of Cardiology, University of Texas Southwestern Medical Center. This time, the men weren't prescribed bed rest. But they were studied to find out how ageing had affected their hearts. Surprisingly, VO_2 max had only declined by 12 per cent over three decades — far less than the 27 per cent nosedive from those original three weeks on their backs. It turns out ageing can be far less catastrophic for your heart than idleness.

And when these men trained again — albeit at a gentler pace and for longer duration — they regained nearly all their cardiovascular fitness from their younger days. Ageing hadn't robbed them of their heart's capacity to bounce back. It had just made the climb steeper.

They were followed up after another ten years and, now in their 60s, things had started to unravel. Hypertension had crept in, arrhythmias emerged and one had undiagnosed cancer. The lesson here is crystal clear — the earlier you intervene, the more you preserve the heart's plasticity.

The modern-day heart reboot

Let's jump ahead to 2018, when the same research group from the University of Texas Southwestern Medical Center decided to answer a burning question: can we actually reverse the cardiac ageing caused by years of sitting and stressing and skipping workouts, especially in middle age?

This time, they recruited 61 healthy but sedentary middle-aged adults and split them into two groups. One got two years of light stretching and yoga — the 'do no harm' control group. The other group got a structured, periodised exercise regime that included:

◆ four to five days per week of training

◆ moderate aerobic work at zone 2 (the backbone of endurance — more on that later in this chapter)

◆ high-intensity intervals in the form of the heavily researched Norwegian-style 4×4 protocol (four minutes of high-intensity exercise getting the heart rate to 90 to 95 per cent of maximum, followed by three-minute light recovery, repeated for four intervals — more on this also later in the chapter)

◆ long endurance sessions

◆ strength training (twice per week).

This wasn't a quick-fix boot camp. It was a two-year study of pretty serious training. And after two years, the results were pretty bloody impressive. The exercise group saw an 18 per cent increase in VO_2 max — a massive win in middle age, and a definite boost to their longevity potential. (As a measure of oxygen use and cardiovascular health, your VO_2 max is the single biggest predictor of how long you're going to live.) But the real prize was deeper: their hearts became more compliant, more elastic and more youthful. Left ventricular stiffness, a key indicator of heart health, dropped.

Heart size increased. Stroke volume improved. Resting heart rate decreased. They didn't just feel younger—they were younger, at a cardiac level.

The control group? Nada. In fact, they edged closer to frailty with increased left ventricular stiffness and declining function. It's a stark reminder to use it or lose it.

Cardiac stiffness is a key driver of heart failure and a common and devastating condition in older adults. Once stiffness sets in, the heart can't relax properly or fill efficiently. You tire easily. You puff going up stairs. And, eventually, your quality of life shrinks to match your cardiovascular reserve.

But here's the kicker: if you intervene in middle age, you can prevent this trajectory. The heart, it turns out, is still beautifully plastic in your 40s and 50s—if you give it the right nudge.

And that nudge doesn't have to be a marathon. This study's protocol mirrored public health guidelines of 150 to 180 minutes of exercise per week—plus a dash of high-intensity magic. It was doable and sustainable. And it worked.

Now let's widen the net and go from focusing on the heart to the bigger topic of ageing and anti-ageing therapies. Things have to get technical here, because I'm going to outline the mechanisms by which we age and how exercise counters all of these mechanisms to emerge as the single best anti-ageing intervention available—by a country mile.

The 12 hallmarks of ageing—and the exercise antidote

Back in 2013, a group of elite ageing researchers published a landmark paper in the high-quality academic journal *Cell* that shifted the whole paradigm. Instead of ageing being seen as some vague, inevitable decline, they broke it down into nine specific cellular processes that deteriorate over time and drive the ageing train. Fast-forward to 2023, and the same research group added three more processes. Now, we have a full roster of 12 interconnected biological hallmarks that together define how we age — and why we get frail, slow, stiff, foggy and sick.

But here's the kicker: exercise fights back against every single one. And it doesn't just throw a punch — it rewrites the playbook. Let's break these processes down, without putting you to sleep. (For the details of the research that supports the findings outlined in the following sections, see the references list at the end of this book.)

Genomic instability

Your DNA is the instruction manual for your body. But, over time, it gets battered — by UV light, pollution, stress and even just normal metabolism. Damaged DNA means typos in that instruction manual, which can lead to diseases such as cancer.

Exercise helps fight this process by stimulating DNA repair enzymes, such as poly (ADP-ribose) polymerase (PARP), and enhancing your endogenous (internal) antioxidant defence systems — superoxide dismutase, catalase and glutathione. These antioxidant enzymes are basically your cellular clean-up crew. I call them the Special Forces of your antioxidant defence system — as against the antioxidants you might pop in a pill, which are closer to Dad's Army. These enzymes reduce oxidative damage and help fix broken DNA, which slows down the genomic 'wear and tear'.

Translation: Exercise makes your cells better at fixing the damage life throws at them.

Telomere attrition

Telomeres are like the plastic tips on shoelaces that stop them fraying, except, in this case, they're on the ends of chromosomes. Every time your cells divide, those tips get shorter. Eventually, they get too short and the cell gives up — either dying or turning into a grumpy zombie cell called a senescent cell. I go into more detail on senescent cells later in this chapter. For now, if you've seen *Game of Thrones*, these cells are the White Walkers!

Exercise boosts telomerase, the enzyme that maintains telomeres. It also reduces inflammation and oxidative stress, which are like acid rain for your telomeres. In essence, it slows the fraying of the shoelaces.

Translation: Regular movement helps keep your cellular 'shoelaces' intact so your cells live longer and healthier.

Epigenetic alterations

Epigenetics controls which genes are switched on or off — similar to dimmer switches in a genetic light system. Ageing messes this up. Helpful genes (such as those involved in repair) get silenced, while dodgy ones can get cranked up.

Exercise modifies DNA methylation and histone acetylation — fancy terms for how genes are wrapped and presented. These changes restore youthful gene expression, turning down the bad stuff and upregulating genes involved in repair, metabolism and resilience.

Translation: Exercise resets your genetic playlist — fewer sad songs, more get-up-and-go tracks.

Loss of proteostasis

Proteins are your body's Lego bricks. They need to be built correctly, clicked into the right shapes and recycled when damaged, through a dynamic process known as proteostasis. With age, this process goes sideways, leading to clumps of misfolded proteins — think of Alzheimer's plaques and other gunk.

Exercise has been shown to boost heat shock proteins (molecular chaperones that help proteins fold properly) and autophagy (your cell's rubbish removal service). Autophagy clears out broken proteins and organelles, maintaining cellular tidiness.

Translation: Exercise tells your cells to take out the trash and re-fold the crumpled laundry.

Deregulated nutrient sensing

Your cells use sensors to gauge energy availability via systems such as insulin, mTOR, AMPK and sirtuins. With age, these sensors get out of whack — like a thermostat that doesn't know how hot or cold it is — leading to weight gain, fatigue and metabolic disease.

Exercise hits the reset button through the following:

◆ improving insulin sensitivity (so your cells actually use glucose efficiently)

◆ activating AMPK, which promotes fat burning and repair

◆ inhibiting mTOR slightly (which promotes longevity when not overactive)

◆ boosting sirtuins, enzymes linked to DNA repair and mitochondrial health.

Translation: Exercise helps your cells read the energy room better and respond intelligently — burning fat, not crashing.

Mitochondrial dysfunction

Mitochondria are the power plants in your cells (and, as covered later in this chapter, so much more). Ageing turns them into sluggish, pollution-spewing factories, with less energy, more reactive oxygen species (ROS), and more problems.

Exercise lights a fire under them. It increases PGC-1α, a master switch for mitochondrial creation and efficiency. You build more mitochondria, and they work better. You get more energy and less cellular smog.

Translation: Exercise upgrades your cell's battery and throws in a few spares.

Cellular senescence

Senescent cells are like undead zombies — the White Walkers I mentioned earlier in this chapter. They don't die, but they also don't function. Worse, they secrete nasty inflammatory chemicals called cytokines that damage nearby cells. They're like that rotting strawberry in the bottom of the punnet.

Exercise reduces the zombie load, enhancing immune surveillance (natural killer cells and macrophages), which tags and removes senescent cells. Exercise also reduces the inflammatory soup senescent cells secrete — the senescence-associated secretory phenotype (SASP).

Translation: Exercise helps evict cellular squatters and stops them poisoning the neighbourhood.

Stem cell exhaustion

Stem cells are your body's repair team. With age, however, they burn out, go into hiding or stop working effectively.

Exercise reboots them. It increases the production of growth factors such as BDNF (for brain cells) and IGF-1 (for muscle and bones), and stimulates myokines from muscles that keep stem cells active and responsive.

Translation: Exercise calls the repair crew back to the job site.

Altered intercellular communication

Cells constantly talk to each other. With age, this communication becomes garbled, with more stress signals, more inflammation and less collaboration.

Exercise clears the lines. It reduces chronic inflammation and improves hormonal signalling (including insulin and cortisol). Muscles also release beneficial 'talking molecules' called myokines, which send anti-inflammatory and regenerative signals throughout the body.

Translation: Exercise gets your cells speaking fluent, productive biology again.

Disabled macroautophagy

Autophagy is a mouthful, but it just means 'self-eating'. This process is how your cells recycle damaged components, but it slows with age and, without it, junk piles up fast.

Exercise reactivates this cellular recycling, helping cells chew up broken mitochondria and misfolded proteins, repurpose the pieces and keep things humming.

Translation: Exercise keeps the recycling truck coming regularly.

Chronic inflammation

Known as inflammaging, chronic inflammation is a low-level smoulder that worsens everything from arthritis and dementia to diabetes and heart disease.

Exercise is anti-inflammatory medicine. It reduces pro-inflammatory cytokines (such as IL-6 and TNF-α) and boosts anti-inflammatory signals such as IL-10. It also improves gut health, which is a major player in inflammation.

Translation: Exercise extinguishes the slow-burning fire that's cooking your insides.

Dysbiosis

Your gut microbiome isn't just about digestion — It's a control centre for immunity, mood and metabolism. Ageing shrinks its diversity and boosts harmful bugs, which can lead to dysbiosis, or a gut microbiome imbalance.

Exercise fertilises your internal garden. It boosts microbial diversity and increases production of short-chain fatty acids (SCFAs) such as butyrate, which strengthen your gut barrier and reduce inflammation.

Translation: Move more, poop better and feel sharper.

Exercise as medicine

The impact of exercise on these hallmarks of ageing isn't just an interesting observation — it also translates into real-world, crystal-clear benefits. Perhaps the most staggering evidence of its power comes from a sweeping review published by researchers Bente Pedersen and Bengt Saltin, which made an almost biblical pronouncement: exercise is medicine. And not just for one or two conditions, but for a whopping 26 different chronic diseases.

Their landmark paper showed that regular physical activity not only reduces symptoms but also, in many cases, addresses the root pathology. Take depression, for example. While we've long suspected that exercise can boost mood, the evidence now shows it can be as effective as antidepressants for some people — without the side effects and with a bunch of added bonuses such as stronger muscles, better sleep and reduced risk of nearly every chronic disease.

For metabolic syndrome and type 2 diabetes, the story is even more compelling. Exercise doesn't just improve insulin sensitivity but can also reverse the condition in some cases, especially when started early. Pedersen and Saltin also highlighted that hypertension, once thought to be the territory of salt restriction and statins, responds brilliantly to structured physical activity. Measurable drops were seen in systolic and diastolic pressure — better than or equal to some drugs.

What's remarkable is that these effects span so many systems of the body. From strengthening the hippocampus in people with early dementia to easing stiffness in osteoarthritis and improving survival outcomes in people with cancer, exercise appears to be nature's universal prescription pad.

The effects of cardiovascular fitness and muscle strength

In recent years, a number of large-scale studies have confirmed what the fittest among us might already suspect: your VO_2 max and muscle strength are more than measures of performance. They're also two of the most powerful predictors of how long you'll live.

Let's start with aerobic fitness. One landmark study from 2018 by Kyle Mandsager and colleagues analysed over 122 000 adults who underwent treadmill testing at a major US medical centre.

The participants, who had a median follow-up of over eight years, were divided into five fitness levels based on their performance. The findings were nothing short of jaw-dropping: the higher your fitness, the lower your risk of death — regardless of age, sex or pre-existing conditions. Even more compelling, the benefit had no 'upper limit'. Being in the top 2.3 per cent of fitness scorers (the so-called elite group) reduced your risk of death by a staggering 80 per cent compared to those in the lowest bracket. Here's a summary of the study and its findings:

- The study tracked 122 007 adults, with a mean age of 53.4, for around eight years.

- Elite performers were found to have an 80 per cent lower mortality risk than the least fit.

- Moving from the lowest category of fitness to below average reduced the risk of death by almost half — a huge effect.

- Risk reduction continued with each increase in fitness category.

- The benefits from improved fitness exceeded those of avoiding smoking, diabetes or heart disease.

Another even larger study from 2022 drove the point home. Peter Kokkinos and colleagues studied over 750 000 US veterans ranging in age from their 30s to their 90s. They found a similar graded, inverse relationship between cardiorespiratory fitness and mortality risk. What's particularly striking is that even in septuagenarians and octogenarians, the fittest individuals had significantly lower mortality risks than their less fit peers. This wasn't just a 'young man's game' — the benefits of fitness extended into old age, across genders, races and health statuses. Here are some further details on this study and its findings:

- The study tracked 750 302 US veterans, aged between 30 and 95.

- A 76 per cent lower mortality risk was found in the highest fitness group versus the bottom 20 per cent.

- Consistent benefits were seen across sex, age and race.

- Again, a clear dose response was highlighted — that is, every extra level of fitness was better.

Now let's consider muscular strength — the oft-overlooked sibling of aerobic capacity. A massive 2018 meta-analysis pooled data from nearly two million people across 38 studies and found that greater handgrip and leg strength were independently associated with reduced risk of early death. (Note that handgrip strength is used as a proxy of overall muscle strength.) In fact, women with strong grip strength had up to a 40 per cent lower mortality risk. Other reviews confirmed that these effects persist even when you control for how aerobically fit someone is. Muscle strength isn't just a nice-to-have — it's a survival metric. The study details are as follows:

- The analysis pooled 1.9 million participants across 38 studies.

- High handgrip strength was found to indicate 31 per cent lower all-cause mortality.

- Women benefited most, with a 40 per cent reduction in mortality.

- Higher knee extension strength, an indicator of increased power and stability in the legs, indicates a 14 per cent lower death risk.

Another ten-year observational study of around 4500 US adults aged 50 and older from Ran Li and colleagues found that those with low muscle mass had a 40 to 50 per cent greater risk of all-cause mortality than the control group over the study period. They also found that the strength of the muscles was more important than the size of the muscles.

Adding to this body of evidence, a 2022 systematic review by Haruki Momma and colleagues examined data from 16 cohort studies involving over 263 000 participants. Their meta-analysis showed that muscle-strengthening activities, such as resistance training, were associated with significant reductions in the risk of all-cause mortality, cardiovascular disease, cancer, diabetes and even lung cancer.

And the importance of strength just keeps rising. In a 2011 study, researchers followed a group of around 1500 men for nearly two decades and found that even if they were in the lower half of cardiorespiratory fitness, participants' risk of dying by any cause was still around 48 per cent lower if they were in the top third of the group in terms of strength versus the bottom third — so being strong gives you a fair chunk of protection if you're unfit.

The case for both cardiovascular fitness (VO_2 max) *and* good muscle strength is clearly compelling. I outline how to get there in more detail at the end of this chapter.

Let's first dig into the main driver of all of these benefits — your very own magical myokines.

Myokines: The hardiness hormones of movement

If exercise is medicine, myokines are its active ingredients.

When I did my master's degree in exercise science in the mid-1990s, we were taught that muscles were important for daily function and health, but the mechanisms on why weren't fully understood. But around that time, a few clever researchers started noticing something interesting — when people exercised, their muscles began secreting chemical messengers. These messengers were not only dealing with the muscle itself but also travelling through the bloodstream, tapping on the doors of distant organs such as the brain, liver, pancreas, fat cells and even bone—and stimulating them all to function better.

These secreted substances were dubbed myokines—literally 'muscle cytokines'. (Cytokines are small signalling proteins that regulate the growth and activity of immune cells and blood cells.) Small but mighty, myokines are the hormones of hardiness, and their discovery rewrote the playbook on how exercise influences whole-body health.

The origins: From cytokines to myokines

The first breakthrough came with interleukin-6 (IL-6). Once thought to be just an inflammatory molecule, IL-6 was found to skyrocket in the bloodstream after exercise, even when no injury or inflammation was present. Rather than being a warning signal, this was a signal of adaptation. The muscle contractions themselves were found to be triggering its release.

And with that, the muscle's secret life as an endocrine (hormonal) organ was revealed. Muscles don't just respond to your will. They whisper biochemical instructions to the rest of your body every time they contract.

Fast-forward to today, and researchers have catalogued over 600 potential myokines, with a shortlist of well-understood heavy hitters that includes BDNF, irisin, IL-15, myostatin, apelin, BAIBA and IGF-1. And each one has its own job and systemic influence.

Cross-organ whisperers

Myokines operate through three channels of communication:

1. *Autocrine:* Talking to the muscle cell itself.

2. *Paracrine:* Chatting with neighbouring cells.

3. *Endocrine:* Dialling up distant organs via the bloodstream.

As shown in figure 7.1, this means that your muscles are basically sending text messages to your immune system, fat cells, gastrointestinal system, liver, pancreas, bones, brain and more, every time you work out.

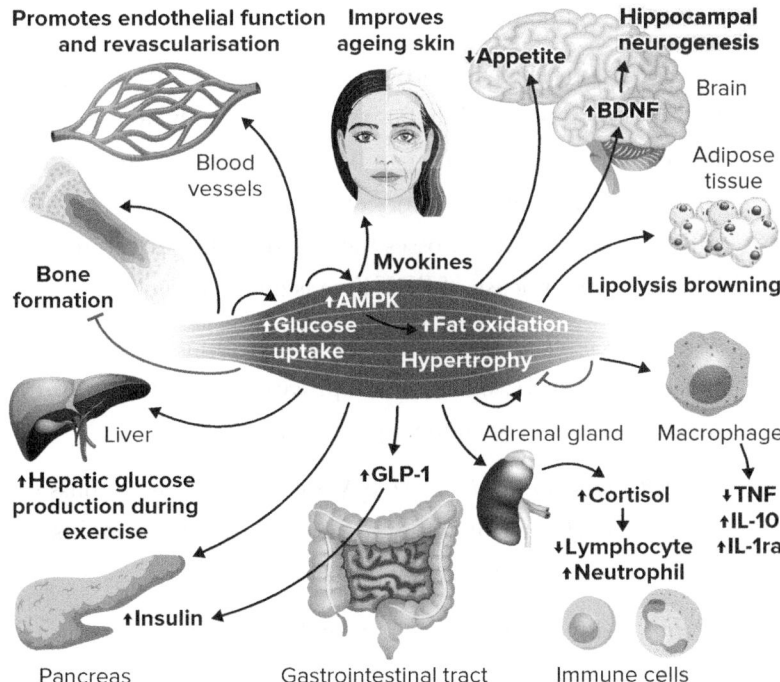

Figure 7.1: The different systems in the body myokines communicate with

Source: © Endocrine Society 2020

This cross-talk forms the biochemical basis of the 'exercise effect' — and is one of the reasons moving your body has such widespread benefits, from sharper cognition to stronger bones to lower *[name your disease]* risk. Experts now know at least 35 diseases are prevented or attenuated by myokines.

What's remarkable is how directly myokines intervene in the ageing process, and especially in the 12 hallmarks of ageing discussed earlier in this chapter. Here's a whistle-stop tour:

◆ *BDNF (brain-derived neurotrophic factor):* Often called 'Miracle-Gro for the brain', BDNF supports neurogenesis, synaptic plasticity and mental clarity. It's a myokine that helps fend off dementia, depression and brain fog.

◆ *Irisin:* Famous for its fat-browning, metabolism-boosting powers, irisin turns white fat into metabolically active beige fat (meaning the fat can be used as energy rather than stored), increases energy expenditure and reduces inflammation. It also crosses the blood-brain barrier and stimulates the release of BDNF, so is neuroprotective.

◆ *IL-6 (in its myokine form):* Unlike the inflammatory version, muscle-derived IL-6 actually improves glucose metabolism, fat oxidation and immune regulation.

◆ *BAIBA (β-aminoisobutyric acid):* A tiny molecule with massive impact, BAIBA regulates fat metabolism, protects against oxidative stress and even supports bone integrity.

◆ *Apelin:* A star in cardiovascular health, apelin improves blood pressure regulation, boosts muscle regeneration and might help fight age-related sarcopenia.

◆ *IGF-1 (insulin-like growth factor-1):* This is a growth-promoting powerhouse that boosts protein synthesis, supports bone and muscle strength, and has been implicated in cellular repair.

♦ *Myostatin:* The villain of the group, myostatin suppresses muscle growth. Fortunately, exercise suppresses this myokine, allowing muscle maintenance and growth. The pharmaceutical companies that make the successful weight-loss drugs have just created new drugs that target the myostatin pathway, so people don't lose muscle on their drugs (a major side effect). Think about buying shares in that drug when it comes out!

These molecules influence all of the 12 ageing hallmarks, from improving mitochondrial function and reducing inflammation, to enhancing autophagy, stabilising genomic function and revitalising stem cell activity.

In simple terms, when you move, your muscles become your body's biochemical defence squad, firing off signals that promote regeneration, repair and resilience.

The mitochondrial link

Many myokines are powered by PGC-1α, the same transcription coactivator discussed earlier in relation to mitochondrial biogenesis. When you exercise, PGC-1α gets activated in muscle cells, kicking off a cascade of benefits, including more mitochondria, cleaner energy production and the creation of myokines such as irisin and BAIBA.

And here's the twist: mitochondria themselves may help modulate the release of these myokines. This means a beautiful feedback loop is created—healthy mitochondria help make more myokines, which in turn help preserve mitochondrial function, particularly in the brain.

Myokine medicine

Different types of exercise stimulate different myokines, as follows:

◆ *Aerobic (endurance):* Upregulates irisin, BDNF, BAIBA, IL-6 (anti-inflammatory form), apelin and SPARC.

◆ *Anaerobic (including strength training):* Boosts BDNF, IGF-1, IL-15, decorin, BMP-7 and more.

◆ *Both:* Reduces myostatin (good!), increases VEGF (vascular growth) and supports neuromuscular health.

Each muscle contraction sends a little chemical telegram of resilience to the rest of your body. Every time you exercise, you're turning muscle into a factory of hardiness hormones — dispatching myokines to protect your brain, boost metabolism, quiet inflammation, build stronger bones, regulate fat and even reboot your stem cells. You're chemically re-engineering your body. These molecules counter disease and shape the arc of ageing.

Imagine if 'Big Pharma' invented something that could target all 12 hallmarks of ageing, while simultaneously reducing your risk of 26 chronic diseases and significantly extending your lifespan and healthspan (the part of your life when you are generally in good health). It would likely cost a fortune and be splashed across every billboard. But nature has already given the solution to you.

It's cheap. It's ridiculously effective. And it's available right now.

So move daily. Contract deliberately. And remember: inside every bicep curl and squat lies a cellular whisper that says, 'Not today, ageing. Not today.'

Getting physical: Exercise recommendations

The research studies highlighted through this chapter clearly indicate that cardiorespiratory fitness (VO_2 max) and muscle strength and mass have independent and synergistic effects on health. And here's the point — you need both. In terms of optimal effects on lifespan and healthspan, the bodybuilder is generally not fit enough cardiovascularly while the marathon runner generally doesn't have enough muscle mass and upper body strength.

In the following section, I outline what you can do to improve in both areas.

A dual focus is required

When it comes to healthspan and lifespan, the combination of a high VO_2 max and good muscle strength is king. For the cardiorespiratory portion, comprehensive research by Roy Shephard in 2008 suggests that to continue to live independently, older men need a VO_2 max of at least 18 ml/kg/min while older women need 15 ml/kg/min. (As a comparison, an active adult male might have a VO_2 max of around 45 ml/kg/min.) We all lose it with age, so it's important that you build up a buffer. But even in the elderly, Shephard reports that an increase of at least 10 ml/kg/min is absolutely achievable — but starting early is better. (Remember, your cardiac elasticity really drops off when you hit your 60s.)

The gold standard way to train your cardiorespiratory system has been shown to us by Dr Benjamin Levine and his team who conducted the Dallas studies mentioned at the start of the chapter. The most comprehensive and time-efficient way is to combine both lower intensity steady-state exercise in zone 2 (of the five heart-rate training zones) and high-intensity Norwegian 4×4 intervals.

A great basis for a training program includes the following:

◆ *Start with zone 2:* Exercising in the zone 2 range means you're at 60 to 70 per cent of your maximum heart rate. You can talk, but you can't sing. You should be able to hold a conversation with a little difficulty. With a reasonable level of fitness, you should be able to stay in this zone non-stop for 30 minutes or more. Aim to include at least one of these sessions per week, because this zone is wonderful for mitochondrial function.

◆ *Add in Norwegian 4 × 4:* This protocol breaks your workout into set times and sessions. After a warm-up, go as hard as you can with a cardio exercise (such as running, cycling or rowing) for four minutes. Aim to get your heart-rate to 90 to 95 per cent of your maximum by the end of the interval. On your RPE (rating of perceived exertion), you should be at 9 or 10 out of 10 at the end (very hard to maximum effort). Then you bring the pace way down and recover (while still moving) for three minutes. You need to complete four intervals for a total workout time of 25 minutes (no recovery after the final four-minute intensity), plus warm-up and cool-down. It's hard, but very efficient. Aim to include one session per week of this protocol.

◆ *Lift heavy shit:* As demonstrated, the benefits of strength and cardio are different and complementary, so you also need to incorporate muscle strengthening activities — lifting heavy shit — at least twice a week. Two full-body workouts per week will give you a huge lifespan and healthspan boost, especially when combined with the cardio already outlined. You can do these sessions in around 30 minutes if you do circuit-style training, or 45 to 60 minutes for the more traditional style with rest periods between sets.

◆ *Ramp up on your weak points:* For the remaining exercise sessions — ideally you're exercising five or six times a week — focus on your deficits. If your VO$_2$ max is pretty good, do more strength training; if you're strong but not that fit, do more cardio.

As an alternative to going it alone, sign up to a CrossFit, F-45 or similar combined training gym in your area — these types of classes target both strength and cardiovascular fitness in one workout, and provide the added benefit of doing it with other humans. Going to a regular class where you get to know people helps you form a bit of a tribe, and can massively increase your enjoyment and commitment. I know this from my own experience. I had not been a member of a gym since my military days, and instead had always had a home gym and trained there — because I always thought that I'd leave joining a gym until I lost the motivation to train by myself. Last year, when I learned that I needed open-heart surgery, I decided to join the local CrossFit gym which my wife, Carly, and kids, Ceara and Oscar, trained at. And I have absolutely loved it — and will not go back to training on my own. Maybe I'm very lucky with my local CrossFit gym, but the culture is brilliant, with elite athletes training alongside old buggers like me and Carly — and some even older. Finding something that you enjoy is key.

Strength training considerations

Subtle differences exist in how you train if aiming for increasing muscle strength versus training for increasing muscle mass (known as hypertrophy training). But the outcome we're focusing on here is healthspan — to be in good health and daily function in old age.

This means you should be orienting your training towards increasing muscle strength through functional strength exercises. To do so, focus on the following:

- compound lifts (such as squats and deadlifts) over single joint exercises (such as knee extensions and hamstring curls)

- free weights over machines (once you pass novice phase)

- both upper and lower body, as well as back and front of the body

- incorporating single-leg exercises and balance training (to prevent falls — a massive killer of older adults)

- progressive overload — increasing the weight and volume over time

- higher reps and lighter weights for the first six weeks.

For variation and to keep your muscles responding, you can do one session per week with higher, hypertrophy-focused rep ranges — where you use heavier weights with fewer reps — and the other session focused on strength. See appendix B for a full weekly exercise program, broken into sessions and exercises to focus on.

Putting it all together: Anti-ageing isn't in a pill, but in the gym

Let's kill the myth once and for all: ageing is not a one-way ticket to decline. Inactivity is. The data is clear — your cardiovascular system is less a ticking time bomb and more a garden. Neglect it and it wilts. Train it and it blooms.

Three weeks of bed rest at 20 is as bad for your heart as 30 years of ageing. But the flip side? Just months of smart, progressive exercise can reverse decades of decline.

The best anti-ageing therapy isn't collagen or cryotherapy or some guru's supplement stack. It's consistent strength and cardiovascular training, with both bringing something different to the party. Your heart, brain and other organs don't care if you've been sedentary—they care if you stay that way.

Start now. Go hard (intermittently). Stay consistent. And give your cells the power to slow the march of Father Time.

8
Feed your ecosystem

Let food be thy medicine and medicine be thy food.

Unknown (commonly misattributed to Hippocrates)

Let's start with a truth bomb: if someone tells you one perfect diet exists for everyone, they're either a) deluded, b) trying to sell you something, or c) a card-carrying member of a dietary cult. Possibly all three. The truth is the idea of a universal diet is outdated, unscientific and borderline dangerous.

The evidence for this is clear in the field of nutrigenomics — the science showing how our genes interact with different foods. The best diet for you might make me bloated, sluggish or strangely emotional. So when someone insists that everyone should eat nothing but raw foods or just meat or drink yak butter tea, you can confidently tell them to go piss up a rope!

And here's the uncomfortable truth: the modern diet is not only making us fat and sick but also ageing us faster. Chronically inflamed, metabolically broken and nutrient-starved bodies are the new norm in high-income countries. But it doesn't have to be this way. This chapter offers a solution. We're going to cut through the noise and focus on evidence-based nutrition approaches that can help slow the ageing process and extend not just your lifespan, but also your healthspan — when you are generally still healthy and able to enjoy life. I explore how certain foods and nutrients directly impact the 12 biological hallmarks of ageing discussed in the previous chapter.

You'll discover why most dietary guidelines might not be telling the whole story (for example, with saturated fat), why ultra-processed foods are creating a global health crisis, how omega-3 fatty acids are working at the cellular level to keep you biologically younger and why protein becomes increasingly critical as you age. I then wrap up with some practical tips on increasing your nutritional intake with supplements.

The nutrition information in this chapter is for educational purposes only and may not be suitable for everyone. Always seek the advice of your physician or other qualified health provider before implementing any health suggestions.

Let's start by questioning some of the largely accepted wisdoms about nutrition, beginning with one of the most persistent dietary dogmas of the past half-century.

The great fat misconception

Before diving into what you should eat, let's address one pervasive misconception that has shaped dietary guidelines for decades. This deep dive into the saturated fat debate reveals why we should be sceptical of even official dietary recommendations. Governments across the Western world have been shouting 'cut the fat!' since the 1970s. But now, the science is whispering something different. Let's start by outlining the current dietary guidelines on saturated fats across the United States, the United Kingdom and Australia.

- In the United States, the Dietary Guidelines for Americans recommend that saturated fat intake should be less than 10 per cent of total daily calories.

- The United Kingdom's NHS follows suit, advising to keep saturated fat to a minimum, ideally below 10 per cent.

- Australia's National Health and Medical Research Council also echoes this, emphasising a limit on saturated fat as part of heart-healthy eating.

But here's the kicker — a growing body of research is now challenging these long-standing views.

A brief history of the diet-heart hypothesis

Back in the 1950s, a physiologist named Ancel Keys proposed the 'diet-heart hypothesis', suggesting that saturated fat raises total serum cholesterol, which increases the risk for heart disease. This idea took off, especially after the now infamous Seven Countries Study, led by Keys, which linked saturated fat consumption to heart disease across populations.

But here's something important: the Seven Countries Study was not a clinical trial. It was observational, and only collected detailed dietary data on fewer than 5 per cent of participants, or fewer than 100 per country. And Keys didn't study seven countries — researchers found later that he actually studied 22 countries, but 15 of them didn't suit his hypothesis, so he got rid of their data. That's not misleading research — it's fraudulent research. And it set up the case for demonising fat, and saturated fat in particular. In other words, it wasn't exactly a strong foundation for decades of global nutrition policy.

In 1955, around the same time Keys was proposing his theories, the sitting US President, Dwight Eisenhower, suffered a heart attack. This caused an intense focus on heart disease. Combine this with Keys's subsequent study and stated findings, and saturated fat becomes public enemy number one. In 1980, the first Dietary Guidelines for Americans recommended limiting it; by 1990, a hard cap of 10 per cent was introduced, which remains to this day.

Revisiting ignored evidence

The 1960s and '70s saw several large randomised controlled trials (RCTs) testing the diet-heart hypothesis. Combined, these included around 67 000 participants and ran for up to seven years — long enough to track 'hard' outcomes such as heart attacks and death.

And what did these trials show? Well, not what you'd expect. The totality of evidence did not support the idea that lowering saturated fat reduces cardiovascular risk. Yet — and this is crucial — these trials were largely ignored in shaping the official dietary guidelines.

In fact, a 2018 citation network analysis showed clear bias in the literature, with 82 per cent of supportive reviews only citing the one positive trial, while ignoring others with contradictory findings.

Fast-forward to more recent times and, since 2010, we've seen a wave of systematic reviews and meta-analyses, including from research heavyweights such as the Cochrane Collaboration (a global independent network of researchers, professionals, patients and carers). These reviews found that reducing saturated fats does not significantly impact mortality, heart attacks or strokes.

Even the 2020 Cochrane review — led by researcher Lee Hooper and considered by most academics to be the most rigorous — found no significant benefit when trials that successfully reduced saturated fat were analysed separately. On the observational front? Out of at least eight large meta-analyses, most found no association between saturated fat intake and coronary heart disease.

One 2019 umbrella review of 17 studies ('Fat or fiction: The diet-heart hypothesis') concluded: '[We] must consider that the diet-heart hypothesis is invalid or requires modification.'

The flawed reliance on LDL-cholesterol

So why does the idea persist? A big reason is that saturated fat increases LDL-cholesterol ('bad' cholesterol). But not all LDL particles are equal. Saturated fats mainly raise large LDL particles, but it's the small, dense ones that drive heart disease. Saturated fat also raises HDL cholesterol (the 'good' kind) — and your Triglyceride/HDL ratio is a way more powerful indicator for developing cardiovascular disease, as well as diabetes and metabolic syndrome.

In short: using LDL-cholesterol as a proxy for heart disease risk in people is overly simplistic and potentially misleading.

The 2020 guidelines: Still not reflecting the science

The 2020 Dietary Guidelines for Americans committee excluded nearly 20 review papers by external scientists, and instead relied on in-house United States Department of Agriculture (USDA) reviews. Of the 39 studies they cited, 88 per cent had null or negative findings, yet the guidelines still recommend capping saturated fat at 10 per cent of total calories.

And what about specific types of food? They found that dairy — including butter — was either neutral or beneficial for heart disease risk. Meat had mixed findings. But, again, most studies showed no consistent harm from foods rich in saturated fat.

Also noteworthy was the influential Prospective Urban Rural Epidemiology (PURE) study, which followed over 135 000 people across five continents. This study found no link between saturated fat and heart disease, and even found a lower risk of stroke from those with a higher saturated fat consumption.

Bottom line: our war on saturated fat is based on outdated, oversimplified and selective science. It's time to stop treating it as dietary public enemy number one.

Understanding the food matrix and dietary context

Here's a crucial takeaway. We eat foods, not nutrients. The food matrix (how nutrients are packaged together) plays a big role in health effects. For example, saturated fat in cheese behaves differently than in processed meats.

Even more important is the overall diet. In low-carb diets, for instance, saturated fat is burned for fuel rather than stored and can lead to improved cardiometabolic health.

The move away from isolated nutrient targets has been embraced for total fat and dietary cholesterol, yet saturated fat remains stuck in the past.

So, is it time to retire the 10 per cent saturated fat limit?

The answer, based on the totality of RCTs, meta-analyses and real-world observational studies, is yes, or at least to re-evaluate this limit. As the authors of the comprehensive 2021 review 'Dietary saturated fats and health: Are the US guidelines evidence-based?' put it:

Making a 'strong' recommendation based on weak and contradictory evidence does not meet scientific standards for guidelines.

That pretty much says it all.

Having dismantled one of nutrition's biggest myths about saturated fat, let's now get into the nitty-gritty of what I think are the most important aspects of nutrition, when viewed through the lens of increasing healthspan and lifespan. I'm going to make this as simple as possible and focus on five areas, starting with what may be the most pervasive and dangerous aspect of modern eating: ultra-processed foods. While we've been arguing about fat percentages, our food system has been fundamentally transformed.

Nutrition rule #1: Limit ultra-processed foods

Let me open with a bold claim: ultra-processed foods (UPFs) are one of the greatest threats to human health since the Black Plague. That might sound like hyperbole, but once you grasp just how pervasive these products have become, and how devastating their health consequences are, you might agree.

So let's do a deep dive into what UPFs are, why they're so harmful and what an extraordinary new umbrella review has uncovered about their relationship with chronic disease. I also look at why these foods dominate our global food system and, most importantly, what you can do about it.

Defining ultra-processed foods—and how they took over our diets

UPFs are not just 'junk food' or 'packaged snacks'. They're an entire category of modern industrial food products that have fundamentally altered the way we eat, and the way our bodies function.

The term 'ultra-processed food' comes from the NOVA classification, developed by Brazilian public health researchers. The NOVA system divides all food into four categories:

1. *Unprocessed or minimally processed foods:* This includes fresh vegetables, fruits, meat, eggs and milk.

2. *Processed culinary ingredients:* Ingredients such as salt, sugar and oils, used in home cooking.

3. *Processed foods:* These are simple products made from combining foods and ingredients, such as canned tomatoes, sourdough bread or traditionally cured meats.

4. *Ultra-processed foods:* These are industrial formulations made mostly from ingredients not found in a home kitchen. They're often made from cheap commodity crops (such as corn, wheat and soy) and refined and recombined with additives such as emulsifiers, colourings, preservatives, flavour enhancers and artificial sweeteners.

UPFs are designed for shelf-life, convenience, taste and profit — not for nourishment.

To put it simply: if it was never alive or if it doesn't resemble the food it once was, it's probably ultra-processed. A sweet potato is real food. Sweet potato fries from a fast-food outlet, deep-fried in cheap oil and plastered with stabilisers and salt, are not.

How UPFs hijack the human body

So, what's the problem? Why are UPFs so bad for you?

Well, first, they are nutritionally unbalanced. They're typically high in refined carbohydrates, added sugars, processed seed oils and sodium, while being low in fibre, antioxidants and essential micronutrients.

But it goes deeper than that. UPFs are designed to override your brain's satiety signals, making you eat more than you need. They're often hyper-palatable, stimulating reward pathways in the brain — and bypassing more rational control centres — in a way that mimics addictive substances. This is not accidental at all. A whole army of flavour scientists literally engineer these foods to keep you coming back for more.

Additionally, many UPFs contain additives such as emulsifiers and synthetic sweeteners that disrupt gut bacteria, impair intestinal barriers and drive systemic inflammation.

And when these foods become a regular part of your diet, they displace whole foods and fibre, contributing to a cascade of metabolic dysfunctions — including weight gain, insulin resistance, lipid abnormalities and oxidative stress.

The final research nail in the coffin

Now, nutrition research is notoriously difficult. Running long-term, controlled studies is hard, and isolating single food items in real-world diets is even harder. But a new umbrella review published in *The British Medical Journal* (now simply *The BMJ*) in 2024 may provide the most damning evidence yet against UPFs.

This review analysed 45 meta-analyses, covering data from nearly 10 million people. It's the largest and most comprehensive review to date, synthesising decades of research to determine what links, if any, exist between UPFs and health outcomes.

The verdict? UPFs are unequivocally harmful.

The authors, led by researcher Melissa Lane, graded the strength of evidence using rigorous criteria. In the world of nutrition science, where most evidence is conflicting or merely suggestive, finding what's termed 'Class I' (convincing; the highest standard) or 'Class II' (highly suggestive) evidence is incredibly rare. And yet, this review found it. Let's look at some of the most striking findings.

Class I evidence was found for links between UPF consumption and:

◆ cardiovascular disease-related death — a 50 per cent higher risk in those with the highest UPF intake

◆ type 2 diabetes — a 12 per cent increase in risk for every 10 per cent increase in UPFs

◆ anxiety — a 48 per cent higher risk

◆ common mental disorders — a 53 per cent increase in likelihood.

Class II evidence linked UPFs to:

◆ all-cause mortality — a 21 per cent higher risk of dying from any cause

◆ heart disease mortality — a 66 per cent increased risk

◆ obesity — a 55 per cent higher risk of developing obesity

◆ depression — a 22 per cent higher risk

◆ other conditions such as sleep disturbances and asthma symptoms — significant associations also shown.

These are not small effects. They're large, population-level risks, attributable not to smoking or alcohol, but to what we're eating every day. In fact, the authors noted that these findings 'may represent one of the most significant public health discoveries in nutrition science to date'.

UPFs as accelerators of the hallmarks of ageing

The reason that UPFs have such negative impacts on our health is that they are drivers of many of the hallmarks of ageing. They may taste great, but they are bad ju-ju for your cellular processes. Table 8.1 provides a quick summary of their impacts on some of the main hallmarks of ageing, as outlined in chapter 7. (See the references at the end of the book for full details of studies that outline these impacts.)

Table 8.1: How ultra-processed foods accelerate different hallmarks of ageing

Hallmark of ageing	Effect of UPFs
Genomic instability	• Increase oxidative DNA damage • Impair DNA repair mechanisms • Lack protective phytonutrients that maintain genomic integrity
Epigenetic alterations	• Lack methyl donors (folate, B12, choline) needed for DNA methylation • Contain endocrine disruptors that alter gene expression • Accelerate epigenetic changes associated with ageing
Loss of proteostasis	• Impair cellular stress response pathways such as Nrf2 • Lack protective antioxidants found in whole foods • Promote accumulation of misfolded proteins and cellular dysfunction
Deregulated nutrient sensing	• Disrupt insulin signalling and increase mTOR activation • Create conflicting cellular signals: excess energy amid nutritional poverty • Promote insulin resistance and dysregulated growth factor signalling

(continued)

Table 8.1: How ultra-processed foods accelerate different hallmarks of ageing *(cont'd)*

Hallmark of ageing	Effect of UPFs
Mitochondrial dysfunction	• Fructose in UPFs bypasses normal regulation, depleting ATP and creating energy crisis • Increase reactive oxygen species and deplete NAD+ • Damage mitochondrial efficiency, impair calcium signalling and lipid metabolism
Cellular senescence	• Promote accumulation of 'zombie cells' through oxidative damage • Senescent cells secrete inflammatory compounds (SASP) • Create cascading effect accelerating tissue ageing
Stem cell exhaustion	• Create metabolic environment that accelerates stem cell senescence • Reduce tissue regenerative capacity • Chronic inflammation exhausts stem cell population
Altered intercellular communication	• Disrupt hormone and neurotransmitter signalling • AGEs damage cell surface receptors • Impairs normal cellular recognition and response patterns
Inflammaging	• Processed oils, advanced glycation end-products (AGEs) and additives act as danger signals to immune cells • Trigger chronic production of pro-inflammatory cytokines (TNF-α, IL-6, IL-1β) • Create self-perpetuating cycle of systemic inflammation
Dysbiosis	• Reduce gut microbiome diversity and promote pathogenic bacteria • Disrupt intestinal barrier leading to 'leaky gut' • Emulsifiers directly damage protective mucus layer

The global takeover of UPFs

You might be wondering, if UPFs are so bad, how did we let this happen?

The rise of UPFs is not a natural evolution. It's the result of a systemic transformation of the global food economy, driven by transnational food corporations seeking shelf-stable, highly profitable products that require little refrigeration or transportation costs.

Reports from the Pan American Health Organization and research from 2013 by Dr Carlos Monteiro and colleagues show how rapidly UPFs have come to dominate global food markets. In high-income countries, they now make up 50 to 70 per cent (or more) of food sold in supermarkets. But in middle- and low-income nations, the intake is rising quickly — especially among children and the urban poor.

We are witnessing the wholesale replacement of traditional diets (which are based on minimally processed foods, local ingredients and cooking skills) with industrially engineered products that are displacing food cultures that have existed for millennia.

It's not hyperbolic to call this one of the greatest public health threats of our time. The last time we saw a mortality threat on this scale was during the Black Death — and this time, the threat isn't a virus. It's a food system.

Switching out UPFs

To move away from UPFs, and their serious health impact, here's a simple principle I use: eat a low human-interference diet — what I call a low-HI diet.

If a food once grew in the ground, swam or ran on four legs or two, and it's been minimally interfered with, you're probably safe. These are your foundation foods: fruits, vegetables, eggs, fish, unprocessed meats, beans, legumes and whole grains in their intact forms.

If the food has never been alive, or it's been broken down and reconstituted in a lab or factory, it belongs in your treat food category — not your daily foundational fare.

Here are some quick ways to make the switch:

♦ Swap processed breakfast cereals for steel-cut oats with berries, nuts and seeds, or for eggs and artisan sourdough toast with avocado and smoked salmon or nitrate-free bacon.

♦ Choose sourdough bread from a traditional bakery over mass-produced supermarket loaves.

♦ Avoid so-called health bars, protein cookies and flavoured yoghurts, opting instead for snacks of home-made trail mix (nuts, seeds, dried cranberries and dark chocolate) or high-protein unflavoured yoghurts with berries or raw honey.

♦ Cook more often — and make your own lunch (leftover dinners work well) — so you can regain control of your ingredients.

This is not about perfection. It's about awareness. Once you start reading labels, once you start noticing the number of synthetic ingredients in so many products, you'll realise just how far we've drifted from real nourishment.

UPFs have infiltrated nearly every corner of our diets, masquerading as convenience, affordability and even health through clever marketing strategies. But the science is clear, and it's growing stronger by the day: these products are making us sicker, fatter, more anxious and more inflamed.

We've just lived through a pandemic that reminded us of how vulnerable we are. The next public health crisis is already here and it's sitting quietly on our shelves, in plastic wrappers, engineered for bliss.

Let's not be victims of death by shit food. Let's choose to pull back the curtain and reclaim real food — food that supports not just our biology, but also our communities, our mental health and our future.

Nutrition rule #2: Eat an anti-ageing diet

Beyond just avoiding UPFs, experts now understand that specific nutrients and dietary patterns can directly impact the biological hallmarks of ageing outlined in chapter 7. Nutrition has been shown to be a powerful tool to slow down the ageing clock at the cellular level. The following sections explain how, outlining how nutrition provides powerful tools to target some of the main hallmarks of ageing directly. (See the references at the end of the book for full research details.)

Genomic stability and DNA protection

Damage to our DNA accumulates over time, driving the ageing process. Nutrients can help maintain genomic stability in several ways:

◆ Antioxidant-rich foods protect DNA from oxidative damage. Colourful fruits and vegetables provide polyphenols, flavonoids, carotenoids and other compounds that neutralise free radicals before they can damage DNA.

◆ Cruciferous vegetables (broccoli, cauliflower, brussels sprouts) contain sulforaphane, which activates DNA repair pathways and enhances detoxification of carcinogens.

◆ Mediterranean diet patterns have been shown to reduce DNA damage markers by up to 30 per cent compared to Western diets. The combination of olive oil, fish, fruits and vegetables appears to create a synergistic DNA-protective effect.

Telomere maintenance

Telomeres, those protective caps on our chromosomes, shorten with each cell division. Several nutritional factors affect telomere length:

◆ Omega-3 fatty acids are associated with longer telomeres and slower telomere attrition rates.

◆ Antioxidant-rich diets protect telomeres from oxidative damage. Vitamins C and E, and polyphenols from fruits and vegetables have all been linked to better telomere maintenance.

◆ Mediterranean dietary patterns consistently show associations with longer telomeres. For example, in the Nurses' Health Study (an ongoing large-scale, long-term study tracking the health of over 120 000 US nurses since 1976), greater adherence to a Mediterranean diet was associated with longer telomeres equivalent to about 4.5 fewer years of ageing, which is pretty bloody significant!

Epigenetic optimisation

As outlined in chapter 7, our epigenome — the system that controls which genes are expressed — becomes dysregulated with age. Nutrition has a profound effect on epigenetic patterns through the following:

◆ Methyl donors such as folate, vitamin B12, betaine and choline help maintain proper DNA methylation patterns. These nutrients are found in leafy greens, eggs, liver and legumes.

◆ Polyphenols including resveratrol, quercetin and curcumin can modify histone proteins and influence gene expression patterns related to longevity.

◆ Fasting and caloric restriction trigger epigenetic changes that promote stress resistance and longevity, partly through activating sirtuins, a class of proteins that regulate gene expression.

Proteostasis support

As also covered in chapter 7, our cells lose the ability to maintain protein quality control as we age, leading to the accumulation of damaged proteins. Nutrition can support the proteostasis process in the following ways:

◆ Protein intake provides the amino acids necessary for new protein synthesis.

◆ Spices such as turmeric contain curcumin, which activates heat shock proteins that help refold misfolded proteins.

◆ Plant compounds such as sulforaphane, EGCG from green tea and resveratrol can activate the proteasome — our cellular protein recycling system.

Nutrient sensing regulation

Nutrient sensing pathways, especially insulin/IGF-1, mTOR and AMPK, play crucial roles in ageing. These pathways can be modulated by the following:

- ◆ Intermittent fasting and time-restricted eating improve insulin sensitivity and reduce IGF-1 signalling.

- ◆ Avoiding excess calories can reduce excessive mTOR activation, which, when chronically stimulated, can accelerate ageing.

- ◆ Polyphenols from berries, tea and cocoa activate AMPK, a cellular energy sensor that promotes autophagy and stress resistance.

Mitochondrial support

Mitochondrial dysfunction is a hallmark of ageing that nutrition can directly address:

- ◆ Coenzyme Q10 levels decline with age but can be boosted through consumption of organ meats, fatty fish and whole grains.

- ◆ Polyphenols such as resveratrol and quercetin improve mitochondrial biogenesis through activation of PGC-1α.

- ◆ Alpha-lipoic acid found in spinach, broccoli and organ meats helps regenerate other antioxidants and protects mitochondrial membranes.

Combating inflammation

Several lifestyle factors can drive systemic inflammation, including our choices around nutrition. Certain foods have known anti-inflammatory effects in the body, as follows:

◆ Sugar and processed carbohydrates promote the creation of advanced glycation end-products (ironically called AGEs), so limiting them is important.

◆ Omega-3 fatty acids are particularly good at combating inflammation. (See later in this chapter for more on the importance of omega-3 fatty acids.)

◆ Extra-virgin olive oil contains oleocanthal, a compound with anti-inflammatory properties similar to ibuprofen. Regular consumption is associated with reduced inflammation and lower risk of chronic diseases.

◆ Berries (including strawberries, blueberries, raspberries and blackberries) are high in antioxidants such as anthocyanins, which have anti-inflammatory effects and may reduce the risk of disease.

◆ Leafy greens such as spinach, kale and collards are rich in vitamins and antioxidants that help lower inflammation.

◆ The spice turmeric contains curcumin, a powerful anti-inflammatory compound. Consuming turmeric with black pepper enhances curcumin absorption.

◆ Green, white and black teas are rich in polyphenols and antioxidants that can help reduce inflammation and protect against cellular damage.

The power of food synergy

What makes a truly anti-ageing diet so powerful is not just individual nutrients but also the synergy between them. Research increasingly shows that whole food patterns such as the Mediterranean, traditional Okinawan (from Japan) or modified DASH (dietary approaches to stop hypertension) diets have greater anti-ageing effects than any single nutrient supplement.

The key principles of these successful dietary patterns include:

- abundance of colourful plant foods (eight to ten servings daily)
- adequate protein from diverse sources
- healthy fats from olive oil, avocados, nuts and fish
- limited refined carbohydrates and added sugars
- phytochemical diversity (eating the rainbow)
- fermented foods for gut microbiome health
- herbs and spices for their anti-inflammatory compounds.

By incorporating these principles, you're not just preventing disease. You're also actively protecting your cellular machinery and promoting biological resilience at every level.

Nutrition rule #3: Optimise your omega-3 fatty acids

When it comes to slowing the ageing process and designing a diet that enhances lifespan and healthspan, one nutritional compound stands tall above the rest: omega-3 fatty acids.

If you're already a fan of omega-3s, some fascinating new research might just reinforce why these fats are essential. And if you're not, well, you might be by the end of this section.

The omega-3 deficiency crisis

First things first, let's look at the numbers. Around 80 per cent of the world, and a whopping 90 per cent of Americans, aren't getting enough omega-3s. That's a big deal, because low omega-3 levels are now being linked to a five-year decrease in life expectancy, putting them in the same health risk category as smoking.

Omega-3 fatty acids are essential fats, meaning our bodies don't produce them, so we need to get them from food or supplements. They play vital roles in neurodevelopment, cognitive function, inflammation control, cardiovascular health, immune response and even cancer prevention. When it comes to ageing, they might be one of our most powerful biological tools.

Omega-3s and the war on inflammaging

One major reason omega-3s are so critical for healthy ageing is their ability to combat inflammaging—the low-grade, chronic inflammation that underpins many age-related diseases, including cardiovascular disease, Alzheimer's disease and type 2 diabetes, and is one of the major hallmarks of ageing discussed in chapter 7.

A 2019 study led by Joel Ramirez showed that omega-3s increase levels of specialised pro-resolving mediators (SPMs), which are not your average anti-inflammatories. They're bioactive molecules that help *resolve* inflammation, which is a key difference. Omega-3s don't just suppress the fire—they help extinguish it and clear out the smoke.

The Omega-3 Index: A clear indicator of longevity

The Omega-3 Index is a marker of long-term omega-3 intake. It measures the percentage of omega-3 fatty acids, specifically EPA and DHA, in red blood cell membranes. Levels over 8 per cent are associated with the lowest risk of disease and longest life expectancy, while levels below 4 per cent are considered dangerously low.

A major study from 2004 by William Harris and Clemens Von Schacky found that people with an Omega-3 Index of 8 per cent or more lived, on average, five years longer than those with an index of 4 per cent or less. Five years! That's a PhD, a decent sabbatical, or the time it takes the average bloke to finally finish cleaning out the garage (I'm not there yet!).

Interestingly, the average Japanese person has an Omega-3 Index over 8 per cent, thanks to their seafood-rich diet. The average American sits under 5 per cent. And, lo and behold, the Japanese also outlive Americans, on average, by about five years. Coincidence? I think not!

Cardiovascular and cognitive perks

Omega-3s have been shown in research studies to reduce the risk of sudden cardiac death by up to 45 per cent and overall coronary heart disease mortality by 25 per cent. That's on par with some of the best heart medications out there, without the long list of side effects.

In the brain, the DHA type of omega-3 fatty acid helps maintain the structure and fluidity of neurons. This means omega-3s reduce the risk of cognitive decline, and higher intakes are associated with slower brain ageing. One study found that older adults with higher omega-3 levels had younger-looking brain scans than their same-age peers.

Slowing the clock: Omega-3s and biological ageing

Multiple studies using DNA methylation clocks that measure biological age (such as GrimAge and PhenoAge) show that higher omega-3 intakes are associated with slower biological ageing. In one

2025 study published in *Nature Aging*, consuming around 1.1 grams of omega-3s daily was associated with a slower pace of ageing across multiple biomarkers.

This isn't just about living longer — it's about staying functional longer. Higher omega-3 levels are linked to better mobility, lower frailty scores and improved quality of life into older age.

Interestingly, the same study found that women, older adults (over 60) and people with high blood pressure seem to benefit the most from omega-3s.

Omega-3s versus the hallmarks of ageing: Fats with fight

If you thought omega-3s were just good for your heart and maybe helping you remember where you put your keys, think again. These fatty acids don't just play defence — they're out on the biological battlefield engaging with several of our hallmarks of ageing. (See the references at the end of the book for full study details.)

GENOMIC INSTABILITY

Our DNA takes a beating over the years. Oxidative stress, poor diet, toxins, dickheads at work — all of it chips away at genomic integrity. Omega-3s help reduce that damage by lowering systemic inflammation and oxidative stress, both major drivers of DNA mutation and damage.

TELOMERE SHORTENING

Research shows that Omega-3s also seem to support telomere maintenance, protecting those shoelace caps that keep chromosomes from unravelling.

LOSS OF PROTEOSTASIS

Misfolded proteins? Plaques? Neurodegeneration? Yep—omega-3s help here too. They've been shown to enhance autophagy, the cells' way of cleaning up old junk. This matters big time for brain health and for preventing the kind of toxic protein build-up that's seen in conditions such as Alzheimer's disease.

MITOCHONDRIAL DYSFUNCTION

You likely remember from chapter 7 that mitochondria are the power plants of the cell that tend to start puffing out more smoke than energy as we age. Well, omega-3s help keep them running clean. The fatty acids DHA and EPA improve mitochondrial efficiency and reduce the leakage of reactive oxygen species (ROS)—those nasty little sparks of oxidative damage that fry cellular machinery from the inside. Some studies even suggest omega-3s support the creation of new mitochondria through activation of the PGC-1α pathway. In other words, they create more power, less rust.

INFLAMMAGING (AKA CHRONIC INFLAMMATION)

One of the most potent weapons omega-3s bring to the longevity table is their ability to resolve inflammation. As mentioned earlier, they boost production of SPMs, which don't just suppress inflammation but end it—clearing out immune cells, repairing tissues and hitting the 'reset' button on chronic inflammatory loops. This is crucial, because inflammaging is like having a permanent, low-grade fire in your tissues, and omega-3s are your internal fire brigade.

Omega-6 to omega-3: The modern imbalance

Modern diets are a mess when it comes to fat ratios. Many people consume 10 to 20 times more omega-6 than omega-3, thanks to vegetable oils and processed foods. Omega-6 has been shown to fuel inflammation and displace omega-3s from cell membranes.

Evolutionarily, our ancestors had a roughly 1:1 ratio of omega-6 to omega-3. Even 100 years ago, the ratio was around 4:1 or less. Today, many people are closer to 16:1, which is a ratio that drives chronic disease.

Optimising your omega-3s

To increase omega-3s in your diet, take a food-first approach and focus on the following:

◆ salmon, sardines, mackerel, anchovies, and other fatty fish — aim for three or four servings per week if you want to be optimal

◆ flax or chia seeds — these are decent sources of ALA, a type of omega-3 fatty acid, but provide poor conversion to EPA or DHA fatty acids.

You can then supplement with the following:

◆ Aim for 2 to 3 grams of EPA + DHA per day via fish oil supplements (or algae oil for vegetarians and vegans).

◆ Look for triglyceride or phospholipid forms for better absorption.

◆ Avoid oxidised oils. (Oils with low TOTOX values, indicating a fresher and higher quality oil, are ideal — aim for below 10.)

◆ Check third-party testing websites to compare the purity of different supplements (for example, the websites for IFOS (International Fish Oil Standards), Nutrasource and the NSF (National Science Foundation).

You can test your own Omega-3 Index at omegaquant.com and track changes over time. It's inexpensive (around $50 per test) and could just help you add up to five years to your life by optimising it!

Omega-3s are most certainly not 'snake oil' options. They are well-researched, widely deficient, and critical for healthspan and lifespan. They lower inflammation, protect the heart and brain, and might just keep you biologically younger for longer.

They aren't a magic pill—but along with exercise, they're about as close as we've come so far.

So, if you haven't made omega-3s a cornerstone of your nutrition strategy yet, now is the time.

Nutrition rule #4: Optimise your protein intake

While protein has long been a staple for bodybuilders and athletes, emerging research suggests that adequate protein intake is crucial for maintaining muscle mass, function and overall health for everyone. The truth is many of us simply aren't getting enough protein, especially as we grow older.

The age-related protein paradox

Here's the paradox: as we age, our bodies become less efficient at using protein (a phenomenon called anabolic resistance), yet most older adults consume less protein than their younger counterparts. It's a perfect storm for accelerated muscle loss and functional decline.

Research now indicates that older adults need significantly more protein than the standard recommended dietary allowance (RDA) of 0.8g per kilogram of body weight per day. In fact, for adults over 60, the optimal range appears to be 1.4 to 1.6g/kg/day or more — nearly double the standard recommendation.

A 2022 meta-analysis led by Hélio José Coelho-Júnior found that higher protein intake in older adults was associated with increased muscle mass, strength and physical performance. But protein's benefits extend far beyond muscle.

Protein's role in combating multiple hallmarks of ageing

Adequate protein intake tackles several of the hallmarks of ageing discussed in chapter 7 and through this chapter. The key findings are as follows:

◆ *Supporting proteostasis:* Amino acids are essential for the synthesis of new proteins to replace damaged ones.

◆ *Combating cellular senescence:* Protein-rich diets support immune function, which helps clear senescent cells.

◆ *Maintaining stem cell function:* Protein provides the building blocks for stem cell proliferation and differentiation.

◆ *Reducing inflammaging:* Several amino acids play direct roles in immune regulation and reducing chronic inflammation.

Protein and longevity: Striking the balance

You might have heard that restricting protein extends lifespan in some animal models, mainly due to inhibition of mTOR, a protein kinase that influences five of the 12 hallmarks of ageing. However, the idea that low protein equals reduced mTOR activation equals longer lifespan does not take into account the differences between chronic mTOR activation and the acute mTOR activation that occurs in response to eating protein.

While suppressing chronic mTOR activation may well extend lifespan, simply no evidence suggests that suppressing acute protein-induced mTOR activation would have the same effect. Consider exercise, which increases blood pressure and heart-rate acutely, but lowers them chronically.

For me, the best way to hedge your bets is to consume adequate protein in your main meals but don't snack between meals (note that both carbohydrate and protein activate mTOR signalling). The best way to not snack between meals? Consume adequate bloody protein in your main meals, which increases satiety!

Additionally, while studies in laboratory mice show that suppressing mTOR helps them live longer, most laboratory mice die of cancer, and low mTOR inhibits cancer. However, frailty and its effects kill many humans, but doesn't kill laboratory mice. Additionally, human research suggests that higher protein intake in later life is associated with better outcomes, including reduced all-cause mortality.

My reading on this? If you're a lab mouse, limit your protein intake, but if you're a human, ensure you eat enough.

Another way to hedge your bets may be to vary protein intake across the lifespan to account for changes in muscle protein synthesis: moderate consumption (but ensuring you're at least 1.4 grams per kilogram of bodyweight) in early and middle adulthood, followed by increased intake when you hit your 50s to get on the front foot and prevent sarcopenia and frailty kicking in when you hit your 60s and 70s. Ideally, at this stage you're hitting around 2 grams per kilogram of bodyweight to offset the decline in muscle protein synthesis that kicks in around your 50s and 60s.

As always, the quality of protein matters tremendously. Highly processed protein sources loaded with additives, preservatives and sodium (such as protein bars) don't confer the same benefits as minimally processed options. This brings us back to the low-HI principle — so choose proteins that have undergone minimal human interference.

Some practical tips for protein optimisation

So how should you incorporate protein into your daily eating pattern?

First, aim for 25 to 30 grams of high-quality protein per meal, spaced throughout the day. This approach maximises muscle protein synthesis and overcomes age-related anabolic resistance.

Second, prioritise complete protein sources that contain all essential amino acids, such as the following:

- animal proteins (eggs, dairy, meat, fish)
- complete plant combinations (rice and beans, hummus and wholegrain pita)
- complete plant proteins (quinoa, soy).

Third, timing matters — particularly breakfast, which is typically the most protein-deficient meal for most adults. Starting your day with a protein-rich breakfast (including, for example, Greek yoghurt, eggs or a protein smoothie) sets a metabolic tone for the entire day. Aim for at least 25 to 30 grams of high-quality protein at breakfast. Yes, this is a lot. You'll have to deliberately prioritise protein to achieve this, and I have some suggestions for how to do so in appendix C.

If you're concerned about animal protein consumption, research shows that plant-based proteins can be equally effective when consumed in slightly higher amounts to account for lower digestibility and amino acid profiles.

Nutrition rule #5: Take targeted supplements

While I'm a big fan of getting the vast majority of your nutrients through food, modern farming practices mean that most foods are not as nutritious as they used to be. This is where supplements can be helpful — and here is my personal top 10 list of anti-ageing supplements. I consider the top seven to be very important, especially if you're over 40, and the rest are optional if you have the money to spend. Please consult with your doctor before adding any of these supplements to your health plan.

1. *Vitamin D:* As you'll see in the next chapter, vitamin D positively affects most of the major hallmarks of ageing and also plays a crucial role in mood regulation — so it is right at the top of my list of required supplements if your levels are suboptimal. (Most researchers consider optimal levels to be 100 to 150 nmol/l (40 to 60ng/dl). For most adults, starting with supplements of 2000 to 4000 international units (IU) daily makes sense, but many people need 5000 to 8000 IU daily to reach optimal blood levels.

2. *Omega-3:* I've talked a lot about the benefits of omega-3 earlier in this chapter. Aim for a high-quality fish oil or algae oil if you're exclusively plant-based. You can get your omega-3 index tested at omegaquant.com and the aim is to get your score above 8 for clear longevity benefits.

3. *Creatine:* This is probably the best researched and safest sports supplement, but it also has proven brain benefits as well. The only potential issue is if you have existing kidney problems, so pass on this if you do. If not, aim for 3 to 5 grams of pure creatine monohydrate per day.

4. *GlyNac:* This combination of N-acetyl cysteine (NAC) and the amino acid glycine has been shown to enhance longevity by reducing inflammation, oxidative stress and mitochondrial function in mice. Research has shown that it affects the same processes in older adults, so for me, that's enough to take it if you're over 50.

5. *Alpha-ketoglutarate (AKG):* This supplement is showing promising health and longevity benefits across multiple species, with robust mechanistic foundations. Early studies in humans are showing promise — a recent pilot study in using a sustained-release calcium-AKG supplement showed an average 7-8 year reduction in biological age over just seven months, with larger trials now underway.

6. *Magnesium glycinate:* Magnesium is involved in so many processes in the body and many people have deficiencies due to lower levels in the soil these days. Many forms of magnesium are available, but magnesium glycinate is the most bio-available version.

7. *Circumin:* This is the active ingredient in turmeric, a popular spice used in cooking and for traditional benefits. Many studies demonstrate the anti-inflammatory properties of curcumin, so it deserves a place on this list.

8. *Hardy's Daily Essentials:* These are the best researched nutrients on the planet when it comes to the impact on the brain and nervous system, and I take this supplement

as insurance. If you are on psychiatric medication, make sure you talk to your doctor as the product can up-regulate the effects of the medication. Use the code Hardiness25 at checkout to get a 25 per cent discount. (Note that this is my discount, and I do not receive any money from the company.)

9. *Ubiquinol:* This is the most bioactive form of co-enzyme Q-10 (CoQ10) and it plays an important role in the electron transport chain, thus benefiting your mitochondria. It's also great for the heart and a must if you're taking a statin.

10. *Watch list – nicotinamide riboside (NR), nicotinamide mononucleotide (NMN), Spermidine:* These supplements are creating a bit of hype in anti-ageing circles for their purported longevity benefits, but most of the research at the time of writing is animal based, with the few studies on humans being small and often with conflicts of interest. That said, the logic is sound, so watch this space!

See the references at the end of the book for details of the research supporting this list, and see appendix C for anti-ageing meal plans that limit UPFs, increase omega-3 intake and provide adequate protein.

Putting it all together: Your personalised nutrition approach

As we wrap up this exploration of nutrition for healthy ageing, let's summarise the key principles:

◆ Minimise ultra-processed foods by adopting a low human-interference diet, focused on whole foods that look like they came from nature.

◆ Incorporate anti-ageing nutrients that target the hallmarks of ageing by eating a diverse, colourful diet rich in phytonutrients, antioxidants and anti-inflammatory compounds.

◆ Optimise your omega-3 intake from fatty fish, algae sources or high-quality supplements to combat inflammaging and support brain, heart and cellular health.

◆ Prioritise adequate protein to maintain muscle mass, support metabolic function, and provide the building blocks for cellular repair and immune function.

◆ Remember that nutrition isn't 'one-size-fits-all'. The best diet for you might be different from what works for someone else. Pay attention to how different foods make you feel, and don't be afraid to adjust your approach based on your own experience.

The beautiful thing about these principles is their flexibility. Whether you prefer Mediterranean-style eating, low-carb, vegetarian or something in-between, you can adapt these guidelines to fit your preferences, cultural background and lifestyle.

What matters most is consistency, not perfection. Small, sustainable changes to your daily eating patterns will compound over time, potentially adding years to your life and life to your years.

Food is more than fuel—it's information for your cells, instructions for your genes and the foundation on which your health is built. By making mindful choices based on evidence rather than fads, you're investing in your future self, one meal at a time.

Start where you are, use what you have and do what you can. Your cells will thank you.

9

Harness
the healing
power of light

Go to the rising sun; I am already setting.

Marcus Aurelius

To have a proper conversation about light and its healing powers, we need to talk about the electromagnetic spectrum — your knowledge of which may be buried somewhere deep in your mind from high school physics.

The electromagnetic spectrum is basically the full range of electromagnetic radiation that surrounds us all the time, on a spectrum of wavelengths. The wavelengths determine how they are produced, how they interact with matter and their practical applications. As shown in figure 9.1 (overleaf), this spectrum includes everything from gamma rays (which can cause cancer) on one end of the scale, through x-rays to microwaves and then radio waves at the other end of the scale. Somewhere in the middle is the good stuff: ultraviolet (UV) rays, visible light, and the red to near-infrared light I rave about in this chapter.

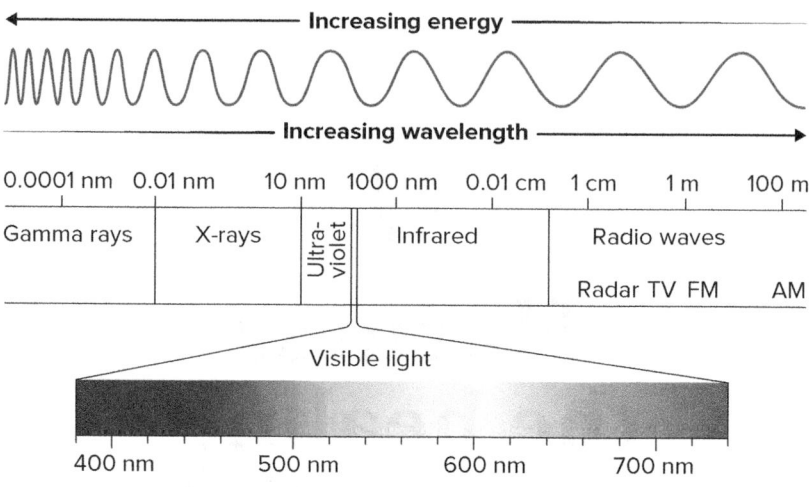

Figure 9.1: The electromagnetic spectrum

Source: © CBD Secretariat

Here's the cheat sheet about the light around the middle of the spectrum:

♦ Ultraviolet light (wavelength 10 to 400 nanometers, or nm) comes in three flavours: UVA, UVB and UVC. UVA (320 to 400 nm) makes you tan and age faster; UVB (280 to 320 nm), while also associated with sunburn and cancer, is your body's natural vitamin D switch; and UVC (100 to 280 nm) is basically sterilising death rays but, thankfully, the ozone layer filters these rays out.

♦ Visible light (400 to 700 nm) is what you see with your eyeballs and what plants use to grow via photosynthesis. It's also what drives your circadian rhythms.

♦ Red light (around 620 to 750 nm) helps your skin look younger, reduces acne and helps with burns and wound-healing.

◆ Near-infrared light (750–1100 nm) is like a cellular espresso shot — it penetrates deeper into tissues and organs, supercharging your mitochondria without burning you to a crisp.

Sunlight contains these kinds of light — UV (which you can't see), visible (including red) and infrared (which you can't see, unless you're a viper or using military-issued night vision goggles). It's our original and still most underrated medicine. But, as you'll see, not all light is created equal. Some of it heals; some of it hurts.

Why the ancient Egyptians were right

Ra (also spelled Re) was the ancient Egyptian deity of the sun. By the Fifth Dynasty of ancient Egypt (25th and 24th centuries BC), he was one of their most important gods — and I think they were definitely onto something.

When I was growing up in Northern Ireland, the sun was something of a mythical creature — rumoured to exist but rarely spotted in the wild. And when it did show its face, even half-heartedly, it was worshipped by the locals just like the ancient Egyptians. At the smallest glimpse, people would spontaneously start sunbathing. If the temperature hit 17 °C or above and the sun was out, shirts came off, ice-cream vans did endless laps of housing estates, and the nearest pub with outdoor seating became the most sought-after piece of real estate in the country. SPF? That was a concept reserved solely for gingers.

When I moved to Australia, it was like living on a different planet. Here, the national anthem may as well be 'Slip, Slop, Slap', a decades-long public health campaign encouraging people to slip on a shirt, slop on sunscreen and slap on a hat—due to the relatively high rates of skin cancer in this country. The campaign has been so successful that some Aussies now have levels of vitamin D deficiency similar to residents of Northern Ireland and Scandinavia!

So in one hemisphere, the sun is a precious, fleeting miracle. In the other, it's a daily threat to be negotiated with scientific precision. As someone who's lived in both worlds, I now find myself torn between these two instincts. Thankfully, a middle ground exists—and it involves understanding which parts of light are your friends, and which ones are trying to sneakily age you.

It turns out that the giant ball of nuclear fusion 93 million miles away is actually crucial to your wellbeing. Welcome to the world of heliotherapy—or, as normal humans call it, getting some sunshine. Think of it this way: our bodies literally evolved under the sun for hundreds of thousands of years, and it governed the way that we live. Our ancestors woke with the sun and slept when it set, and that's how human biology has evolved to work best.

Your internal clock is watching (even if you're not)

The magic of much of your bodily systems happens through your circadian rhythm—your body's internal 24-hour clock that regulates everything from hormone release to body temperature to when you should stop doom-scrolling and actually go to sleep. When morning sunlight hits your eyeballs (specifically the retinal ganglion cells), it tells your brain to suppress melatonin (the sleepy hormone) and release cortisol (the wake-up hormone). It's like someone flipping all the light switches in your body's control room to 'ON'. Here's a more detailed breakdown:

◆ Morning light = cortisol spike = alertness, energy.

◆ Midday light = serotonin boost = mood regulation.

◆ Evening darkness = melatonin release = deep sleep.

Without this daily reset, your internal systems start operating suboptimally. Research from 2014, led by Mohamed Boubekri, shows that office workers with windows sleep 46 minutes more per night than their windowless colleagues. Imagine what you could do with those extra 46 minutes. Actually, the answer should be 'sleep more', which is exactly what your body wants.

Your circadian rhythm getting disrupted doesn't just leave you tired but also sets you up for a carnival of health problems. These include:

◆ sleep disorders (ranging in severity from a little difficulty to full-blown insomnia)

◆ depression and anxiety (yes, the sun is literally an antidepressant)

◆ weakened immune function (making you that person who catches every office cold)

◆ metabolic issues (your body starts storing fat like you're preparing for a decade-long famine)

◆ higher risk of heart disease (your heart literally works better when you see daylight regularly)

◆ increased cancer risk (turns out cells like knowing what time it is)

◆ brain fog (explaining why you can't remember why you walked into a room).

Mood lighting: Your brain on sunshine

Likely you've heard of seasonal affective disorder, appropriately abbreviated as SAD—that winter blues phenomenon that makes you want to hibernate under a weighted blanket until spring.

But sunlight's effect on mood goes way beyond preventing you from becoming a grump during winter months.

Sunlight stimulates your brain to produce serotonin, the 'happiness molecule' that regulates everything from mood to memory to mating to sleeping. Low serotonin affects both mood and sleep. Studies show that hospital patients in sunny rooms require less pain medication and check out sooner than those in darker rooms. It's almost like humans weren't meant to recover in windowless boxes under artificial lighting — and I can certainly attest to that, given my recent surgery.

Even a brief ten-minute morning sunbath is enough to measurably improve your mood throughout the day, so the benefits of physical activity are amplified if they're done outdoors.

The vitamin with an identity crisis

When your understanding of biology increases, it becomes pretty clear that vitamin D suffers from a bit of an identity crisis. Despite its name, calling vitamin D a 'vitamin' is like calling a tiger 'just a big cat' — technically true but dramatically understating its power. Vitamin D actually functions as a hormone that influences hundreds of processes throughout your body.

If omega-3s are playing lead guitar in your longevity band (refer to the previous chapter), then vitamin D is undoubtedly on lead vocals. This humble hormone has emerged as one of the most powerful tools in your hardiness toolkit, and yet most of us aren't getting nearly enough.

When UVB rays from the sun hit your skin, they trigger a series of reactions that convert a cholesterol-like compound in your skin (7-dehydrocholesterol) into vitamin D3. This pre-vitamin then travels to your liver for the first transformation, and finally to your kidneys for the final activation. The result is a powerful hormone that can access nearly every cell in your body.

This natural production system is impressively efficient. Just 15 to 30 minutes of midday sun can generate 10 000 to 25 000 international units (IU) of vitamin D if you have fair skin — that's up to 30 times the minimum recommended daily amount. Your skin basically has its own little vitamin D factory that works overtime when it sees the sun.

Of course, various factors affect this production:

♦ *Skin pigmentation:* Melanin is like sunscreen, so darker skin needs more sun exposure for the same vitamin D production.

♦ *Age:* Like everything else, production of vitamin D declines with age.

♦ *Geography:* Living in my birthplace Northern Ireland or further north? Good luck making vitamin D in winter.

♦ *Time of day:* UVB rays peak at solar noon — not necessarily 12 pm thanks to changing time zones and daylight savings.

♦ *Weather and pollution:* Clouds and smog are the uninvited party-crashers of vitamin D production.

♦ *Sunscreen:* SPF 15 blocks about 95 per cent of vitamin D production. This is great for preventing skin cancer, but not so great for vitamin D levels.

The Swiss Army knife against ageing

A 2024 review, 'Targeting the hallmarks of aging with vitamin D: Starting to decode the myth', confirmed what many longevity researchers have suspected: vitamin D impacts nearly every single one of the 12 biological hallmarks of ageing discussed in chapters 7 and 8. As shown in table 9.1, vitamin D is like a Swiss Army knife for your cells in the fight against ageing.

Table 9.1: The impact of vitamin D on different hallmarks of ageing

Ageing hallmark	How vitamin D helps
Genomic instability	Improves DNA repair mechanisms and reduces oxidative stress.
Telomere attrition	Higher levels are associated with longer telomeres, essentially providing a buffer for your cellular ageing clock.
Epigenetic alterations	Influences gene expression across hundreds of genes, activating beneficial pathways while suppressing harmful ones.
Loss of proteostasis	Promotes proper protein folding and cellular clean-up, preventing toxic protein aggregates associated with neurodegeneration.
Deregulated nutrient sensing	Speculated to influence mTOR and IGF-1, though evidence is still emerging.
Mitochondrial dysfunction	Enhances mitochondrial performance and protects these cellular powerhouses against oxidative stress.
Cellular senescence	Helps inhibit pathways leading to cellular senescence and may reduce accumulated 'zombie cells'.
Stem cell exhaustion	Some pre-clinical studies suggest it influences the function of osteoblasts and neural stem cells.
Altered intercellular communication	Acts as an immunomodulatory molecule, counteracting the natural decline in immune surveillance.
Disabled macroautophagy	Drives autophagy through genomic and non-genomic signalling pathways.
Chronic inflammation	Modulates inflammatory cytokines such as IL-6 and TNF-α, supporting balanced immune regulation.
Dysbiosis	Improves gut microbiome diversity and composition, which regulates systemic inflammation.

That ranks Vitamin D right up there, and close to exercise in terms of its impact on the ageing hallmarks.

Vitamin D's day job: Pretty much everything

If vitamin D were a LinkedIn profile, it would be that annoyingly accomplished person with 50+ skills and endorsements in everything from 'immune system regulation' to 'making your bones not snap like twigs'. Its receptors are found in nearly every human tissue, which explains why it's involved in so many bodily processes, including in the following roles:

◆ *Immune system superhero:* Enhances white blood cells' pathogen-fighting abilities while keeping inflammation in check. Studies show adequate vitamin D levels may reduce susceptibility to respiratory infections, including colds, flu and even COVID-19. It's like having an internal mask, but without the ear chafing.

◆ *Cancer's arch-nemesis:* Helps regulate cellular division, potentially preventing the cellular hyperactivity that defines cancer. Research suggests optimal vitamin D levels are associated with reduced risk of colorectal, breast, prostate and other cancers. It can even induce cancer cell death (apoptosis) and prevent tumours from forming new blood vessels.

◆ *Heart helper:* Influences blood pressure regulation through the renin-angiotensin system. It also maintains the health of endothelial cells lining your blood vessels and may reduce arterial calcification. Multiple studies have linked vitamin D deficiency with increased risk of hypertension, heart attack, heart failure and stroke.

◆ *Brain booster:* Your brain contains significant vitamin D receptors, particularly in areas involved in memory and planning. Research suggests optimal vitamin D levels may help maintain cognitive function as you age and could protect against dementia and Alzheimer's disease.

◆ *Metabolism manager:* Influences insulin secretion and sensitivity, potentially affecting diabetes risk. Observational studies have linked higher vitamin D levels with reduced risk of type 2 diabetes, and some intervention studies suggest vitamin D supplementation may improve glycaemic control in pre-diabetic individuals.

◆ *Muscle maintainer:* Beyond its well-established role in bone health, vitamin D also supports muscle function. Maintaining adequate vitamin D levels has been shown to improve muscle strength and reduce fall risk in older adults.

◆ *Autoimmune peacekeeper:* Helps regulate the immune system and may protect against autoimmune diseases, where your immune system mistakenly attacks your own tissues like a dog barking at its reflection. It essentially helps your immune system distinguish between actual threats and your own body parts.

See the reference list at the end of the book for details of the studies that support these findings.

Brain chemistry benefits

Beyond its anti-ageing effects, vitamin D also plays a crucial role in mood regulation. A 2024 systematic review and dose-response meta-analysis, from Shadi Ghaemi and colleagues, reviewed 31 randomised controlled trials and found that vitamin D supplementation significantly reduced depressive symptoms, especially in those already experiencing depression.

Every 1000 IU/day increase led to measurable improvements, with the most substantial benefits seen at around 8000 IU/day. The effect appears to work through anti-inflammatory pathways, immune modulation and even direct action on serotonin production—essentially functioning like nature's antidepressant (anyone from the United Kingdom or further north can attest to this), minus the common side effects of pharmaceutical options.

The ultimate test: Does vitamin D help you stay alive?

Perhaps the most compelling evidence for vitamin D's importance comes from studies examining all-cause mortality—science-speak for 'death from anything'. A comprehensive meta-analysis from 2014 and published in the *American Journal of Public Health* analysed 32 studies involving over 566 583 participants and found that people with the lowest vitamin D levels had nearly twice the risk of death compared to those with the highest levels. Think about that—twice the risk!

Another systematic review examining 12 studies with 32 142 mostly elderly participants found that a 20 nmol/L increase (or 8 ng/ml) in vitamin D was associated with an 8 per cent lower mortality risk. This relationship followed a dose-response pattern, with mortality rates declining as vitamin D levels increased, until reaching a plateau at approximately 75 to 100 nmol/L (30 to 40 ng/ml)—suggesting this may represent the optimal range for not dying, which I think we can all agree is a pretty compelling health goal.

The pandemic nobody's talking about: Vitamin D deficiency

Despite its importance, vitamin D deficiency is staggeringly common worldwide. Depending on the threshold used (and different organisations and countries have different ones), estimates suggest that 30 to 80 per cent of various populations have insufficient levels. It's like a critical nutrient has been identified that almost everyone needs more of, but instead of focusing on it, we're arguing about whether oat milk or almond milk is more sustainable.

This deficiency hits certain populations particularly hard, including the following:

◆ older adults, especially those in care facilities — who often see less sunlight than Dracula

◆ people with darker skin living in northern latitudes — a double whammy of melanin and geography

◆ individuals with obesity — vitamin D gets trapped in fat tissue and can't carry out its functions

◆ people with conditions affecting vitamin D absorption — such as Crohn's disease and celiac disease

◆ those who cover their skin for religious or cultural reasons — suggesting spiritual devotion and boosting vitamin D levels aren't necessarily aligned.

How much D do you need?

Defining optimal vitamin D levels remains somewhat controversial, with different organisations suggesting different targets:

◆ The US Institute of Medicine suggests a 25(OH)D level (a blood test that measures the level of vitamin D in your blood) of at least 20 ng/ml (50 nmol/L) is sufficient for bone health — the bare minimum 'your bones won't shatter' approach.

◆ The Endocrine Society recommends a minimum level of 30 ng/ml (75 nmol/L) for optimal health benefits — the 'actually thriving, not just surviving' level.

◆ The Vitamin D Council and some researchers suggest optimal levels may be between 40 and 60 ng/ml (100 and 150 nmol/L), based on evolutionary biology and levels observed in populations with traditional outdoor lifestyles. I'm with this camp.

The reality is stark: if you're not testing, you're guessing. And most people who guess are wrong. Research suggests that optimal blood levels falling between 40 and 60 ng/ml is associated with better outcomes in everything from immunity to inflammation to mood and, yes, ageing.

Getting your vitamin D levels up

Maintaining healthy vitamin D levels requires a strategic approach that may include sunlight exposure, dietary sources and, in many cases, supplementation. Always consult with your health professional about what approach is right for you. Here's how it can all come together:

◆ Practise responsible sun exposure:

- Aim for 15 to 30 minutes of midday sun exposure to face, arms and legs two to three times weekly (without sunscreen) if you have fair skin, and longer if you have darker skin.

- Consider your latitude — if you live above 37° north or below 37° south, you need to accept that winter is basically a vitamin D desert.

- Avoid sunburn, because it increases skin cancer risk without producing additional vitamin D.

◆ Add in dietary sources, using the following as your supporting cast:

- Fatty fish (salmon, mackerel, sardines) — provides 400 to 1000 IU per 100-gram serving.

- Cod liver oil—provides about 400 to 1000 IU per teaspoon (but tastes exactly like you'd expect liquefied fish liver to taste).

- Egg yolks—about 40 IU each (from pasture-raised hens who actually see the sun).

- Mushrooms exposed to UV light—variable amounts of vitamin D2.

◆ Use supplementation when nature needs a boost and:

  - you don't get much sun (especially in winter or at high latitudes)

  - you're over 60

  - your blood levels test below 100 nmol/L (40 ng/ml)

  - you want to support multiple aspects of healthy ageing with a simple, safe intervention.

For most adults, starting with 2000 to 4000 IU as a daily supplement makes sense, but many people need 5000 to 8000 IU daily to reach optimal blood levels. Always try to pair with vitamin K2 (particularly the MK-7 form) to ensure calcium ends up in your bones rather than your arteries. Vitamin D is fat-soluble, so supplements are best absorbed when taken with meals containing some fat. Blood level testing is recommended before starting high-dose supplementation and periodically thereafter (because more isn't always better—you can get vitamin D toxicity).

Vitamin D is inexpensive, safe at appropriate doses and affects nearly every system in your body. From bones to brain, and from genes to gut, it's a central player in your physiological hardiness machinery. If your levels are suboptimal, no amount of other health optimisation will fully compensate.

Remembering sunlight is health care, not just a weather report

Our ancient connection to the sun is biologically hardwired. From regulating our circadian rhythms to enabling vitamin D production, sunlight plays a fundamental role in human health that your SAD lamp, however expensive, can't fully replace.

The evidence overwhelmingly suggests that maintaining optimal vitamin D levels — ideally through a combination of sensible sun exposure, dietary sources and judicious supplementation when needed — may significantly reduce disease risk and potentially extend lifespan. It turns out that 'getting some sun' isn't just something your granny randomly suggested — it's legitimate health advice.

Rather than fearing the sun, we should develop a new relationship with it — one that acknowledges both its life-giving benefits and potential risks. By incorporating appropriate sun exposure into our daily routines, we reconnect with one of nature's most powerful health resources, and one that has sustained human wellbeing throughout our evolutionary history.

In an age where we have apps to track our steps, heart rate, sleep quality, meditation minutes and water intake, it's worth remembering that sometimes the most powerful medicine is also the most accessible.

Just don't forget the sunscreen after your vitamin D production time is up. Finding the balance between sun benefits and skin cancer risk is tricky and you need to take into consideration your skin type (look up the Fitzpatrick skin type scale, a scientific way of classifying skin types, to get started), where you live and the current state of your skin.

So now we've established that sunlight is basically nature's multivitamin — with a bit of a dark side if you overdo it or forget your sunscreen. But what if you could extract the best bits of sunlight — such as the ones that help your cells heal, your brain fire on all cylinders and your mitochondria to act like they're on steroids — without the whole sunburn and skin cancer risk? Enter red and near-infrared light. These wavelengths are like the nerdy cousins of UV: less flashy, but much more helpful over the long haul. And, unlike UV rays, they won't turn you into a raisin with skin damage. What they will do, however, is quite astonishing.

Shining a light on healing (literally)

Welcome to the world of photobiomodulation (PBM). In plain language, PBM is the use of red and near-infrared light to make your cells function better. Think of this light as giving your mitochondria a much-needed espresso shot.

The magic happens when specific wavelengths of red and near-infrared light (typically between 600 and 850 nm, but higher for some applications) penetrate your skin. The light can either directly affect your skin or reach below the skin to affect cells, tissues and organs, depending on the wavelength of the light.

The light then gets absorbed by a component in your cells called cytochrome c oxidase. This is an enzyme in your mitochondria, which, as already discussed, are the little energy factories inside your cells with other hidden superpowers. When this light hits these cellular components, it's like flipping on a power switch. Your cells start producing more adenosine triphosphate (ATP), which is your cellular energy currency. More ATP means more energy for healing, regeneration and optimal function.

The light also triggers a brief burst of reactive oxygen species (ROS)—which sounds bad, but in small, controlled amounts actually triggers positive cellular responses. Think about this in terms of exercise: no exercise means no stimulation and so is bad, a little stress from regular exercise makes you stronger, but too much stress such as running ultramarathons regularly can damage your heart and cause widespread inflammation. In this way, it follows the typical hormetic curve discussed in chapter 6.

The result of this mild hormetic stress caused by red and near-infrared light is reduced inflammation, accelerated healing, increased collagen production and even improved brain function. Not bad for just sitting under a light, right?

Wound healing: Moving beyond bandaids

Studies show that red light therapy can significantly accelerate wound healing, including cuts, burns and even more stubborn cases such as diabetic ulcers. The healing magic happens because red light PBM boosts circulation, stimulates collagen production, reduces inflammation and increases the proliferation of fibroblasts—the cells responsible for rebuilding damaged tissue. PBM makes them work overtime.

I can also add my own experiment to the increasing amount of peer-reviewed research studies showing the healing benefits of light. I used a combined red and near-infrared panel every day in the days following my open-heart surgery (in conjunction with collagen, targeted supplements and progressively increasing the weight that I lifted in my rehab). As a result, I was attending CrossFit (at reduced capacity) and bench-pressing 60 kilograms six weeks after my surgery, when the official recovery guide said I would likely be ready to make the bed, hang the washing and play darts.

Moving beyond my sample-size-of-one study, let's look at what the research reveals on diabetic wounds — which normally heal about as quickly as government bureaucracy works. Red light therapy at specific wavelengths (around 660 nm) has been shown to significantly improve healing rates of these wounds in a number of studies and is now used as part of best practice in their treatment. The light activates a cellular pathway called the Ras/MAPK pathway that makes those fibroblasts more viable, helps them multiply faster, and gets them moving to the wound site like there's a two-for-one sale on tissue repair.

Even burn wounds, which are notoriously difficult to treat and prone to scarring, respond surprisingly well to PBM. The light helps activate a protein called TGF-β1, which is crucial for healing and tissue regeneration. Research shows that PBM significantly accelerates recovery, and light therapy is now also part of best practice for treating burns victims.

Your brain on near-infrared light

Perhaps the most exciting application of PBM is its potential effect on brain health. When directed at the head, near-infrared light (particularly around 810 nm, but also 1050 nm) can actually penetrate the skull and reach brain tissue, resulting in a range of positive effects. In studies on stroke recovery, applying transcranial laser therapy within 24 hours of a stroke has been shown to produce significant improvements in neurological outcomes. The light helps reduce inflammation, stimulates cellular processes to prevent neurons from dying, and generally results in quicker and fuller recovery.

For neurodegenerative conditions such as Parkinson's and Alzheimer's, the research is still emerging but looks promising. In Parkinson's disease, where dopamine-producing neurons die off and mitochondria function about as well as a car with sugar in the gas tank, PBM seems to protect those neurons and boost mitochondrial function. Some studies combining PBM with hydrogen therapy (for its antioxidant effects) showed improvements in Parkinson's symptoms after just two weeks of daily treatment.

For those with early Alzheimer's or mild cognitive impairment, emerging evidence shows that transcranial PBM may improve cognition by boosting cerebral blood flow and mitochondrial function. While it is certainly not a cure for Alzheimer's disease, it shows more promise than many of the failed drugs that cost millions to develop and had no impact whatsoever.

Inflammation: The fire within (that won't go out)

One of the most consistently reported effects of PBM is a reduction in inflammation, which contributes to everything from heart disease to arthritis to that mysterious pain in your knee when it rains. While anti-inflammatory medications can come with side effects ranging from stomach ulcers to liver damage, red light therapy modulates inflammation without these unpleasant bonuses.

And here's where it gets interesting: PBM actually has different effects depending on the state of the cells it's treating. In normal cells, it might briefly activate inflammatory pathways (which is why you shouldn't spend all day under a panel), but in already inflamed cells, it dials down inflammatory markers. The light also helps reduce oxidative stress — the cellular equivalent of rust. While a small amount of ROS can be beneficial (as mentioned at the start of this section), chronic oxidative stress is like having your car engine run at 6000 revs constantly — eventually, something's going to break. PBM helps balance the production of oxidants and antioxidants, giving your cells a fighting chance.

The mitochondria: Tiny powerhouses, big impact

If cells were cities, mitochondria would be the power plants. When they're running efficiently, everything works well. When they're struggling, the whole city experiences blackouts. PBM essentially helps these cellular power plants work better. By stimulating cytochrome c oxidase (a component of the mitochondrial respiratory chain), PBM facilitates electron transport and increases the production of ATP — your body's energy currency. Even a small increase in ATP can significantly enhance cellular function and have positive effects.

This improvement in mitochondrial function has wide-ranging effects. For your skin, it means more collagen and elastin production (hello, anti-ageing effects). For your muscles, it means better recovery after exercise. For your brain, it means more efficient neural function. It's like giving every system in your body a tune-up simultaneously.

Researchers have identified the specific wavelengths that are most effective for mitochondrial stimulation are between around 620 nm and 680 nm for red light, and between 810 nm and 830 nm for near-infrared. These wavelengths are like the perfect keys that fit the mitochondrial locks, while other wavelengths just jiggle around ineffectively.

Knowing how to actually use this stuff

So hopefully you're now convinced that red light isn't just for photographers' darkrooms and sketchy nightclubs. Now let's talk about how you actually benefit from it.

The good news is that **PBM** devices have become much more accessible. You can find everything from handheld devices to full-body panels, masks for your face, or caps for your head. The bad news is that with this accessibility comes a wide variation in quality and effectiveness. Make sure to check with your doctor first to see if **PBM** is suitable for you. For effective treatment, you need to consider several factors:

◆ *Wavelength:* Effective ranges are typically 630 nm to 680 nm (red) and 800 nm to 850 nm, but in some cases up to 1050 (near-infrared).

◆ *Power density:* Too little won't do anything; too much might be inhibitory. For skin, aim for around 50 to 100 watts; for pain relief and recovery, 100 to 150 watts; and for deeper tissues, above 150 watts.

◆ *Treatment time:* Usually 5 to 20 minutes per session works best.

◆ *Frequency:* Often daily or several times weekly.

The 'Goldilocks zone' for **PBM** is real—too little energy won't trigger the beneficial cellular responses, while too much can actually inhibit them. It's like caffeine: one cup of coffee makes you alert, but chug three or four espressos and you'll be a jittery mess.

For general wellness and skin health, devices that combine red (about 660 nm) and near-infrared (about 850 nm) seem to offer the broadest benefits—and that's what I have. For improving skin tone or combating teenage acne, red light is what you're after, while for deeper tissue issues such as muscle recovery, joint pain or stimulation of mitochondria in deeper tissues, near-infrared is the way to go because it penetrates deeper.

Understanding what red light therapy is not

Before you throw away all your medications and set up a red light shrine in your living room, running the risk of making your house look like it's a brothel, let's be clear about what PBM isn't:

- ◆ It's not a miracle cure for everything. Despite its impressive range of benefits, it won't replace the gym.

- ◆ It's not the same as ultraviolet light therapy. UV light can damage DNA and cause skin ageing — exactly what you're trying to avoid.

- ◆ It's not instantaneous. Like most good things in life, it takes consistency and patience to see results.

- ◆ It's not a replacement for medical treatment. If you have a serious condition, please consult an actual medical professional before attempting to self-treat with any form of light.

The bottom line: Should you give red light a green light?

After sifting through the science, PBM clearly isn't just another wellness fad destined for the same graveyard as oxygen bars and shake weights — and it's why I invested in a combined red and near-infrared panel. I love it, and I'm convinced it accelerated my healing from my surgery. The biological mechanisms are sound, the research is increasingly robust and the potential applications are impressively broad.

From accelerating wound healing, boosting cellular energy and reducing inflammation to potentially slowing neurodegenerative processes, red and near-infrared light therapy offers a unique approach to health that works with your body's own systems rather than overriding them.

Is it worth trying? For most people, absolutely — and thankfully lots of wellness spas, gyms and recovery places are offering paid sessions so you don't have to break the bank investing in a panel. The side effects are minimal to non-existent when used correctly (and not over-used), and the potential benefits are significant. Just remember that like any health intervention, quality matters, consistency is key and realistic expectations will keep you from disappointment.

Putting it all together: Embracing the power of light

From ancient sun worship to cutting-edge red and near-infrared light panels, this chapter has shown that light isn't just something to read by — it's something to heal by. Whether it's the natural sunlight that sets your circadian rhythm and fuels your body's vitamin D factory, or the targeted application of red and near-infrared light to supercharge your mitochondria, light is an underrated but powerful component of your hardiness arsenal.

In an age where we obsess over steps, supplements and sleep scores, it's worth remembering that a walk in the sunshine might do more for your health than another biohacking gadget. And when nature doesn't cooperate — or when you need a deeper, more targeted intervention — PBM steps in to offer the benefits of light without the risks of sunburn or skin damage.

So instead of fearing the sun or ignoring its importance, learn to work with it and with its high-tech cousins to harness its biological benefits safely and effectively.

10
Master strategic recovery

*You should sit in meditation for 20 minutes a day,
unless you're too busy — then you should sit for an hour.*

Zen Koan

Our bodies aren't built for the nonstop, always-on lifestyle of the modern world. We evolved as hunter-gatherers who would sprint after prey or forage intensely, and then rest. This intermittent pattern of exertion and recovery is literally baked into our genome — it's how we're wired to function optimally.

Yet most of us operate like perpetual motion machines, grinding through hour after hour of work with barely a pause, wondering why our energy, focus and productivity tank by mid-afternoon. We reach for another coffee or sugary snack, or just power through on willpower until we collapse into our evening Netflix binges, too exhausted to do anything more meaningful with our precious free time.

What if there was a better way? A science-backed approach to working and living that honours your biology instead of fighting against it? That's what this chapter is all about: strategic recovery — the missing link in most people's performance equation.

Cognitive gears: Working with your brain, not against it

Before diving into recovery techniques, let's talk about matching your tasks to your mental state. Think of your brain as having three distinct gears:

♦ *Gear 1 – administrative work:* This is your low mental effort gear for relatively straightforward tasks that don't require deep thought or creativity. For example:

  • processing emails

  • routine administrative tasks

  • organising your workspace

  • light reading

  • scheduling meetings.

♦ *Gear 2 – collaborative work:* This middle gear involves more cognitive effort, particularly in a social context. This work might include the following:

  • meetings (especially when you need to contribute)

  • problem-solving conversations

  • mentoring or coaching sessions

  • team brainstorming sessions

  • client calls.

◆ *Gear 3 – deep work:* This is your highest cognitive gear, requiring intense focus and mental horsepower. You need the gear for the following:

- strategic planning

- writing (reports, articles, books)

- complex problem-solving

- creative work

- learning difficult new skills

- data analysis.

As Professor Cal Newport explains in his excellent book *Deep Work*, the ability to focus intensely without distraction on cognitively demanding tasks remains extremely valuable in our economy. Yet most of us squander our best mental energy on low-value 'gear 1' tasks.

The key is to match the gear to your energy state throughout the day. Most people experience peak cognitive function in the morning (typically two to four hours after waking), with a smaller second peak in the early evening. A significant dip usually occurs after lunch, and that's biology, not laziness.

So rather than fighting these natural rhythms, work with them:

◆ Schedule your gear 3 deep work during your peak cognitive hours.

◆ Use your afternoon energy dip for gear 1 administrative tasks.

◆ Save gear 2 collaborative work for your middle-energy periods.

As Newport highlights, the ability to perform deep work is becoming increasingly rare at exactly the same time it is becoming increasingly valuable in our economy. As a consequence, the few who cultivate this skill will thrive.

As well as structuring your working hours based on your natural rhythms, science is also recognising the importance of micro-breaks through your day, which I cover later in this chapter. Before jumping into this, however, let's talk about some technical aspects of the thing you do 20000 times a day without thinking. I'm talking about breathing, and it turns out that how we perform it can damage our performance and health, or be performance enhancing and brain boosting.

The science of breathing right

Now, let me start with a bit of personal history. Back in my boxing days, I had my nose both broken and fractured, which left me with a deviated septum. (Yes, I know — a neuroscientist who boxes must be a pretty stupid neuroscientist.) After my injuries, breathing through my nose was nigh on impossible. Unsurprisingly, I became a chronic mouth breather. And, let me tell you, the effects were not subtle. They included poor sleep, suboptimal energy, mouth as dry as a cat's tongue — and my wife, Carly, will tell you all about my (alleged) snoring. Eventually, I bit the bullet and got my septum surgically fixed. The result was a total game-changer. It was like someone turned on the oxygen supply. A couple of years ago, I also started mouth-taping at night (which I still do religiously), and the quality of my sleep and recovery improved even more.

The benefits of nasal breathing

So, what's the deal with nasal breathing versus mouth breathing?

Nasal breathing isn't just about elegance or avoiding drool on your pillow. It actually engages an entirely different set of physiological systems compared to mouth breathing. When you breathe through your nose, you activate the diaphragm more effectively, stimulating the vagus nerve and enhancing parasympathetic (rest-and-digest) nervous system activity.

Research has shown that nasal breathing is linked to the following:

◆ lower diastolic blood pressure and enhanced parasympathetic tone, which translates into a more relaxed, recovery-prone physiological state

◆ improved cognitive function through a surprising mechanism: inhaling through the nose actually enhances brain rhythms and synchronises neural activity across regions involved in attention and memory

◆ better sleep and reduced risk of conditions such as sleep apnoea — a known performance and longevity killer.

Meanwhile, mouth breathing has been associated with:

◆ increased oral acidity, leading to tooth decay and gum disease

◆ biased sympathetic nervous system activation — essentially keeping you in a low-level state of stress

◆ structural changes in developing children's faces and jaws (yep, mouth breathing can literally change your face).

In fact, just five minutes of nasal breathing can begin to shift heart rate variability — a proxy for recovery and stress resilience — in the right direction.

And it's not just physiological. Studies suggest nasal breathing is even rhythmically tied to how we think. One study, led by Ofer Perl and published in *Nature Human Behaviour*, showed that people perform better on tasks involving memory and visuospatial perception when they're inhaling through their nose at the moment of task onset. Let that sink in — your brain is literally timing its cognitive processes with your breathing cycle.

The bottom line (and a bit of tape)

So here's what I recommend as a reformed mouth-breather:

◆ *Mouth tape at night:* This may feel weird at first, but it will transform your sleep. (Don't attempt this if you have any physical conditions that impede breathing through your nose, such as my old injury, a deviated septum, or a blocked nose due to sickness. And, pro tip, don't use duct tape! Use hypo-allogenic tape.)

◆ *Conscious nasal breathing during the day:* Practise this especially during moments of stress or recovery — your body and brain will thank you.

◆ *Nasal-focused breathwork:* Try slow, diaphragmatic nasal breathing — I provide a few protocols for how to do this in the next section.

Breathing may be automatic, but doing it right takes awareness. And if your snout is busted like mine was, get it fixed as soon as possible. Trust me, your performance, mood, immune function and sleep will all level up.

Micro-recovery: The power of strategic renewal

Micro-recovery periods are strategic renewal periods incorporated throughout your workday that help maintain high performance. This isn't about being lazy — it's about being smart with your biological resources.

Research from elite sports shows us that it's not just the volume of training that creates champions but also the quality of recovery between training sessions. The same principle applies to knowledge work. The most productive people aren't those who work the longest hours but those who work intensely and then recover effectively. In this section, I outline some simple techniques so you can be one of those people.

The Pomodoro Technique: Work–recovery cycles

The Pomodoro Technique, developed by Francesco Cirillo, is a simple but powerful method for maintaining focus and energy. Here's how it works:

1. Set a timer for 25 minutes of focused work (one 'Pomodoro').

2. Work on a single task without interruption until the timer rings.

3. Take a five-minute break (micro-recovery).

4. Complete four Pomodoro cycles (totalling two hours), and then take a longer 15- to 30-minute break.

This structured approach creates boundaries around your work periods, preventing the mental fatigue that comes from endless, unfocused effort. The short breaks are also critical — they're not just time-fillers but active recovery periods.

These five-minute micro-recovery sessions can also be broken down, and I recommend the following sequence.

MOVEMENT SNACK (30 TO 60 SECONDS)

Your body was designed to move, not sit in a chair all day staring at screens. Extended sitting not only creates physical problems but also impairs cognitive function. When you sit for more than 30 minutes, gene expression changes occur that negatively affect blood pressure, glucose metabolism and blood flow to the brain.

A quick 'movement snack' of intense movement for 30 to 60 seconds counteracts these effects brilliantly. My favourites include:

- kettlebell swings (if you don't have kettlebells, get some!)
- jumping jacks
- sprint on the spot
- air squats
- push-ups
- burpees
- walk quickly up a couple of flights of stairs.

You don't need to make this complicated. Even 30 to 60 seconds of movement gets your blood flowing, increases oxygen to your brain and burns off stress hormones. If you're in an office and feel self-conscious, duck into a stairwell or bathroom stall — nobody's judging your squats in there.

VISUAL RESET (30 SECONDS)

After your movement snack, it's time to give your visual system a break. Research from neuroscientist Andrew Huberman's lab shows that focusing at a near distance (such as a computer screen) for prolonged periods activates stress responses in the brain.

Counteract this by:

♦ looking out a window at the furthest point you can see

♦ if no window is available, simply expanding your gaze to take in the entire room

♦ focusing on distant objects, then middle-distance, and then close objects.

This visual reset helps deactivate the sympathetic (fight-or-flight) response that builds up during concentrated screen work.

HYDRATION (30 SECONDS)

Next, drink a glass of water. Most of us operate in a mild but chronic state of dehydration, which impairs cognitive performance, decision-making and mood. Your brain is about 75 per cent water and needs proper hydration to function optimally.

Keep a water bottle at your desk and empty it during your micro-recovery sessions. This simple habit will ensure you stay properly hydrated throughout the day. (And make you get up from your desk for refills and toilet breaks — win–win!)

BREATHWORK RESET (2 TO 3 MINUTES)

Finally, use strategic breathwork to reset your nervous system (or meditate, which is equally effective). Depending on your current state and needs, you can either downregulate (calming your system when you feel anxious or stressed) or upregulate (energising your system when you feel sluggish or foggy).

Try the following techniques (also illustrated in figure 10.1) for downregulation:

♦ *Box breathing:* This technique is used by Navy SEALs to control arousal in high-stress situations. Here's the process:

1. Inhale through your nose for a count of four.

2. Hold your breath for a count of four.

3. Exhale through your nose for a count of four.

4. Hold the exhale (empty lungs) for a count of four.

5. Repeat for four to eight cycles.

♦ *Resonant frequency breathing:* This powerful technique helps synchronise your heart rate with your breathing cycle. Here's how:

1. Inhale through your nose for four seconds.

2. Exhale through your nose for six seconds.

3. Maintain this ten-second cycle for one or two minutes.

This aligns with six breaths per minute, and studies show this pattern optimises heart rate variability, a key marker of stress resilience and autonomic nervous system health.

♦ *Physiological sigh:* When you need quick stress relief, try this technique used by lots of animals when stressed (including your pets). A study by Huberman's lab identified sighing as the quickest way to activate your parasympathetic nervous system (and hence the relaxation response). Here's how to sigh with intent:

1. Take two quick inhales through your nose (one right after the other).

2. Exhale in one long sigh through your mouth.

3. Repeat two to three times.

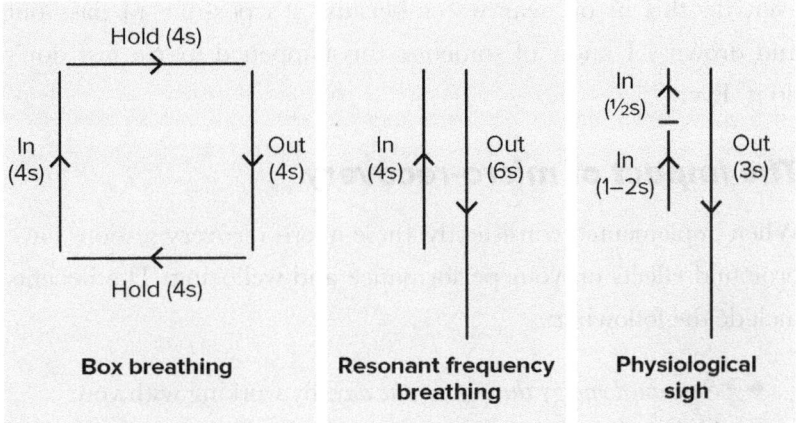

Figure 10.1: The three types of downregulating breathwork

If upregulation is required, you can try controlled cyclic hyperventilation. (If you're familiar with the Wim Hof Method, you're probably all over this like a spider monkey.) To give yourself an energy boost without caffeine, complete the following:

1. Take 30 powerful breaths through the mouth. Your inhale should be similar to when blowing up a balloon. Your exhales should be quick, with your inhales about twice as long as your exhales.

2. After the 30th breath, exhale fully and hold the empty lungs as long as comfortable.

3. Take one deep recovery breath and hold for 15 seconds.

4. Resume normal breathing.

This technique temporarily increases adrenaline and noradrenaline (naturally, without caffeine), providing a rapid energy boost. It also increases alkalinity in the blood, which many people report creates a sense of mental clarity.

Warning: Do not perform this technique while driving or standing. It can cause lightheadedness, so it's best done sitting. And never,

ever, do this in or near water because it's possible to pass out and drown — I know of someone this happened to. So just don't do it. Ever.

The impact of micro-recovery

When implemented consistently, these micro-recovery sessions have profound effects on your performance and wellbeing. The benefits include the following:

- *Sustained energy throughout the day:* By working with your biology instead of against it, you avoid the afternoon energy crash.

- *Improved cognitive performance:* Research shows that brief recovery periods enhance problem-solving, creativity and decision-making.

- *Reduced stress and burnout risk:* Regular nervous system resets prevent the accumulation of stress hormones.

- *Better evening quality of life:* By managing your energy effectively at work, you have more to give to your personal life.

The executives I have worked with who implemented these strategies report not only improved productivity but also higher wellbeing. They also tell me that they have more energy when they get home, allowing for greater quality time with loved ones — and who doesn't want that?

Macro-recovery: The sleep solution

While micro-recovery is essential for daily performance, macro-recovery — getting quality sleep — is the foundation of long-term health, cognitive function and longevity. Sleep isn't just rest; it's also a complex biological process essential for cellular repair, memory consolidation and metabolic health.

Sleep and the hallmarks of ageing

Remember those hallmarks of ageing discussed in chapters 7 and 8? Poor sleep accelerates nearly all of them:

◆ *Genomic instability:* Sleep deprivation damages DNA and impairs repair mechanisms. Even one night of poor sleep can increase DNA breaks and reduce the expression of DNA repair genes.

◆ *Telomere attrition:* Studies show chronic insomnia is associated with shorter telomere length, particularly in older adults (70 to 88 years).

◆ *Epigenetic alterations:* Sleep loss alters gene expression through changes in DNA methylation and other epigenetic mechanisms, causing cells to functionally 'age' faster.

◆ *Loss of proteostasis:* Sleep is crucial for removing misfolded proteins from the brain and body. The glymphatic system (the brain's waste clearance pathway) is primarily active during sleep. Disrupted sleep contributes to protein accumulation associated with neurodegenerative diseases.

◆ *Deregulated nutrient sensing:* Poor sleep disrupts insulin sensitivity and metabolic regulation. One study, led by Xuewen Wang, showed that three nights of slightly less sleep than normal significantly raised blood glucose levels and impaired insulin sensitivity.

◆ *Mitochondrial dysfunction:* Sleep deprivation damages mitochondria and reduces ATP production. This contributes to fatigue and cognitive impairment, and accelerated ageing.

- *Cellular senescence:* Inadequate sleep increases markers of cellular senescence — those zombie-like cells that secrete inflammatory compounds. Even partial sleep deprivation activates the senescence-associated secretory phenotype (SASP).

- *Stem cell exhaustion:* Sleep disruption impairs stem cell function and regenerative capacity. Studies show that REM sleep deprivation reduces neurogenesis (the birth of new brain cells) in the hippocampus.

- *Altered intercellular communication:* Sleep loss promotes chronic inflammation and disrupts hormonal signalling pathways, creating system-wide dysfunction.

The evidence is clear (and you can check the references at the end of the book for details of the studies that demonstrate this). Chronic poor sleep doesn't just make you tired, but also fundamentally accelerates ageing at the cellular level.

Sleep architecture: Understanding the cycles

To optimise sleep, it helps to understand its structure. Sleep isn't a uniform state but instead cycles through distinct stages, as follows:

- *Stage N1 (light sleep):* Heart rate and breathing begin to slow, muscles relax and brain waves transition from waking alpha waves to theta waves.

- *Stage N2 (stable sleep):* Body temperature drops, eye movements stop, and brain waves show characteristic 'sleep spindles' and 'K-complexes'.

- *Stage N3 (deep sleep):* Also called slow-wave sleep, this is when your brain produces delta waves. Growth hormone is released, physical restoration occurs and the glymphatic system clears metabolic waste from the brain.

◆ *REM sleep:* Your brain becomes highly active (similar to wakefulness), muscles are paralysed (to prevent acting out dreams) and intense dreaming occurs. This stage is crucial for emotional processing and memory consolidation, and poor REM sleep can cause anxiety to develop.

You cycle through these stages approximately every 90 minutes, with more deep sleep in the first half of the night and more REM sleep in the second half. For optimal cognitive and physical health, you need adequate amounts of all these sleep stages.

Practical strategies for developing your sleep muscle

Your sleep quality can be improved through some simple, practical steps, which I outline here.

MAINTAIN CONSISTENT SLEEP TIMING

Your circadian rhythm—that is, your internal biological clock—thrives on consistency. Going to bed and waking up at roughly the same time (even on weekends) strengthens your sleep–wake cycle.

This might be hard advice to follow if you love a weekend lie-in, but it's one of the most impactful changes you can make. Your body starts preparing for sleep several hours before bedtime, releasing hormones and adjusting temperature to optimise sleep onset. When you maintain consistent timing, this preparation becomes more efficient.

CONTROL LIGHT EXPOSURE

Light is the primary controller of your circadian rhythm. The following tips help you utilise it to your advantage, based on the time of day:

- *Morning:* Get bright light exposure within 30 to 60 minutes of waking. This suppresses melatonin (the sleep hormone) and increases cortisol and serotonin, signalling to your brain that it's time to be awake and alert. Ideally, get outside in natural sunlight for at least 10 to 15 minutes.

- *Evening:* Reduce blue light exposure at least an hour before bed. Blue light from screens suppresses melatonin production by up to 50 per cent, making it harder to fall asleep. Use blue-light blocking glasses, install f.lux on your computer, or activate night shift or night mode on your devices.

- *Bedroom:* Make your sleeping environment as dark as possible. Even small amounts of light (such as from a digital clock) can disrupt sleep quality.

MANAGE TEMPERATURE

Your body temperature needs to drop for optimal sleep. The ideal sleeping temperature is cooler than most people expect — between 16 and 19 °C (or 61 and 66 °F).

Counterintuitively, taking a warm bath or shower or sauna before bed can improve sleep onset. This works because when you emerge from the warm water, your core temperature drops rapidly, mimicking the natural pre-sleep temperature decline.

BE STRATEGIC ABOUT CAFFEINE

Caffeine has a half-life of approximately six hours in the average adult, meaning half the caffeine from your 3 pm coffee is still active at 9 pm. However, this varies widely between individuals based on genetics and other factors.

If you're having sleep troubles, try limiting caffeine to before noon, or at minimum eight hours before your bedtime. Remember that coffee, tea, chocolate and many sodas and supplements contain caffeine. Some people are faster processors of caffeine — meaning they can have a double-espresso and go straight to sleep. However, the research shows that even though these people may get to sleep okay, they spend less time in restorative deep sleep.

RETHINK EVENING ALCOHOL

While alcohol might help you fall asleep faster, it significantly disrupts sleep architecture, particularly REM sleep. The 'nightcap' is actually a sleep quality destroyer. Dutch researchers led by Rick Wassing found in 2019 that inhibiting REM sleep can induce anxiety. They found that in REM sleep you process memories while the brain blocks the release of stress hormones — meaning REM sleep is like nightly therapy for the brain. Simply, more alcohol = less therapy.

If you do drink, ideally try to finish at least three hours before bedtime, and limit consumption to one to two standard drinks to minimise sleep disruption.

CREATE A WIND-DOWN ROUTINE

Your brain needs transition time between the stimulation of the day and the stillness of sleep. Develop a 30- to 60-minute pre-sleep routine that signals to your body and mind that it's time to wind down.

Effective wind-down activities include:

- reading (fiction works particularly well)
- gentle stretching or yoga

- meditation or breathing exercises

- journaling

- taking a warm bath

- listening to calming music.

Avoid work, news, social media, intense exercise or emotionally charged conversations right before bed.

MAKE YOUR BEDROOM A SLEEP SANCTUARY

Your bedroom should be associated primarily with sleep (and a bit of oofty-magoofty if you're lucky!). Ditch the TV, and remove work materials and other non-sleep-related items that might create mental associations with wakefulness.

Invest in a quality mattress, pillows and bedding. Consider blackout curtains, white noise machines or earplugs if your environment has light pollution or is noisy.

USE MOUTH TAPE

Using mouth tape can not only improve your physiology but, if you're a snorer, also massively reduce this or eliminate it.

One caveat, though. For some people, mouth breathing at night can be an indication of a serious medical condition such as obstructive sleep apnoea. While tape that forces you to breathe through your nose can be transformative for some people, sufficient research isn't yet available on its use with sleep apnoea, and it could make problems worse. Make sure you check with your doctor before using mouth tape, and it's a good idea to leave a little bit of the sides of your mouth uncovered, in case you do need to breathe through it.

Evidence-based sleep supplements

While improving sleep habits should be your first approach, certain supplements can support sleep quality (though check with your doctor before adding any supplements to your sleep regime). These include the following:

◆ *Magnesium:* This plays a critical role in GABA production (a calming neurotransmitter) and helps regulate the sympathetic nervous system. Magnesium deficiency is common in Western diets and may contribute to sleep issues.

   Dosage: 200 to 400 mg of magnesium glycinate, taken one to two hours before bed. Magnesium glycinate is generally better absorbed and less likely to cause digestive issues than other forms of magnesium.

◆ *Ashwagandha:* This adaptogenic herb (a natural substance that helps your body maintain balance) has been used for centuries in Ayurvedic medicine to combat stress and improve sleep. Modern research confirms its ability to reduce cortisol levels and anxiety.

   Dosage: 300 to 600 mg of root extract (standardised to contain at least 5 per cent withanolides), taken one to two hours before bed.

◆ *L-theanine:* Found naturally in green tea, L-theanine promotes relaxation without sedation by increasing alpha brain waves (associated with calm alertness) and GABA production.

   Dosage: 200 to 400 mg, taken 30 to 60 minutes before bed.

◆ *Glycine:* This amino acid reduces core body temperature, which helps induce sleep. It may also improve subjective sleep quality and reduce daytime sleepiness after sleep restriction.

   Dosage: 3 g, taken one hour before bed.

◆ *Tart cherry juice:* Rich in natural melatonin and anti-inflammatory compounds, tart cherry juice has been shown to improve sleep duration and quality in clinical trials.

Dosage: 240 ml, consumed one to two hours before bed.

◆ *Low-dose melatonin:* While often overused and overdosed, appropriate melatonin supplementation can be helpful, particularly for shift workers or those with jet lag. (Note that in Australia melatonin is available without prescription if you're over 55.)

Dosage: 0.3 to 1 mg (much lower than commonly sold doses), taken 30 to 60 minutes before bed.

Important: Use the supplement that is right for you, rather than a combination of all the listed options. Always consult with a healthcare provider before starting any supplement regimen, especially if you have existing health conditions or take medications.

The business case for recovery

If all this talk of recovery seems self-indulgent in our hustle culture, consider the bottom-line impact. In research conducted by Leslie Perlow and Jessica Porter at the Boston Consulting Group, consultants were required to take predictable time off (complete disconnection from work) every week. The results included the following:

◆ higher job satisfaction

◆ better communication within teams

◆ improved work products delivered to clients

◆ greater overall productivity.

Similarly, a 2022 study from Zhanna Lyubykh and colleagues found that forcing employees to take breaks actually increased their productivity and creativity.

The lesson is clear: strategic recovery is good for your wellbeing and it's good for business. In fact, it might be the most under-utilised performance enhancement strategy in the modern workplace.

Putting it all together: Your recovery challenge

Here's my two-part challenge if you want to experience the power of strategic recovery:

1. Implement the Pomodoro Technique with micro-recovery for two weeks, tracking your energy levels and productivity as you go. Remember to incorporate the following:

    *   25 minutes of focused work

    *   5 minutes of micro-recovery (movement + vision reset + hydration + breathwork).

2. Choose three sleep hygiene practices to implement consistently for the two weeks. These practices could be consistent sleep timing, morning light exposure or a 30-minute wind-down routine. Note any changes in sleep quality, morning energy, and daytime performance.

At the end of the two weeks, I'm confident you'll notice significant improvements in both your professional performance and personal wellbeing. And if not ... well, feel free to troll me on social media! Remember, the most productive people aren't those who work the longest hours — they're those who work with intensity and purpose, and then recover with equal intention. By working in synch with your biology instead of fighting against it, you'll not only perform better but actually enjoy the process more.

(continued)

As the popular Zen saying goes, 'You should sit in meditation for 20 minutes a day, unless you're too busy—then you should sit for an hour.'

The same wisdom applies to recovery: the busier and more demanding your life, the more essential strategic recovery becomes.

11

Rewild your biology

Look deep, deep into nature, and then you will understand everything better.

Albert Einstein

Humans used to be wild. We used to track prey, forage for berries, stare at the stars and run barefoot over the Earth with the occasional tick bite. Now? We stare at glowing rectangles under fluorescent lighting for 8 to 12 hours a day, while Uber Eats and Deliveroo do our foraging.

Modern humans have become what I like to call *Homo fluorescentus* — biologically still human, but behaviourally more like hamsters with Outlook calendars. According to statistics from 2022, the average Australian spends around 90 per cent of their time indoors. That means we live, work, exercise, shop and socialise in environments that are temperature-controlled, Wi-Fi drenched and almost entirely cut off from nature.

And it's not going well.

We are sicker, sadder and more stressed than ever. Rates of depression and anxiety are soaring. Sleep problems are epidemic. Our immune systems are hyper-reactive and under-performing. And we're starting to see the evidence that our disconnection from nature is one of the root causes. In this chapter, I get to the bottom of why — and outline what you can do about it.

Urbanisation: The biological mismatch

Cities are triumphs of human ingenuity, offering proximity, opportunity and a reliable source of smashed avocado on toast. But they are also biological mismatch zones. Urban environments are dense with stimulation through noise, traffic and artificial light, but often lacking in what we evolved to need: green space, natural light, clean air and quiet.

In a 2018 study conducted by Professor Mathias Basner, living in a city was associated with a 56 per cent increased risk of developing major depressive disorder and a 21 per cent increased risk of anxiety disorders. These findings echoed those from 2011 by the World Health Organization, which identified urban noise pollution as a growing public health threat, contributing to sleep disturbance, elevated blood pressure and cognitive impairment, particularly in children.

Urban noise is not only irritating but also biologically disruptive. It keeps our stress systems activated, our sleep fragmented and our nervous systems inflamed. Yet most of us accept this constant background hum as the price of modern life.

Nature as medicine: Evidence from the wild (and the lab)

A massive scoping review led by Julius Freymueller in 2024 synthesised the global literature on the benefits of spending time in nature. This review found that the vast majority of studies reported significant positive impacts of nature exposure on mental health. These included reductions in stress, anxiety, depression and inflammatory biomarkers, along with improvements in cognition, mood and resilience.

As an example of such research, in 2014 Kirsten Beyer and colleagues studied over 2000 participants in the Wisconsin Survey and found that those living near more greenspace had lower levels of depression, anxiety and stress, even after controlling for income, education and other demographic factors. Further studies into the importance of greenspace highlight that even small doses of outdoor time can have measurable effects on psychological wellbeing.

And it's not just the mind that benefits. Research from 2007 led by Qing Li demonstrated that a weekend spent in a forest setting boosted natural killer cell activity by more than 50 per cent, and the effect persisted for up to 30 days. The subjects also showed an increase in anti-cancer proteins as well. Natural killer cells are essential for immune surveillance and cancer prevention — in other words, nature, quite literally, makes us harder to kill.

Nature's mechanisms: How it works without trying

Nature is not a magic bullet, but it does appear to be a powerful multi-system modulator of our physical and mental health. Here's how:

◆ *Attention restoration theory:* First introduced by psychologist Stephen Kaplan in 1995, this theory suggests that nature provides what's called 'soft fascination' — the kind of gentle attention that allows our prefrontal cortex to rest and recover. This is the part of the brain responsible for working memory, decision-making and executive function — all of which get overloaded in our modern, multitasking lives.

◆ *Stress recovery theory:* Another early adopter — and the founder of evidence-based healthcare design — Professor Roger Ulrich proposed in 1991 that natural environments activate the parasympathetic nervous system, shifting us out of fight-or-flight and into rest-and-digest. The result? Lower heart rate, reduced blood pressure, lower cortisol and stress levels, and increased heart-rate variability (all of which is a good thing).

◆ *Phytoncides and fractal patterns:* Trees emit compounds called phytoncides, which have been shown to reduce anxiety and improve immune function. Other studies have found that fractal patterns in nature — the repeating self-similar shapes found in clouds, leaves and coastlines — reduce stress by up to 60 per cent in just minutes. These patterns are processed rapidly and efficiently by the visual system, leading to an almost instant calming effect.

◆ *Natural light and microbial exposure:* Exposure to natural daylight regulates our circadian rhythms, boosts vitamin D and elevates serotonin levels. And when we get our hands dirty in gardens, trails or forests, we're exposed to beneficial soil microbes that help diversify the gut microbiome, influencing everything from inflammation to mood and brain function.

Green spaces and trees: From windows to forests

Even a view of nature makes a difference. Back in 1984, Ulrich found that patients recovering from gallbladder surgery who had a view of trees from their window recovered faster and used less pain medication than those staring at a brick wall. I can certainly vouch for this — when I went through open-heart surgery recently, I was moved out of intensive care and into a cardiac rehab ward on my second day. The air conditioning in the room was noisy and my view out the window was of a concrete wall 15 feet away. After a couple of days, I was moved to another room with a great view of trees and the sky, and I could literally feel the reduction in stress from being able to look out of a window onto nature!

More immersive experiences take it further. In a 2008 study from Marc Berman and colleagues, participants took 50-minute walks in two different areas of study. One group walked in an arboretum (a botanical garden devoted to trees), while the other walked in a city street. The nature walkers showed significant improvements in working memory and mood, while the urban group did not. That's a pretty cool, free brain boost.

In 2012, Ruth Ann Atchley and colleagues conducted a four-day wilderness immersion with 56 participants who unplugged from technology and immersed themselves in natural settings. Their creative problem-solving abilities increased by 50 per cent, indicating that time away from digital distraction — and immersed in natural beauty — can reboot the brain's higher-order processing.

And of course, Lis' 2007 forest bathing study on an increase in natural killer cells and anti-cancer proteins from spending a few hours in nature remains foundational. The research group have more recently conducted a comprehensive review of *shinrin-yoku* (forest bathing) studies and found that time spent in forests also increases serotonin levels in blood, reduces blood pressure, and reduces stress hormones such as adrenaline and cortisol, downregulating the sympathetic (fight-or-flight) nervous system and upregulating the parasympathetic (rest-and-digest) nervous system. They also report that *shinrin-yoku* has been shown to improve sleep and several parameters of health. Finally, in studies that have assessed participants' mood with the validated Profile of Mood States (POMS) questionnaire before and after *shinrin-yoku*, it has been shown to reduce the scores for anxiety, depression, anger, fatigue and confusion, and increase the score for vigour, showing preventive effects on depression. Taken collectively, *shinrin-yoku* acts like anti-depressant, anti-anxiety and anti-hypertensive medications, all rolled into one, with no side effects whatsoever — other than missing out on a selection of funny dog and cat videos on TikTok!

Spending time in green spaces and forests is more than just relaxing. It's also deeply protective and regenerative.

Let them eat dirt: Rewilding the biome

Once upon a time, getting filthy was a childhood rite of passage. We made mud pies, dug holes to try to get to China, and emerged from the garden with twigs in our hair and microbes up our noses. These days, thanks to sanitiser, indoor lifestyles and a cultural obsession with cleanliness, many kids are better acquainted with iPads than insects. The result is a generation with squeaky-clean hands and suboptimal immune systems.

Hygiene versus biodiversity

Excessive cleanliness is the essence of the hygiene hypothesis, first proposed by researcher David Strachan in 1989. He observed that kids in larger families — especially those with older siblings — had lower rates of allergies and immune disorders. He argued this was because they were more likely to swap bacteria through shared toys, sneezes and sibling squabbles. In other words, a bit of filth builds fortitude.

Fast-forward to today, and this theory has evolved into the biodiversity hypothesis — the idea that contact with a rich variety of environmental microbes (especially those found in soil and nature) helps calibrate our immune system, reduce inflammation and even protect against anxiety and depression. And let's be clear: soil is teeming with microbial life. A single teaspoon of healthy soil contains over 8 billion microorganisms — around the same number of humans on the planet — including bacteria, fungi, viruses and tiny invertebrates.

And if you're not into injecting soil bacteria (can't imagine why not), the good news is gardening works too. Finnish researchers transformed urban day care playgrounds by replacing the asphalt and gravel with soil and vegetation from coniferous forests. Within four weeks, the kids showed a measurable improvement in gut and skin microbiome diversity and an uptick in anti-inflammatory immune markers. Other studies have found that families who garden regularly — and especially those with more diverse plant species in their gardens — have healthier gut bacteria and more robust immune profiles.

The soundtrack of nature: Not just pretty noise

It's not just the microbes in nature that can heal us — the auditory experience is important as well. Research from 2017, led by Cassandra Gould van Praag, found that listening to naturalistic soundscapes (such as birdsong or ocean waves) alters default mode network connectivity in the brain, reducing mind-wandering and enhancing present-moment focus. Very good evolutionary reasons are behind this if you think about it. Birds chirping is a signal of safety. If they're singing, no predators are around—so our threat systems relax.

This may also explain why people feel so calm with water nearby. It's not just poetic but also neurological.

Biophilic design: Bringing nature in

As well as spending time outside in nature, bringing nature indoors also provides benefits. Biophilic design—the architectural and interior design approach that incorporates plants, sunlight, natural textures and views—has been shown to:

- increase focus and creativity

- reduce absenteeism

- improve mood and energy.

Office workers exposed to natural light and greenery report fewer sick days and greater job satisfaction. When I interviewed integrative medicine doctor Jenny Brockis on my podcast, she told me about a general practitioner in Perth who transformed his medical clinic with these principles—using natural light, plants and calming design to transform clinical care into a sensory healing experience—and saw dramatic improvements in patient mood and engagement.

Green scripts: Prescribing nature

Thankfully, we are now seeing the medical system belatedly catch on to this convincing research. In the United Kingdom, green social prescribing is being integrated into the National Health Service (NHS). Patients with mental health issues or chronic illness are being prescribed time in nature—a 'green script'—instead of, or in addition to, medication. This is what they used to do in the 1930s in Britain — back to the future, eh?

In Canada, PaRx is an evidence-based, nature prescription program that gives physicians the tools to prescribe outdoor time, based on hundreds of studies conducted on the health benefits of spending time in nature. Through PaRx, people are educated that time in nature busts stress, reduces the risk of chronic disease, controls blood pressure and increases health perception to a similar amount as a $10 000 raise! The program has been shown to improve the immune system of kids and literally make their brains bigger, increasing the size of the areas involved in memory and attention.

In the United States, ParkRx partners with the National Park Service, and has provided more than 500 000 park visits a year to more than 100 000 patients. A systematic review by Phi-Yen Nguyen and colleagues in 2023 found these interventions had led to improvements in mood, physical activity, sleep and cardiometabolic markers — and cost the health system very little. This is what's known as primary and secondary prevention — treating people with lifestyle interventions to prevent or manage health conditions — and it's more effective, cheaper and a shit-load less painful than waiting until people are really sick and treating them with surgical intervention or drugs (tertiary treatment), which is where the vast majority of the government healthcare spending goes.

Grounded: Why your nervous system needs a date with the dirt

We live on a giant, electrically charged rock that most of us spend too little time touching. Instead, we wear rubber-soled shoes, live in high-rise buildings or commute in sealed vehicles like climate-controlled sardine cans. Our skin rarely meets the surface of the Earth.

And, it turns out, that's a problem. Because according to an intriguing body of research, being physically connected to the Earth's surface — aka 'grounding' or 'earthing' — can lead to measurable improvements in inflammation, blood flow, sleep, stress, pain and even immune function.

I used to think grounding was woo-woo horse-shit — until I dug into the research and tried it for myself. Turns out, a plethora of well-conducted studies is available, and this stuff has been tested in real humans with wires, monitors, bloodwork and, in some cases, massage therapists. Let's dig in.

The return of the barefoot human

Grounding is exactly what it sounds like: putting your bare skin in contact with the Earth — through grass, sand, soil, natural rock or any conductive surfaces that channel Earth's electrons. The premise is that the Earth has a subtle negative electrical charge, and our bodies, when disconnected from this charge, build up positive electrical potentials from static electricity, artificial environments and electromagnetic fields.

Modern living insulates us from that negative charge. And, apparently, when we plug back in — quite literally — we recalibrate.

Researchers have tested grounding in a variety of ways, including walking barefoot on grass, using grounding mats connected to the Earth or attaching electrodes to the skin. Most studies are small, but the results have been surprisingly consistent and biologically plausible.

In one randomised controlled trial (RCT) from 2013, Gaétan Chevalier and colleagues found that two hours of grounding increased the zeta potential of red blood cells by a factor of 2.7.

Okay, 'What the hell is zeta potential?' I hear you ask! It means the red blood cells were less sticky, flowed more freely and were less likely to clump together — a massive plus for cardiovascular health. The same study found significantly reduced red blood cell aggregation.

Another study led by Chevalier using thermal imaging showed that just one hour of grounding improved facial blood flow regulation, an effect that's likely linked to autonomic nervous system changes (upregulation of the parasympathetic nervous system) and the associated vasodilation.

And in continued studies from Chevalier and colleagues, in a 2019 double-blind, RCT (a very good study design) involving 16 massage therapists, grounding over four weeks led to reduced pain, improved physical function, lower anxiety and depression scores, better sleep and increased energy levels. That's quite a list of benefits for something that basically involves touching the surfaces of the planet.

And let's not ignore the inflammation angle. A 2010 pilot study on delayed-onset muscle soreness (DOMS) after physical workouts found that grounded participants had lower pain perception and reduced creatine kinase levels within 72 hours. (Elevated creatine kinase levels are a marker of muscle damage.) These biochemical changes suggest reduced muscle damage and inflammation, not just a placebo effect.

Even more intriguing was that when participants in a 2018 study (also led by Chevalier) were ungrounded after four weeks of consistent grounding, their inflammatory markers increased — suggesting that being ungrounded actually made their bodies grumpier. It's like the Earth broke up with them and their immune systems took it personally.

Your nervous system wants to be grounded too

It's not just your blood and immune system that respond to grounding. Your autonomic nervous system (ANS) — the system that governs heart rate, breathing, digestion and stress reactions — also seems to take a chill pill when you touch the Earth. In a crossover RCT from 2010, Chevalier also found that just 40 minutes of grounding changed skin conductance, increased respiratory rate, and altered blood oxygenation and perfusion — all signs of nervous system modulation. Participants essentially flipped from 'fight or flight' to 'rest and digest' while still lying on a surface that connected them to the Earth.

Meanwhile, in 2004 Maurice Ghaly and Dale Teplitz looked at cortisol levels in participants with pain, sleep issues and stress. After eight weeks of sleeping grounded (using a conductive mattress pad), subjects showed normalised circadian cortisol rhythms, improved sleep and less stress. These results aren't bad for something that doesn't require a prescription, co-payment or app login.

Even in a population with known neurological issues, grounding showed promise. In a 12-week RCT from 2022, Chien-Hung Lin and colleagues studied patients with mild Alzheimer's disease. Those who were grounded daily had significantly improved sleep quality and reductions in anxiety and depression scores, suggesting significantly improved quality of life.

How is this even happening? The (shockingly grounded) mechanisms

Grounding may sound like a fringe wellness hack promoted by scantily clad influencers in scenic locations, but the proposed mechanisms are surprisingly well supported by biology.

One mechanism involves the transfer of free electrons from the Earth into the body. These electrons may act as natural antioxidants, neutralising positively charged free radicals involved in chronic inflammation and oxidative stress.

Another mechanism involves improved blood flow. The aforementioned increase in zeta potential means red blood cells repel each other more, improving circulation and reducing the likelihood of microvascular sludging — a known risk factor in everything from fatigue to cardiovascular disease.

The nervous system effects likely come from subtle electrical shifts in skin voltage, as shown in multiple studies. These shifts lead to autonomic rebalancing, increased heart rate variability and lowered sympathetic tone — all of which are associated with better hardiness and reduced stress reactivity.

And then comes the hormonal piece of the puzzle. Grounding seems to help reset circadian rhythms, probably via cortisol modulation (according to the Ghaly and Teplitz research), which in turn affects sleep, mood, immunity and even metabolism.

So, basically, this isn't hippie stuff — it's physics (or electrophysiology, to be exact). The Earth has an electrical field. You have an electrical system. Connecting the two seems to do good things.

Just as we shield sensitive electronics from static build-up, our bodies may benefit from discharging excess charge and syncing with the Earth's baseline. Think of grounding as a neurological reboot — like unplugging your brain, waiting 30 seconds and plugging it back in.

How to ground (without going off-grid)

You don't need to live barefoot on a beach or buy a $400 copper rod to ground yourself and connect back in with the Earth. Most studies used simple methods such as walking barefoot on grass, lying on a grounded mat or placing a grounding patch on the skin.

The key point of all these methods was that you need to connect directly to the Earth—not via a floorboard or your indoor plant. Preferably, you make this connection through actual soil, sand, grass, rock or sea; however, if needed, a grounding mat or patch can also be used. Even 20 to 40 minutes of being grounded can trigger effects in skin conductance, respiratory rate and stress biomarkers. Longer durations—several weeks of daily grounding—seem to have the biggest cumulative effects on pain, sleep, inflammation and cortisol rhythms.

Grounding may seem too simple to matter. But often, so can hydration—until you forget to do it and get a headache, mood swing and existential crisis all in one. Grounding isn't a replacement for allopathic (conventional) medicine, but it may be one of the cheapest, safest and most ancient interventions for modern physiological dysfunction. We evolved with our feet on the ground. It's hardly surprising that pulling the plug on that connection might create systemic static.

So if you're feeling wired, inflamed, achy, anxious or like you've been living too long in the cloud (digitally or metaphorically), go touch the Earth. You might just feel the difference.

Battery kids versus free-range kids: The cost of a life indoors

While the nature interventions discussed so far in this chapter can profoundly affect adult health, the stakes are even higher for children. In developed countries around the world, too many kids are facing a nature-deprivation crisis that threatens to create the first generation of children who are less healthy than their parents.

Children are now being diagnosed with myopia (nearsightedness) at younger ages and in greater numbers than ever before. And it's not just a little blurry vision that we're talking about here — this is a global health issue that's exploding, particularly in urbanised regions such as Singapore and South Korea. In Singapore, myopia affects 65 per cent of primary grade 6 students (around age 12) and a staggering 83 per cent of young adults aged 18 to 25. In South Korea, the numbers are even more alarming, with more than 95 per cent of 19-year-old males enlisting in military service diagnosed with myopia.

Let that sink in, because it's bonkers! Nearly every young adult in Seoul is starting their adult life with compromised vision — and research suggests this isn't genetic destiny, but largely the result of environmental conditions. Specifically, these conditions are reduced outdoor play and insufficient exposure to natural light. According to research from Amanda French and colleagues, just two hours a day outdoors can reduce the risk of myopia by up to 34 per cent.

And this isn't just an eye issue — it's also a brain and body issue. Low sunlight exposure also contributes to widespread vitamin D deficiency, which affects immune function, bone health, mood and sleep (as discussed in chapter 9). Now add in screen fatigue, recycled air and the neurological effects of noise pollution and you have a recipe for physical and cognitive frailty. If we keep going like this, our future generations will be nearsighted, hunched, anxious, physically feeble and vitamin-D deficient.

Instead of raising wild, hardy kids, we're raising battery kids.

Professor Grant Schofield, a public health academic and multiple bestselling author (and good mate of mine), has coined this very idea. He contrasts today's 'battery children' with the 'free-range kids' of previous generations—and the difference is stark. He highlights research showing that in the early 1900s, children as young as eight regularly roamed up to 10 kilometres from home alone or with friends. Today the average is under 300 metres.

The results of this shrinking childhood territory are everywhere: rising rates of obesity, anxiety, depression, attention disorders and, yes, chronic disease. A recent report by the University of Sydney revealed a jaw-dropping statistic: almost half of Australian teenagers now live with a chronic disease or developmental condition such as asthma, obesity, ADHD or autism spectrum disorder (ASD).

Let's think about that: half.

Around the industrialised world, childhood disease rates are soaring. I touch on some of these figures in the introduction to this book and now come back to them, as I'm close to wrapping up. According to 2022 data from the Australian Institute of Health and Welfare, one in four Australian children aged between 2 and 17 are overweight or obese. In the United States, the Centers for Disease Control and Prevention (CDC) report similar figures, with obesity affecting nearly 20 per cent of children aged between 6 and 11. Type-2 diabetes, once dubbed 'adult-onset' diabetes, is now being diagnosed in children as young as eight. In the United Kingdom, the number of children being treated for type-2 diabetes has more than doubled over the last five years.

And then there's mental health. Nearly 39 per cent of Australians aged 16 to 24 now live with a diagnosed mental health disorder (according to 2022 data from the Australian Bureau of Statistics). In the United Kingdom, NHS Digital data shows one in six children aged 5 to 16 had a probable mental health disorder in 2021. In the United States, the CDC reports that 42 per cent of high school students felt persistently sad or hopeless in 2021 — a 50 per cent increase from a decade earlier.

We are raising a generation more fragile, more anxious, more depressed, more overweight and less hardy than any in modern history. And a big part of that is because we've taken away their natural habitat and replaced it with a screen-intensive, sedentary, drab environment.

Research backs this up. A landmark longitudinal study of over 500 preschoolers in Norway led by Vidar Ulset found that the more time children spent outdoors, the better their attention span and behaviour in school — with the benefits still seen even years later. Increased outdoor time was associated with higher digit span scores (a measure of working memory) and fewer hyperactivity-inattention symptoms. In other words, free-range kids are more focused, better behaved and neurologically more robust than their battery-farmed peers.

Other studies support these findings, showing access to green space buffers children from the negative effects of stressful life events, and that urban schoolchildren surrounded by greenery score higher on cognitive function tests and have lower levels of inattentiveness. Even short walks in natural settings improve adolescents' mental wellbeing, reduce stress hormones and increase gratitude.

But as we pave over parks and fill kids' days with screen time and standardised tests, we're replacing nature's neurological benefits with artificial inputs — none of which seem to be working all that well.

So, what's the solution?

We need to let kids roam. We need to rewild our children. Encourage unsupervised outdoor play. Let them get dirty. Give them mud, trees and space. Kick them off their phones and computer games and give them time in nature — which may also mean you need to prise yourself away from your own phone or screen to join them!

Let's shift the conversation from how to treat anxious, overweight and myopic kids to how to prevent these problems in the first place. Nature is not just a 'nice to have' but is essential. It's the original operating system we evolved with.

The choice is stark: raise battery kids or raise wild, healthy, hardy humans. Let's choose wisely.

How much nature is enough?

I'll finish this chapter with some practical tips — and the reassurance that, based on the clear evidence, you don't need to move into a yurt in Mongolia to get the benefits of nature.

Research suggests that just 120 minutes per week in nature is associated with significantly better health and wellbeing outcomes. And whether this time is 17 minutes per day or a big two-hour block once a week doesn't matter — the key is consistency.

In his essay 'Exploring the nature pyramid', Professor Tim Beatley proposed a nature pyramid (using a concept originally developed by Tanya Denckla-Cobb). In this pyramid, being in nature is broken down into hourly and local activities (the base of the pyramid), through weekly and monthly activities, and right up to international and yearly activities (the tip of the pyramid). Dr Rachel Hopman, from the University of Utah, simplified the concept even further and offers a simple 20-5-3 rule:

- Spend 20 minutes a day in a green space.

- Aim for five hours a month in larger parks or reserves.

- Try to get three full days a year immersed in wild nature.

That's it. That's the maintenance plan for your nervous system and immune system.

Putting it all together: Rewilding as a path to physiological hardiness

We are not designed to be *Homo fluorescentus*. Our mitochondria, immune cells, neurotransmitters and emotional centres all evolved in constant dialogue with natural light, microbial soil, birdsong and green complexity.

Rewilding isn't about quitting modern life — it's about rebalancing it. It's about remembering that beneath the job title and the inbox and the ergonomic keyboard, mouse and chair, you are still an animal. And animals do better when they spend time in their natural habitat.

So go outside. Breathe. Touch a tree. Lie in the grass. Watch the clouds. Walk in the rain. Get your bare feet in contact with the surfaces of the Earth. Reclaim your *Homo sapiens* birthright.

Rewild yourself and your children — one step, one sunbeam, one deep breath at a time.

Conclusion

The modern choice of Hercules

Waste no more time arguing what a good man should be. Be one.

Marcus Aurelius

As well as the stories about Hercules, the ancient Greeks had another myth. Okay, they had plenty, but this one also speaks directly to our modern predicament. Long before Hercules faced his crossroads, humanity itself stood at a similar juncture in the tale of Prometheus. When Prometheus stole fire from the gods to give to humanity, he didn't just gift us technology—he set us on a path that would eventually divorce us from the natural world that created us.

After chaining Prometheus to a rock in the mountains so his liver could be devoured daily by an eagle, the punishment Zeus devised for humanity was revealing. He created Pandora and gave her a box containing all the world's evils. But here's what often gets lost in the retelling—the last spirit trapped in that box was hope. Not despair, not resignation, but hope is what remained with humanity even as we ventured further from our origins.

Today, we face our own Promethean moment. We've mastered fire and much more — we've created artificial environments, digital worlds, processed foods and thermo-neutral indoor lifestyles that would have seemed like magic to our ancestors. We've traded the uncertainty of nature for the illusion of complete control. But like the myth suggests, our 'progress' has unleashed its own evils: chronic disease, mental illness, disconnection and a profound sense of something missing.

Yet hope remains, just as it did for the ancient Greeks. That hope lies in recognising that building hardiness isn't a retreat but a reclamation. It's choosing, like Hercules did, the harder path that leads to true excellence.

The modern labours of hardiness

If Hercules had 12 labours to complete his transformation, perhaps we have our own set of modern labours to reclaim our hardy birthright:

1. *Forging the hardiness mindset:* Choose to see change as opportunity for growth, just as Hercules viewed his impossible tasks as the forge where heroes are made.

2. *Embracing life's challenges:* Welcome adversity as a worthy opponent that sharpens your character, rather than retreat into comfort.

3. *Mastering what you can control:* Focus your attention like a laser on your responses and actions, and let go of what lies beyond your influence.

4. *Committing fully to life:* Complete your values and tombstone exercises so that you're engaging deeply with purpose and meaning, rather than drifting as a passive consumer of experiences.

5. *Weaving meaningful connections:* Set aside time to build genuine relationships that sustain you through hardship, recognising that deep social connectedness is a critical part of a life well lived.

6. *Awakening cellular resilience:* Map out a hormetic stress exposure plan (cold showers, anyone?) to make your biology anti-fragile, the way nature intended it to be.

7. *Activating your longevity organ (muscle):* Take your daily movement medicine, understanding that your muscles are endocrine organs that speak to every system in your body. Get out of breath and lift heavy shit regularly.

8. *Nourishing for longevity:* Feed yourself with real food that honours your evolutionary biology, not convenience that poisons slowly.

9. *Bathing in beneficial light:* Align yourself with natural rhythms of sun and darkness, harnessing light as medicine for every cell.

10. *Mastering strategic recovery:* Cycle between deep work and restoration, making rest active rather than passive.

11. *Returning to the wild:* Reclaim your birthright as a creature of nature, touching the Earth, breathing free air and feeding the microbiome within.

12. *Choosing daily excellence:* Recommit each day to the path of Aretê, understanding that hardiness is not a destination but a way of being.

Like Hercules, you don't have to complete these labours alone or perfectly. You simply need to choose to be on the path.

If you are looking for an impactful starting point, start with dialling up your exercise, and getting your omega 3 score up to 8 (test it at omegaquant.com) and your vitamin D between 100 and150 mmol/L. They all independently impact the 12 hallmarks of ageing discussed through this book. Add in your tombstone statement, get clear on your values and train yourself to see adversity as challenges and you'll be well on your way.

The choice is still yours

At the beginning of this book, we met Hercules at his crossroads, torn between the easy path of Kakia and the challenging way of Aretê. Now, having journeyed through both psychological and physiological hardiness, we return to that same timeless choice.

Kakia still beckons with her promises of comfort: climate-controlled environments, processed convenience foods, endless entertainment and the illusion that we can outsmart our biology indefinitely. She offers a life of ease but, as outlined throughout this book, that ease comes at a staggering cost to our health, vitality and sense of meaning.

Aretê's path — the path of hardiness — remains arduous. It asks us to step outside, get dirty, feel uncomfortable, test ourselves physically and psychologically, and remember what it means to be fully alive. But this path leads somewhere worth going: toward robust health, genuine connection, and the deep satisfaction of living in alignment with our values and purpose.

The following pages illustrates how this choice between the path of ease and the path of hardiness can play out through the decades of your life.

30s

PATH OF KAKIA	PATH OF ARETÊ
The (un)comfortable decline	**The hardiness effect**

PATH OF KAKIA
The (un)comfortable decline

- **Diet:** Dominated by ultra-processed, convenience foods.

- **Activity:** Minimal exercise, mostly sedentary.

- **Stress management/recovery:** Streaming services, alcohol, junk food, avoidance.

- **Sunlight and nature:** Rarely ventures outside.

- **Sleep:** Late nights, poor sleep hygiene, phone in bed.

- **Mental health:** Diagnosed with mild depression and/or anxiety, prescribed medication.

- **Physical health:** Weight gain, fatigue, early signs of metabolic dysfunction.

PATH OF ARETÊ
The hardiness effect

Reads *The Hardiness Effect* and vows to change.

- **Diet:** Whole foods, high in phytochemicals, reduced processed intake.

- **Activity:** Weekly strength and cardio routines, lots of movement 'snacks'.

- **Stress management/recovery:** Exercise, breathwork, cold exposure, sauna, red-near-infrared light, journaling.

- **Sunlight and nature:** Prioritises daily sunlight, weekly nature immersion.

- **Sleep:** Ditches screens, adopts circadian rhythm habits, invests in sleep hygiene.

- **Mental health:** Strengthens mindset through the four Cs — control, challenge, commitment, connection.

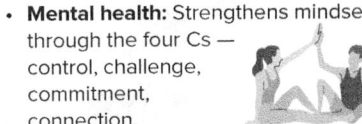

- **Physical health:** Gets fitter, has more energy.

PATH OF KAKIA
The (un)comfortable decline

- **Chronic stress** becomes unmanageable.

- **Gains more weight**, develops high blood pressure and starts medication.

- **Relationships feel shallow**, energy and motivation decline.

PATH OF ARETÊ
The hardiness effect

- **Hormetic stressors** (heat, cold, fasting) enhance resilience.

- **Body fat lowers**, strength and VO2 max increases with training.

- **Targeted supplements** optimise health and performance — no need for medications.

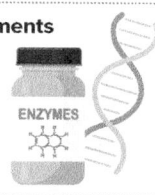

- **Purposeful work** and strong social ties deepen wellbeing.

PATH OF KAKIA	PATH OF ARETÊ
The (un)comfortable decline	**The hardiness effect**

- **Diagnosed** with Type 2 diabetes and/or high blood pressure.

- **Still biologically vibrant:** low inflammation, high energy, sharp cognition.

- **On a cocktail of medications** including SSRIs, statins, blood pressure and diabetes drugs.

- **Trains** for a masters-level athletic competition.

- **Physical pain** and emotional numbness become daily companions.

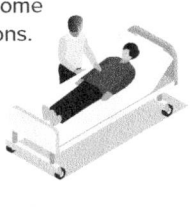

- **Coaches others** on the path of Aretê.

60s
... and beyond

PATH OF KAKIA	PATH OF ARETÊ
The (un)comfortable decline	**The hardiness effect**
• **Retires** into the abyss.	• **Retires** in radiant health.
• **Life becomes a cycle of doctor's appointments**, drug management and limitation.	• **Travels, hikes and mentors** and life is full of vitality and meaning.
• **Despite living longer**, life is a slow, pharmacologically managed decline.	• **Supplements maintain cellular resilience.** No, or few, meds required.
	• **Ageing with grace;** not just adding years to life, but life to years.

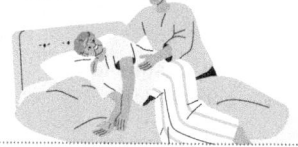

The beauty is that we don't have to choose between modern life and primitive existence. A life committed to hardiness isn't about abandoning technology or civilisation. It's about integrating the wisdom of nature into our contemporary lives. It's about becoming more human, not less civilised.

As the Stoic philosopher Seneca wrote:

> *Every new beginning comes from some other beginning's end. Fire is the test of gold; adversity, of strong men.*

This is the essence of hardiness — understanding that you are tested and strengthened by the very challenges you once sought to avoid. The modern world will keep offering short cuts, comfort and ease. But deep within, where your wild nature still remembers, you know these are mirages. While the path of Kakia appears to be easier at first, the long-term outcome is very different (and the alternative prescriptions for mental health outlined in appendix A are a great reminder of this).

Like Hercules, when you choose the harder path, you don't just save yourself. You become an example for others, creating ripples that can transform not just your own life but also the lives of generations to come. You show your children that humans are meant to be strong, connected and deeply engaged with life.

So the choice remains, as it always has: will you choose the path of easy comfort or the path of excellent hardiness? Will you remain *Homo fluorescentus*, living under artificial light and recycled air? Or will you reclaim your birthright as the wild, hardy human you were born to be?

For further help along the way, make sure you access these online resources:

- *www.paultaylor.biz/hardiness:* For lots of hardiness resources, as well as information on the hardiness challenge you can sign up to through the hardiness app I have created.

- *www.hardinesslab.com:* To see the hardiness research I'm conducting with my partner-in-crime, Professor Grant Schofield.

The labours of hardiness aren't easy. But, like Hercules, you might just find they're exactly what transform you into who you were meant to become. The fire is still burning. The only question is will you step into it or away from it?

Appendix A

The crossroads: Alternative prescriptions for mental health

Every day, we stand at the crossroad, facing the choice between the seductive comforts of Kakia's way and the modern path of Aretê and hardiness. As already stressed, this approach doesn't reject medication when truly needed, but does place equal emphasis on addressing the fundamental biological, psychological, environmental and social factors that shape your physical and mental health. In table AA.1 (overleaf), I pull together these aspects to offer my alternative mental health prescription. (See the reference list for the details of the studies that outline the findings included.)

Please check with your GP or health provider before considering any changes to existing medications.

Table AA.1: Comparing alternative mental health prescriptions

Prescription	Possible side-effects	Withdrawal effects	Effectiveness	
Anti-depressant medication (SSRI)	• 61% chance of ten or more side effects • 71% chance of emotional numbness • 70% chance of feeling foggy or detached • 66% chance of feeling 'not like myself' • 60% chance of a reduction in positive feelings • 50% chance of suicidal thoughts from the medication • 40% chance of feeling addicted to the drugs	• More than half (56%) of people who attempt to come off antidepressants experience withdrawal effects • Nearly half (46%) of people experiencing withdrawal effects describe them as severe • They often last for weeks or months	• Small effect size • Estimated to work for around 15% of people, according to the *Maudsley Deprescribing Guidelines*	**Kakia**
Exercise	• Risk of injury • Reduced risk of 26 common diseases • Counters all the hallmarks of ageing	N/A	Moderate to large effect size; all exercise types more effective than SSRIs	**Areté**
Vitamin D	• Toxic if levels get too high • Counters most of the hallmarks of ageing	N/A	Small to large effect size in a systematic review	
Nutritious diet	• Can be more expensive than ultra-processed food • Counters most of the hallmarks of ageing	N/A	Small to very large effect size in seven studies of 49 000 people	
Nature prescription	• Chance of getting wet, hot or cold if you venture outside • Good for your microbiome	N/A	An 8–17% lower risk of depression with more green space exposure in numerous studies	

Appendix B

Sample exercise programs

As I mention in chapter 7, bodybuilders are usually not fit enough, and marathon runners are usually not strong enough. You need both a good VO$_2$ max and good muscle strength for optimal longevity. So I've provided here two sample seven-day workout plans—the first for if you're looking to have more of a focus on cardiorespiratory fitness (but still some focus on strength) and the second for the opposite.

Focus on cardiorespiratory fitness

In the following sample program (outlined in table AB.1, overleaf), for the Norwegian 4×4 intervals, you can run, row, use an echo bike or a normal bike—the idea is that at the end of the four minutes, your heart rate is at 90 to 95 per cent of your maximum, or a perceived exertion of 9 out of 10 (very, very hard). The session of ten times one-minute intervals is at an all-out pace for one minute.

Table AB.1: Sample seven-day exercise program—focus on cardiovascular fitness

Day	Focus	Duration	Key Activities
Monday	VO$_2$ max HIIT	30 min	Norwegian 4×4 intervals (4 minutes @ 90–95% max heart rate, 3 minutes slow-paced recovery)
Tuesday	Full-body strength	45–60 min	Compound lifts (heavy)
Wednesday	Active recovery	30 min	Mobility, walking, bike riding or any low-intensity movement
Thursday	Zone 2 aerobic	30–45 min	Steady state zone 2 (can talk but can't sing)
Friday	VO$_2$ max HIIT	30 min	10×1 minute intervals with 1 minute rest + core workout
Saturday	Full-body strength	45–60 min	Compound lifts (moderate volume)
Sunday	Active recovery	30 min	Mobility, walking, bike riding or any low-intensity movement

These VO$_2$ max sessions are both very hard, but the best way to enhance your VO$_2$ max quickly. Your zone 2 aerobic session is an easy session, performed at 60 to 70 per cent of your maximum heart rate, where you can talk but not sing, and helps to build your aerobic base.

Focus on strength

Table AB.2 provides a sample exercise program focusing more on strength. After this table are some sample strength workouts for the different body areas to focus on.

Table AB.2: Sample seven-day exercise program — focus on strength

Day	Focus	Duration	Key activities
Monday	Lower-body strength	30 min	Compound lifts (heavy)
Tuesday	Upper-body strength	45–60 min	Compound lifts (heavy)
Wednesday	Active recovery	30 min	Mobility, walking, bike riding or any low-intensity movement
Thursday	VO$_2$ max HIIT	30–45 min	Norwegian 4 × 4 intervals (4 minutes @ 90–95% max heart rate, 3 minutes slow-paced recovery)
Friday	Lower-body Strength	30 min	Compound lifts (moderate)
Saturday	Upper-body Strength	45–60 min	Compound lifts (moderate)
Sunday	Zone 2 aerobic	30–45 min	Steady state zone 2 (can talk but can't sing)

If you haven't strength trained before, make sure you check with your GP before getting started. I also recommend having four or five sessions with a personal trainer or exercise physiologist to learn the right techniques and to check on any exercises you're not sure about. The following two sample strength workouts (outlined in tables AB.3 and AB.4, both overleaf) are designed as supersets to minimise time in the gym. You can also do them sequentially without supersetting, if you have more time. In that case, rest for 90 seconds to two minutes between sets (note the shorter rest in supersets is because different muscle groups are targeted, so each group gets more rest).

Table AB.3: Workout A

Exercise	Sets/reps	Rest	Notes
Squats (Zercher/back/front) Shoulder press	3 × 5–8RM 3 × 5–8RM	1 min	Superset—go from one exercise to the other, and then rest
Bench press Close-grip seated row	3 × 5–8RM 3 × 5–8RM	1 min	Superset—go from one exercise to the other, and then rest
Cable woodchop	4 × 8–12RM	1 min	Alternate direction each set (two sets to right, two to left)

Note: Zercher squats (where you hold the barbell in the crook of your elbows) are my preferred squats because they allow you to squat deeper and are good if you have any back issues. They work like goblet squats, but you can handle more weight.

Table AB.4: Workout B

Exercise	Sets/reps	Rest	Notes
Deadlifts Rope face pulls	3 × 8–12RM 3 × 8–12RM	1 min	Superset—go from one exercise to the other, and then rest
Incline bench press Lat pulldown/chin-ups	3 × 8–12RM 3 × 8–12RM	1 min	Superset—go from one exercise to the other, and then rest
Side plank	30–60 sec each side	1 min	Perform each side then rest

RM stands for repetition maximum – so 8RM is the heaviest weight you can lift for eight reps. Ideally, do a warm-up set and then pick a weight you can do eight reps for 'to failure' (can't do anymore, or one or two left in the tank if training by yourself for safety reasons). Slightly increase the weight to reach 5RM on your last set of each exercise.

Note the different rep ranges for workout A and workout B—this is to get a blend of strength and hypertrophy. I'd suggest swapping those rep ranges around every week or two to keep providing a slightly different stimulus. Tables AB.5 and AB.6 provide strength exercises for specific body areas.

Table AB.5: Lower-body strength workout A

Exercise	Sets/reps	Rest	Notes
Squats (Zercher/back/front)	3 × 5–8RM	2 min	Zercher squats preferred unless you are proficient
Romanian deadlift Walking lunges	3 × 8–10RM 3 × 12 per leg	2 min	Superset—go from one exercise to the other, and then rest
Leg extension Leg curl	3 × 8–12RM 3 × 8–12RM	2 min	Alternate direction each set (two sets to right, two to left)

Table AB.6: Lower-body strength workout B

Exercise	Sets/reps	Rest	Notes
Deadlifts (straight bar or trap bar if available)	6 × 5–8RM	2 min	Drive with the legs and squeeze your glutes at the top
Bulgarian split squats	4 × 8 each leg	2 min	Back foot raised onto bench—use dumbbells
Standing calf raise drop set	3 × 15–20	2 min	Drop weights twice without rest

For the following upper-body workouts, workout A (outlined in table AB.7, overleaf) focuses mostly on horizontal push/pull plus some arm and shoulder work. Workout B (outlined in table AB.8, overleaf) has more of a focus on vertical push/pull, scapular stability and hanging for grip strength.

Table AB.7: Upper-body strength workout A

Exercise	Sets/reps	Rest	Notes
Bench press Pec deck or dumbbell fly	3-4×5–8RM 3-4×15–20RM	2 min	Superset—go from one exercise to the other, and then rest
Barbell or seated cable row Barbell/EZ bar biceps curl	3-4×5–8RM 3-4×15–20RM	2 min	Superset—go from one exercise to the other, and then rest
Seated dumbbell or Arnold press Cable face pulls	3-4×5–8RM 3-4×15–20RM	2 min	Superset—go from one exercise to the other, and then rest

Table AB.8: Upper-body strength workout B

Exercise	Sets/reps	Rest	Notes
Pull-ups or chin-ups Overhead press (barbell or dumbbell)	3-4×5–8RM 3-4×5–8RM	2 min	Superset—go from one exercise to the other, and then rest
Close-grip lat pulldown Dumbbell pullover on bench	3-4×12–15RM 3-4×8–12RM	2 min	Superset—go from one exercise to the other, and then rest
Hanging on bar Bird dog	3×max hold 3×8–10 per side	2 min	Superset—go from one exercise to the other, and then rest

In workout B, you may need to use a resistance band or machine to assist if you struggle with pull-ups; alternatively, add weight if you can do more than eight reps. For the lat pulldowns, focus on full range and scapular control with a lighter weight.

Appendix C
Anti-ageing meal plans

Chapter 8 covers the key nutritional principles for healthy ageing. In tables AC.1 to AC.4 on the following pages, I put the information together with practical meal plans. Each of these plans incorporates the four requirements of limiting ultra-processed foods (aiming for low human-interference, or low-HI), including anti-ageing nutrients that target the hallmarks of ageing, optimising omega-3 intake and providing adequate protein.

The key here is not to eat these same foods every day, but to replicate the themes, which are:

1. Low-HI, real foods, with lots of polyphenols and flavenoids.

2. Breakfast is high in protein with moderate fat, rather than the high-sugar, low-protein meal that many people eat.

3. Minimal added sugars and only moderate amounts of starchy carbohydrates.

Table AC.1: Meal plan 1: Mediterranean-inspired

Meal	Foods	Comments
Breakfast	• 2 eggs scrambled with spinach, tomatoes and feta cheese • 1 slice sourdough toast with olive oil and avocado • 1/4 cup walnuts • Green/black/white tea	30g protein Omega-3 rich
Lunch	• Mediterranean bowl: 120g grilled salmon over quinoa • Roasted vegetables (capsicum, zucchini, eggplant) • Mixed greens with olive oil, lemon juice and herbs • 1/4 cup hummus with cucumber slices • Small orange	33g protein Anti-ageing nutrients
Dinner	• 140g herb-roasted chicken • Roasted sweet potato with olive oil and rosemary • Sautéed broccoli with garlic • Mixed green salad with olive oil and balsamic vinegar • 30g dark chocolate (85%+ cacao)	35g protein Low-HI focus
Snacks	• Greek yogurt with berries and cinnamon • Handful of mixed nuts and an apple	Optional

Table AC.2: Meal plan 2: Asian-inspired

Meal	Foods	Comments
Breakfast	• Miso soup with silken tofu, wakame seaweed and green onions • 2 scrambled eggs with mushrooms and spinach • 1/2 cup fermented kimchi • Green tea	31g protein Omega-3 rich
Lunch	• Bento box: 120g wild salmon sashimi • 1/2 cup brown rice with sesame seeds • Cucumber and carrot quick-pickles • 1/2 cup edamame • Small handful of nori sheets • Fresh fruit with a sprinkle of sesame seeds	29g protein Anti-ageing nutrients
Dinner	• 140g miso-glazed cod • 1/2 cup black rice • Stir-fried bok choy with ginger and garlic • Shiitake mushrooms • Green/white/black tea	32g protein Mitochondrial support
Snacks	• 1/4 cup edamame • Seaweed snacks • Matcha smoothie with silken tofu and berries	Optional

Table AC.3: Meal plan 3: Low-carb focus

Meal	Foods	Comments
Breakfast	• 2-egg omelette with spinach, mushrooms and goat cheese • Half avocado with sea salt and olive oil • Handful of berries • Green tea or coffee with cinnamon	28g protein Cellular repair nutrients
Lunch	• Large salad with 115g grilled chicken breast • Mixed greens, cucumber, radish and red onion • Olive oil and lemon dressing • 1/4 cup walnuts • 1/4 cup blueberries	32g protein Low inflammatory focus
Dinner	• 140g baked mackerel with herbs and lemon • Cauliflower mash with olive oil and roasted garlic • Roasted brussels sprouts with pecans • Small side salad with extra virgin olive oil • 30g dark chocolate (85%+ cacao)	35g protein Omega-3 rich
Snacks	• Hard-boiled egg with sea salt • Celery with almond butter • Handful of macadamia nuts	Optional

Table AC.4: Meal plan 4: Plant-based

Meal	Foods	Comments
Breakfast	• Smoothie bowl: plant protein powder, berries, ground flaxseed, chia seeds • Topped with walnut pieces and pumpkin seeds • Small banana • Green tea	27g protein Nutrient-dense
Lunch	• Grain bowl: quinoa, lentils, tempeh cubes (115g) • Roasted sweet potato, broccoli and red onion • Tahini-lemon dressing • Sprinkle of pumpkin seeds • Apple slices	30g protein Anti-inflammatory focus
Dinner	• Tofu (140g) stir-fry with vegetables (capsicum, snow peas, mushrooms) • 1/2 cup brown rice or cauliflower rice • Garnish with crushed almonds and sesame seeds • Small side salad with microgreens and olive oil dressing • 30g dark chocolate with handful of walnuts	32g protein Omega-3 optimised
Snacks	• 3/4 cup Greek yoghurt or coconut yoghurt (for vegans) with berries • Hummus with cucumber and carrot sticks • Handful of brazil nuts and an orange	Optional

Adaptations and tips

If following a plant-based diet, follow these adaptations:

◆ Replace eggs with tofu scramble using nutritional yeast and turmeric.

◆ Use tempeh, edamame or legumes instead of animal proteins.

◆ Add extra nuts and seeds for omega-3s.

◆ Consider algal oil supplements for DHA/EPA fatty acids.

◆ Use pea or rice protein powder in smoothies.

And here are my pro tips for implementation:

◆ *You don't need a PhD in nutrition – you need a plan and a chopping board:* Sunday prep is your secret weapon. Grill a stack of chicken thighs, roast some veggies in olive oil and soak your oats overnight.

◆ *Stock essential pantry items:* Keep nuts, seeds, olive oil, spices, herbs and whole grains ready to enhance any meal.

◆ *Use the 'plate method':* Fill half your plate with colourful vegetables, one-quarter with protein, and one-quarter with whole grains or starchy vegetables.

◆ *Create an omega-3 routine:* Designate certain days for fatty fish, and keep walnuts, ground flaxseed and chia seeds accessible for daily use.

◆ *Use the 'no UPF' rule for packaged foods:* If an ingredient list contains items you wouldn't find in a home kitchen, it likely doesn't belong in your regular diet.

◆ *Schedule a monthly review:* Once a month, assess how well you're sticking to these principles and adjust as needed.

References

Introduction

- Menke, A, et al. (2015). 'Prevalence of and trends in diabetes among adults in the United States, 1988–2012'. *JAMA*, 314(10), 1021–1029.
- Emeritus Professor Allen Frances: https://www.theaustralian.com.au/health/mental-health/everloosening-psychiatric-definitions-result-in-diagnosis-overload/news-story/6e510096a22c968be00eb25a40e1d42e
- Moncrieff, J, et al. (2023). 'The serotonin theory of depression: A systematic umbrella review of the evidence'. *Mol Psychiatry*, 28, 3243–3256.
- Read, J, & Williams, J. (2018). 'Adverse effects of antidepressants reported by a large international cohort: Emotional blunting, suicidality, and withdrawal effects'. *Curr Drug Saf*, 13(3), 176–186.
- Read, J, et al. (2014). 'Adverse emotional and interpersonal effects reported by 1829 New Zealanders while taking antidepressants'. *Psychiatry Res*, 216(1), 67–73.

Chapter 1

- Maddi, SR, & Kobasa, S.C. (1984). *The Hardy Executive: Health under Stress*. Dow Jones-Irwin.

- Stockdale, JB. (1993). *Courage Under Fire: Testing Epictetus's Doctrines in a Laboratory of Human Behavior.* Hoover Institution Press.
- Bartone, PT, et al. (2008). 'Psychological hardiness predicts success in US Army Special Forces candidates'. *International Journal of Selection and Assessment,* 16(1), 78–81.
- Johnsen, BH, et al. (2013). 'Psychological hardiness predicts success in a Norwegian Armed Forces border patrol selection course'. *International Journal of Selection and Assessment,* 21(4), 368–375.
- Soccorso, CN, et al. (2019). 'Psychological hardiness predicts successful selection in a law enforcement special operations assessment and selection course'. *International Journal of Selection and Assessment,* 27(3), 291–295.
- Thomassen, ÅG, et al. (2018). 'The effect of hardiness on PTSD symptoms: A prospective mediational approach'. *Military Psychology,* 30(2), 142–151.
- Bartone, PT, & Bowles, SV. (2021). 'Hardiness predicts post-traumatic growth and well-being in severely wounded servicemen and their spouses'. *Military Medicine,* 186(5/6), 500–506.
- Maddi, SR, et al. (2023). 'Hardiness predicts post-traumatic growth in survivors of trauma'. *Journal of Traumatic Stress,* 36(2), 230–239.
- Lambert, VA, et al. (2003). 'Psychological hardiness, workplace stress, and related stress reduction strategies'. *Nursing and Health Sciences,* 5(2), 181–184.
- Senewiratne, S, et al. (2025). 'Cognitive hardiness in the workplace: A systematic review and call for future research'. *Manag Rev Q.*
- Meng, Q, & Jia, W. (2022). 'Influence of psychological hardiness on academic achievement of university students: The mediating effect of academic engagement'. *Work,* 74(4), 1515–1525.
- Yi, S, et al. (2024). 'Sense of belonging, academic self-efficacy and hardiness: Their impacts on student engagement in distance

learning courses'. *British Journal of Educational Technology*, 55(4), 1703–1727.

- Amelia, SR, et al. (2025). 'Fortitude meets perseverance: Unravelling the link between hardiness, grit, and academic burnout among architecture students in Surabaya'. *Educational Psychology Journal*, 13(2).
- Kulikova, T, et al. (2022). 'Relationship between hardiness and maladaptive schemes in students of different age groups.' *Perspectives of Science and Education*, 55(1), 463–476.
- Bartone, PT, & Pastel, R. H. (2008). 'Hardy-resilient style is associated with high-density lipoprotein cholesterol levels'. AMSUS Conference.
- Bartone, PT, et al. (2016). 'Psychological hardiness predicts cardiovascular health'. *Psychology, Health & Medicine*, 21(6), 743–749.
- Sandvik, AM, et al. (2013). 'Psychological hardiness predicts neuroimmunological responses to stress'. *Psychology, Health & Medicine*, 18(6), 705–713.
- Sandvik, AM, et al. (2019). 'Physical fitness and psychological hardiness as predictors of parasympathetic control in response to stress'. *Journal of Police and Criminal Psychology*, 34(3), 215–226.
- King, LA, et al. (1998). 'Resilience-recovery factors in post-traumatic stress disorder among female and male Vietnam veterans: Hardiness, postwar social support, and additional stressful life events'. *Journal of Personality and Social Psychology*, 74(2), 420–434.

Chapter 2

- Kobasa, SC, et al. (1979). 'Who stays healthy under stress?' *Journal of Occupational Medicine*, 21(9), 595–598.
- Crum, AJ, & Langer, EJ. (2007). 'Mind-set matters: Exercise and the placebo effect'. *Psychol Sci*, 18(2), 165–71.

- Luong, G, et al. (2016). 'When bad moods may not be so bad: Valuing negative affect is associated with weakened affect–health links'. *Emotion*, 16(3), 387–401.
- Jamieson, JP, et al. (2010). 'Turning the knots in your stomach into bows: Reappraising arousal improves performance on the GRE'. *Journal of Experimental Social Psychology*, 46(1), 208–12.
- Jamieson, JP, et al. (2016). 'Reappraising stress arousal improves performance and reduces evaluation anxiety in classroom exam situations'. *Social Psychological and Personality Science*, 7(6), 579–87.
- Jamieson, JP, et al. (2012). 'Mind over matter: Reappraising arousal improves cardiovascular and cognitive responses to stress'. *Journal of Experimental Psychology: General*, 141(3), 417.
- Seery, MD. (2013). 'The biopsychosocial model of challenge and threat: Using the heart to measure the mind'. *Social and Personality Psychology Compass*, 7: 637–653.
- Strack, J, et al. (2015). 'Will you thrive under pressure or burn out? Linking anxiety, motivation and emotional exhaustion'. *Cognition and Emotion*, 29(4), 578–91.
- Keller, A, et al. (2012). 'Does the perception that stress affects health matter? The association with health and mortality'. *Health Psychology*, 31(5), 677.
- Hase, A, et al. (2020). 'Threat-related motivational disengagement: Integrating blunted cardiovascular reactivity to stress into the biopsychosocial model of challenge and threat'. *Anxiety, Stress, & Coping*, 33(4), 355–369.
- Goldin, PR, et al. (2019). 'Acceptance versus reappraisal: Behavioral, autonomic, and neural effects'. *Cogn Affect Behav Neurosci.* 19(4), 927–944.

Chapter 3

- LaFreniere, LS, & Newman, MG. (2020). 'Exposing worry's deceit: Percentage of untrue worries in generalized anxiety disorder treatment'. *Behavior Therapy*, 51(3), 413–423.
- Albertella, L, et al. (2023). 'Building a transdisciplinary expert consensus on the cognitive drivers of performance under pressure: An international multi-panel Delphi study'. *Front. Psychol*, 13:1017675.
- Mischel, W, & Ebbesen, EB. (1970). 'Attention in delay of gratification'. *Journal of Personality and Social Psychology*, 16 (2), 329–337.
- Shoda, Y, et al. (1990). 'Predicting adolescent cognitive and self-regulatory competencies from preschool delay of gratification: Identifying diagnostic conditions'. *Developmental Psychology*, 26 (6), 978–986.
- Dunedin Multidisciplinary Health & Development Research Unit. (2011). 'Children with more self-control turn into healthier and wealthier adults'. University of Otago.
- Banfield, J, et al. (2004). 'The cognitive neuroscience of self-regulation'. In Baumeister RF, Vohs KDs (Eds). *The Handbook of Self-Regulation*. Guilford. 62–83.
- Galla, BM, & Duckworth, AL. (2015). 'More than resisting temptation: Beneficial habits mediate the relationship between self-control and positive life outcomes'. *J Pers Soc Psychol*, 109(3), 508–25.
- Davydenko, M, et al. (2021). 'A meta-analysis of financial self-control strategies: Comparing empirical findings with online media and lay person perspectives on what helps individuals curb spending and start saving'. *PLoS ONE* 16(7), e0253938.

Chapter 4

- Aurelius, M. (2002). *Meditations.* Random House.
- Emmons, RA, & McCullough, ME. (2003). 'Counting blessings versus burdens: An experimental investigation of gratitude and subjective well-being in daily life'. *Journal of Personality and Social Psychology,* 84(2), 377–389.
- Keltner, DJ, & Haidt, J. (2003). 'Approaching awe, a moral, spiritual, and aesthetic emotion'. *Cognition and Emotion,* 17(2), 297–314.
- Keltner, D. (2023) *Awe: The New Science of Everyday Wonder and How It Can Transform Your Life.* Penguin Press.
- Frankl, VE. (1963). *Man's Search for Meaning: An Introduction to Logotherapy.* Washington Square Press.
- Keyes, C. (2024). *Languishing: How to Feel Alive Again in a World That Wears You Down.* Crown.

Chapter 5

- Office of the Surgeon General. (2023). 'Our epidemic of loneliness and isolation: The U.S. Surgeon General's advisory on the healing effects of social connection and community'. US Department of Health and Human Services.
- Eisenberger, NI, & Cole, SW. (2012). 'Social neuroscience and health: Neurophysiological mechanisms linking social ties with physical health'. *Nat Neurosci,* 15(5), 669–74.
- Uchino, BN. (2006). 'Social support and health: A review of physiological processes potentially underlying links to disease outcomes'. *J Behav Med,* 29(4), 377–87.
- Cacioppo, JT, et al. (2002). 'Do lonely days invade the nights? Potential social modulation of sleep efficiency'. *Psychol Sci,* 13(4), 384–7.
- McCain, J, & Salter, M. (2008). *Faith of my Fathers.* Harper.

- Holt-Lunstad, J, Smith, TB, & Layton, JB. (2010). 'Social relationships and mortality risk: A meta-analytic review'. *PLoS Med*, 7(7), e1000316.
- Holt-Lunstad, J, et al. (2015). 'Loneliness and social isolation as risk factors for mortality: A meta-analytic review'. *Perspect Psychol Sci*, 10(2), 227–37.
- Cole, SW, et al. (2015). 'Loneliness, eudaimonia, and the human conserved transcriptional response to adversity'. *Psychoneuroendocrinology*, 62, 11–7.
- Hawkley, LC, & Cacioppo, JT. (2010). 'Loneliness matters: A theoretical and empirical review of consequences and mechanisms'. *Ann Behav Med*, 40(2), 218–27.
- Valtorta, NK, et al. (2018). 'Loneliness, social isolation and risk of cardiovascular disease in the English Longitudinal Study of Ageing'. *Eur J Prev Cardiol*, 25(13), 1387–1396.
- Sutin, AR, et al. (2020). 'Loneliness and risk of dementia'. *J Gerontol B Psychol Sci Soc Sci*, 75(7), 1414–1422.
- Cacioppo, JT, et al. (2015). 'The neuroendocrinology of social isolation'. *Annual Review of Psychology*, 66, 733–767.
- Cole, SW, et al. (2007). 'Social regulation of gene expression in human leukocytes'. *Genome Biology*, 8(9), R189.
- Cacioppo, JT, et al. (2002). 'Do lonely days invade the nights? Potential social modulation of sleep efficiency'. *Psychological Science*, 13(4), 384–387.
- Eisenberger, NI, et al. (2003). 'Does rejection hurt? An fMRI study of social exclusion'. *Science*, 302(5643), 290–292.
- Uvnäs-Moberg, K. (1998). 'Oxytocin may mediate the benefits of positive social interaction and emotions'. *Psychoneuroendocrinology*, 23(8), 819–835.
- Krach, S, et al. (2010). 'The rewarding nature of social interactions'. *Frontiers in Behavioral Neuroscience*, 4, 22.

- Cohen, S, & Wills, TA. (1985). 'Stress, social support, and the buffering hypothesis'. *Psychol Bull*, 98(2), 310–57.
- Diener, E, & Seligman, MEP. (2002). 'Very happy people'. *Psychological Science*, 13(1), 81–84.
- Fratiglioni, L, et al. (2000). 'Influence of social network on occurrence of dementia: A community-based longitudinal study'. *The Lancet*, 355(9212), 1315–1319.
- Kulik, JA, & Mahler, HIM. (1989). 'Social support and recovery from surgery'. *Health Psychology*, 8(2), 221–238.
- Stavrova, O, & Luhmann, M. (2016). 'Social connectedness as a source and consequence of meaning in life'. *The Journal of Positive Psychology*, 11(5), 470–479.
- Twenge, JM, et al. (2017). 'Increases in depressive symptoms, suicide-related outcomes, and suicide rates among U.S. adolescents after 2010 and links to increased new media screen time'. *Clinical Psychological Science*, 6(1), 3–17.
- Holtzman, S, et al. (2017). 'Smartphone use undermines enjoyment of face-to-face social interactions'. *Journal of Experimental Social Psychology*, 73, 55–63.
- Gable, SL, et al. (2006). 'Will you be there for me when things go right? Supportive responses to positive event disclosures'. *J Pers Soc Psychol*, 91(5), 904–17.
- Bruess, CJS, & Pearson, JC. (1997). 'Interpersonal rituals in marriage and adult friendship'. *Communication Monographs*, 64(1), 25–46.
- Riess, H, et al. (2012). 'Empathy training for resident physicians: A randomized controlled trial of a neuroscience-informed curriculum'. *Journal of General Internal Medicine*, 27(10), 1280–1286.
- Hampton, KN, et al. (2011). *Social networking sites and our lives*. Pew Research Center.

Chapter 6

- Rattan, SIS, & Kyriazis, M. (Eds). (2018). *The Science of Hormesis in Health and Longevity.* Academic Press.
- Mattson, MP. (2008). 'Hormesis defined'. *Ageing Research Reviews,* 7(1), 1–7.
- Calabrese, EJ, & Baldwin, LA. (2002). 'Hormesis: The dose-response revolution'. *Annual Review of Pharmacology and Toxicology,* 43(1), 175–197.
- Calabrese, EJ, & Mattson, MP. (2011). 'How does hormesis impact biology, toxicology, and medicine?' *Aging and Mechanisms of Disease,* 1(1), 1–8.
- Naviaux, RK. (2020). 'Perspective: Cell danger response biology — the new science that connects environmental health with mitochondria and the rising tide of chronic illness'. *Mitochondrion,* 51, 40–45.
- Sack, MN. (2023). 'Rejuvenation of mitochondrial function by time-controlled fasting'. In Ostojic, SM. (Ed), *Molecular nutrition and mitochondria.* Academic Press, 633–650.
- Fernández-de la Torre, M, et al. (2020). 'Exercise training and neurodegeneration in mitochondrial disorders: Insights from the Harlequin mouse'. *Frontiers in Physiology,* 11, Article 594223.
- Saha, S, et al. (2018). 'Autophagy in health and disease: A comprehensive review'. *Biomedicine & Pharmacotherapy,* 101, 449–459.
- Ichimiya, T, et al. (2020). 'Autophagy and autophagy-related diseases: A review'. *International Journal of Molecular Sciences,* 21(23), 8974.
- Bevere, M, et al. (2022). 'Redox-based disruption of cellular hormesis and promotion of degenerative pathways: Perspectives on aging processes'. *The Journals of Gerontology: Series A,* 77(11), 2195–2206.

- Sharma, V, & Mehdi, MM. (2023). 'Oxidative stress, inflammation and hormesis: The role of dietary and lifestyle modifications on aging'. *Neurochem Int*, 164:105490.
- Calabrese, EJ, & Kozumbo, WJ. (2021). 'The hormetic dose-response mechanism: Nrf2 activation'. *Pharmacol Res*, 167:105526.
- Burtscher, J, & Samaja, M. (2024). 'Healthy aging at moderate altitudes: Hypoxia and hormesis'. *Gerontology*, 70(11), 1152–1160.
- Cuttler, JM, et al. (2021). 'Low doses of ionizing radiation as a treatment for Alzheimer's disease: A pilot study'. *Journal of Alzheimer's Disease*, 80(3), 1119–1128.
- Tapuria, N, et al. (2008). 'Remote ischemic preconditioning: A novel protective method from ischemia reperfusion injury — a review'. *J Surg Res*, 150(2), 304–30.
- Zhu, S, et al. (2022). 'Neuroprotective effect of remote ischemic preconditioning in patients undergoing cardiac surgery: A randomized controlled trial'. *Front Cardiovasc Med*, 9:952033.
- Rattan, SIS, & Demirovic, D. (2010). 'Hormesis can and does work in humans'. *Dose-response*, 8(1), 58–63.
- Mukherjee, S, et al. (2017). 'Exercise-induced hormesis: A possible role in disease prevention and treatment'. *Journal of Exercise Science & Fitness*, 15(1), 1–6.
- Yashin, AI. (2009). 'Hormesis against aging and diseases: Using properties of biological adaptation for health and survival improvement'. *Dose Response*, 8(1), 41–7.
- Calabrese, EJ, et al. (2023). 'Hormesis defines the limits of lifespan'. *Ageing Res Rev*, 91:102074.
- Pruimboom, L, & Muskiet, FAJ. (2018). 'Intermittent living: The use of ancient challenges as a vaccine against the deleterious effects of modern life — A hypothesis'. *Med Hypotheses*, 120:28–42.

Chapter 7

- Mitchell, JH, et al. (2019). 'The Dallas Bed Rest and Training Study: Revisited after 50 Years'. *Circulation*, 14(16), 1293–1295.
- Howden, EJ, et al. (2018). 'Reversing the cardiac effects of sedentary aging in middle age — a randomized controlled trial: Implications for heart failure prevention'. *Circulation*, 137(15), 1549–1560.
- López-Otín, C, et al. (2013). 'The hallmarks of aging'. *Cell*, 153(6), 1194–1217.
- López-Otín, C, et al. (2023). 'Hallmarks of aging: An expanding universe'. *Cell*, 186(2), 243–278.
- Garatachea, N, et al. (2015). 'Exercise attenuates the major hallmarks of aging'. *Rejuvenation Res*, 18(1), 57–89.
- Pedersen, BK, & Saltin, B. (2015). 'Exercise as medicine — evidence for prescribing exercise as therapy in 26 different chronic diseases'. *Scand J Med Sci Sports*, 25 Suppl 3, 1–72.
- Mandsager, K, et al. (2018). 'Association of cardiorespiratory fitness with long-term mortality among adults undergoing exercise treadmill testing'. *JAMA Netw Open*, 1(6), e183605.
- Kokkinos, P, et al. (2022). 'Cardiorespiratory fitness and mortality risk across the spectra of age, race, and sex'. *Journal of the American College of Cardiology*, 80(6), 598–609.
- García-Hermoso, A, et al. (2018). 'Muscular strength as a predictor of all-cause mortality in an apparently healthy population: A systematic review and meta-analysis of data from approximately 2 million men and women'. *Arch Phys Med Rehabil*, 99(10), 2100–2113.e5.
- Li, R, et al. (2018). 'Associations of muscle mass and strength with all-cause mortality among US older adults'. *Med Sci Sports Exerc*, 50(3), 458–467.
- Momma, H, et al. (2022). 'Muscle-strengthening activities are associated with lower risk and mortality in major

non-communicable diseases: A systematic review and meta-analysis of cohort studies'. *Br J Sports Med*, 56, 755–763.

- Artero, EG, et al. (2011). 'A prospective study of muscular strength and all-cause mortality in men with hypertension'. *J Am Coll Cardiol*, 57(18), 1831–7.
- Shephard, RJ. (2008). 'Maximal oxygen intake and independence in old age'. *British Journal of Sports Medicine*, published online April 10.
- Severinsen, MCK, & Pedersen, BK. (2020). 'Muscle–organ crosstalk: The emerging roles of myokines'. *Endocrine Reviews*, 41(4), 594–609.
- Chen, W, et al. (2021). 'Myokines mediate the cross talk between skeletal muscle and other organs'. *J Cell Physiol*, 236(4), 2393–2412.
- Kwon, JH, et al. (2020). 'Exercise-induced myokines can explain the importance of physical activity in the elderly: An overview'. *Healthcare*, 8, 378.

Chapter 8

- Teicholz, N. (2023). 'A short history of saturated fat: The making and unmaking of a scientific consensus'. *Curr Opin Endocrinol Diabetes Obes*, 30(1), 65–71.
- Lane, MM, et al. (2024). 'Ultra-processed food exposure and adverse health outcomes: Umbrella review of epidemiological meta-analyses'. *BMJ*, 384:e077310.
- Esposito, S, et al. (2024). 'Ultra-processed food consumption is associated with the acceleration of biological aging in the Moli-sani Study'. *The American Journal of Clinical Nutrition*, 120, 6, 1432–1440.
- Monteiro, CA, et al. (2013). 'Ultra-processed products are becoming dominant in the global food system'. *Obesity Reviews*, 14(Suppl 2), 21–28.

- Giudici, KV. (2021). 'Nutrition and the hallmarks of aging'. *The Journal of Nutrition, Health And Aging*, 25(9), 1039–1041.
- Rachel, A, et al. (2021). 'Long chain omega-3 fatty acid serum concentrations across life stages in the United States: An analysis of NHANES 2011–2012'. *BMJ Open*, 11, 5.
- Schuchardt, JP, et al. (2023). 'Estimation and predictors of the Omega-3 Index in the UK Biobank'. *Br J Nutr*, 130(2), 312–322.
- Ramirez, JL, et al. (2019). 'Fish oil increases specialized pro-resolving lipid mediators in PAD (The OMEGA-PAD II Trial)'. *J Surg Res*, 238, 164–174.
- McBurney, MI, et al. (2021). 'Using an erythrocyte fatty acid fingerprint to predict risk of all-cause mortality: The Framingham Offspring Cohort'. *Am J Clin Nutr*, 114(4), 1447–1454.
- Harris, WS, et al. (2018). 'Erythrocyte long-chain omega-3 fatty acid levels are inversely associated with mortality and with incident cardiovascular disease: The Framingham Heart Study'. *Journal Of Clinical Lipidology*, 12, 3.
- Harris, WS, & Von Schacky, C. (2004). 'The Omega-3 Index: A new risk factor for death from coronary heart disease?' *Prev Med*, 39(1), 212–20.
- Simopoulos, AP. (2008). 'The importance of the omega-6/omega-3 fatty acid ratio in cardiovascular disease and other chronic diseases'. *Exp Biol Med (Maywood)*, 233(6), 674–88
- Bischoff-Ferrari, HA, et al. (2025). 'Individual and additive effects of vitamin D, omega-3 and exercise on DNA methylation clocks of biological aging in older adults from the DO-HEALTH trial'. *Nat Aging*, 5, 376–385.
- Diwan, B, & Sharma, R. (2022). 'Nutritional components as mitigators of cellular senescence in organismal aging: a comprehensive review'. *Food Sci Biotechnol*, 31, 1089–1109.

- Calder, PC. (2017). 'Omega-3 fatty acids and inflammatory processes: From molecules to man'. *Biochemical Society Transactions*, 45(5), 1105–1115.
- Coelho-Júnior, HJ, et al. (2022). 'Protein intake and physical function in older adults: A systematic review and meta-analysis'. *Ageing Res Rev*, 81:101731.
- Diwan, B, & Sharma, R. (2022). 'Nutritional components as mitigators of cellular senescence in organismal aging: A comprehensive review'. *Food Sci Biotechnol*, 31, 1089–1109.
- Vilchez, D, et al. (2014). 'Proteostasis and aging of stem cells'. *Trends Cell Biol*, 24(3), 161–70.
- Tourkochristou, E, et al. (2021). 'The influence of nutritional factors on immunological outcomes'. *Front Immunol*, 12:665968.
- Odegard, AO, et al. (2013). 'Breakfast frequency and development of metabolic risk'. *Diabetes Care*, 36.
- Phillips, SM, et al. (2016). 'Protein "requirements" beyond the RDA: Implications for optimizing health'. *Appl Physiol Nutr Metab*, 41(5), 565–572.
- Rand, WM, et al. (2003). 'Meta-analysis of nitrogen balance studies for estimating protein requirements in healthy adults'. *Am J Clin Nutr*, (77)1, 109–27.
- Loenneke, JP, et al. (2016). 'Per meal dose and frequency of protein consumption is associated with lean mass and muscle performance'. *Clin Nutr*, 35(6), 1506–1511.
- Hill, CM, & Kaeberlein, M. (2021). 'Anti-ageing effects of protein restriction unpacked'. *Nature*, 589(7842), 357–358.
- Richardson, NE, et al. (2021). 'Lifelong restriction of dietary branched-chain amino acids has sex-specific benefits for frailty and lifespan in mice'. *Nat Aging*, 1(1), 73–86.
- Lipman, RD, et al. (1995). 'Is late-life caloric restriction beneficial?' *Aging (Milano)*, 7(2), 136–9.
- Levine, ME, et al. (2014). 'Low protein intake is associated with a major reduction in IGF-1, cancer, and overall mortality

in the 65 and younger but not older population'. *Cell Metab*, 19(3), 407–17.

- Avgerinos, KI, et al. (2018). 'Effects of creatine supplementation on cognitive function of healthy individuals: A systematic review of randomized controlled trials'. *Exp Gerontol*, 108, 166–173.
- Prokopidis, K, et al. (2023). 'Effects of creatine supplementation on memory in healthy individuals: A systematic review and meta-analysis of randomized controlled trials'. *Nutr Rev*, 81(4), 416–427.
- Kumar, P, et al. (2022). 'GlyNAC supplementation in mice increases length of life by correcting glutathione deficiency, oxidative stress, mitochondrial dysfunction, abnormalities in mitophagy and nutrient sensing, and genomic damage'. *Nutrients*, 14(5), 1114.
- Kumar, P, et al. (2023). 'Supplementing glycine and n-acetylcysteine (GlyNAC) in older adults improves glutathione deficiency, oxidative stress, mitochondrial dysfunction, inflammation, physical function, and aging hallmarks: A randomized clinical trial'. *J Gerontol A Biol Sci Med Sci*, 78(1), 75–89.
- Musso, CG. (2009). 'Magnesium metabolism in health and disease'. *Int Urol Nephrol*, 41(2), 357–62.
- Barbagallo, M, et al. (2009). 'Magnesium homeostasis and aging'. *Magnes Res*, 22(4), 235–46.
- Rowe, WJ. (2012). 'Correcting magnesium deficiencies may prolong life'. *Clin Interv Aging*, 7, 51–4.
- Peng, Y, et al. (2021). 'Anti-inflammatory effects of curcumin in the inflammatory diseases: Status, limitations and countermeasures'. *Drug Des Devel Ther*, 15, 4503–4525.
- Nunes, YC, et al. (2024). 'Curcumin: A golden approach to healthy aging: a systematic review of the evidence'. *Nutrients*, 16(16), 2721.

- Yang, L, et al. (2020). 'Mitochondria as a target for neuroprotection: Role of methylene blue and photobiomodulation'. *Transl Neurodegener*, 9, 19.
- Poudel, SB, et al. (2024). 'Targeting mitochondrial dysfunction using methylene blue or mitoquinone to improve skeletal aging'. *Aging (Albany NY)*, 16(6), 4948–4964
- Tian, G, et al. (2014). 'Ubiquinol-10 supplementation activates mitochondria functions to decelerate senescence in senescence-accelerated mice'. *Antioxid Redox Signal*, 20(16), 2606–20.
- Hernández-Camacho, JD, et al. (2018). 'Coenzyme Q10 supplementation in aging and disease'. *Front Physiol*, 9, 44.

Chapter 9

- Blume, C, et al. (2019). 'Effects of light on human circadian rhythms, sleep and mood'. *Somnologie*, 23(3), 147–156.
- Boubekri, M, et al. (2014). 'Impact of windows and daylight exposure on overall health and sleep quality of office workers: A case-control pilot study'. *Journal of Clinical Sleep Medicine*, 10(6), 603–611.
- Lambert, GW, et al. (2002). 'Effect of sunlight and season on serotonin turnover in the brain'. *The Lancet*, 360(9348), 1840–1842.
- Beauchemin, KM, & Hays, P. (1996). 'Sunny hospital rooms expedite recovery from severe and refractory depressions'. *Journal of Affective Disorders*, 40(1–2), 49–51.
- Wacker, M, & Holick, MF. (2013). 'Sunlight and vitamin D: A global perspective for health'. *Dermato-endocrinology*, 5(1), 51–108.
- Ruggiero, C, et al. (2024). 'Targeting the hallmarks of aging with vitamin D: Starting to decode the myth'. *Nutrients*, 16(6), 906.
- Aranow, C. (2011). 'Vitamin D and the immune system'. *Journal of Investigative Medicine*, 59(6), 881–886.

- Grant, WB, et al. (2020). 'Evidence that vitamin D supplementation could reduce risk of influenza and COVID-19 infections and deaths'. *Nutrients*, 12(4), 988.
- Feldman, D, et al. (2014). 'The role of vitamin D in reducing cancer risk and progression'. *Nature Reviews Cancer*, 14(5), 342–357.
- Judd, SE, & Tangpricha, V. (2009). 'Vitamin D deficiency and risk for cardiovascular disease'. *The American Journal of the Medical Sciences*, 338(1), 40–44.
- Eyles, DW, et al. (2005). 'Distribution of the vitamin D receptor and 1α-hydroxylase in human brain'. *Journal of Chemical Neuroanatomy*, 29(1), 21–30.
- Annweiler, C, et al. (2013). 'Meta-analysis of memory and executive dysfunctions in relation to vitamin D'. *Journal of Alzheimer's Disease*, 37(1), 147–171.
- Littlejohns, TJ, et al. (2014). 'Vitamin D and the risk of dementia and Alzheimer disease'. *Neurology*, 83(10), 920–928.
- Mitri, J, et al. (2011). 'Vitamin D and type 2 diabetes: A systematic review'. *European Journal of Clinical Nutrition*, 65(9), 1005–1015.
- Ghaemi, S, et al. (2024). 'The effect of vitamin D supplementation on depression: A systematic review and dose–response meta-analysis of randomized controlled trials'. *Psychological Medicine*, 54(15), 3999–4008.
- Garland, CF, et al. (2014). 'Meta-analysis of all-cause mortality according to serum 25-hydroxyvitamin D'. *American Journal of Public Health*, 104(8), e43–e50.
- Schöttker, B, et al. (2013). 'Serum 25-hydroxyvitamin D levels and overall mortality. A systematic review and meta-analysis of prospective cohort studies'. *Ageing Research Reviews*, 12(2), 708–718.
- Zittermann, A, et al. (2012). 'Vitamin D deficiency and mortality risk in the general population: A meta-analysis of prospective

cohort studies'. *The American Journal of Clinical Nutrition*, 95(1), 91–100.

- Lips, P. (2010). 'Worldwide status of vitamin D nutrition'. *The Journal of Steroid Biochemistry and Molecular Biology*, 121(1–2), 297–300.

- Ross, AC, et al. (2011). 'The 2011 report on dietary reference intakes for calcium and vitamin D from the Institute of Medicine: What clinicians need to know'. *The Journal of Clinical Endocrinology & Metabolism*, 96(1), 53–58.

- Holick, MF, et al. (2011). 'Evaluation, treatment, and prevention of vitamin D deficiency: An Endocrine Society clinical practice guideline'. *The Journal of Clinical Endocrinology & Metabolism*, 96(7), 1911–1930.

- Pludowski, P, et al. (2018). 'Vitamin D supplementation guidelines'. *The Journal of Steroid Biochemistry and Molecular Biology*, 175, 125–135.

- Tripkovic, L, et al. (2012). 'Comparison of vitamin D2 and vitamin D3 supplementation in raising serum 25-hydroxyvitamin D status: A systematic review and meta-analysis'. *The American Journal of Clinical Nutrition*, 95(6), 1357–1364.

- Bischoff-Ferrari, HA, et al. (2012). 'Oral supplementation with 25(OH)D3 versus vitamin D3: Effects on 25(OH)D levels, lower extremity function, blood pressure, and markers of innate immunity'. *Journal of Bone and Mineral Research*, 27(1), 160–169.

- Schmid, A, & Walther, B. (2013). 'Natural vitamin D content in animal products'. *Advances in Nutrition*, 4(4), 453–462.

- Chung, H, et al. (2012). 'The nuts and bolts of low-level laser (light) therapy'. *Ann Biomed Eng*, 40, 516–533.

- Tsai, SR, & Hamblin, MR. (2017). 'Biological effects and medical applications of infrared radiation'. *J Photochem Photobiol B*, 170:197–207.

- Chaves, ME, et al. (2014). 'Effects of low-power light therapy on wound healing: LASER x LED'. *An Bras Dermatol*, 89(4), 616–23.
- Mathur, RK, et al. (2017). 'Low-level laser therapy as an adjunct to conventional therapy in the treatment of diabetic foot ulcers'. *Lasers Med Sci*, 32(2), 275–282.
- Khan, I, et al. (2021). 'Accelerated burn wound healing with photobiomodulation therapy involves activation of endogenous latent TGF-β1'. *Sci Rep*, 11(1), 13371.
- Hamblin, MR. (2018). 'Photobiomodulation for traumatic brain injury and stroke'. *J Neurosci Res*, 96(4), 731–743.
- Bicknell, B, et al. (2024). 'Parkinson's disease and photobiomodulation: Potential for treatment'. *J Pers Med*, 14(1), 112.
- Su, M, et al. (2023). 'Recent mechanisms of neurodegeneration and photobiomodulation in the context of Alzheimer's disease'. *Int J Mol Sci*, 24(11), 9272.
- Hamblin, MR. (2017). 'Mechanisms and applications of the anti-inflammatory effects of photobiomodulation'. *AIMS Biophys*, 4(3), 337–361.
- Hamblin, MR. (2018). 'Mechanisms and mitochondrial redox signaling in photobiomodulation'. *Photochem Photobiol*, 94(2), 199–212.

Chapter 10

- Newport, C. (2016). *Deep Work: Rules for Focused Success in a Distracted World*. Grand Central Publishing
- Watso, JC, et al. (2023). 'Acute nasal breathing lowers diastolic blood pressure and increases parasympathetic contributions to heart rate variability in young adults'. *Am J Physiol Regul Integr Comp Physiol*, 325(6), R797–R808.

- Zaccaro, A, et al. (2022). 'Neural correlates of non-ordinary states of consciousness in pranayama practitioners: The role of slow nasal breathing'. *Front Syst Neurosci*, 16:803904.
- Zaccaro, A, et al. (2018). 'Breath-control can change your life: A systematic review on psycho-physiological correlates of slow breathing'. *Front Hum Neurosci*, 12:353.
- Perl, O, et al. (2019). 'Human non-olfactory cognition phase-locked with inhalation'. *Nat Hum Behav*, 3, 501–512.
- Ortiz, RO, et al. (2019). 'A systematic review on the effectiveness of active recovery interventions on athletic performance of professional-, collegiate-, and competitive-level adult athletes'. *Journal of Strength and Conditioning Research*, 33(8), 2275–2287.
- Salay, LD, et al. (2018). 'A midline thalamic circuit determines reactions to visual threat'. *Nature*, 557(7704).
- Chaitanya, S, et al. (2022). 'Effect of resonance breathing on heart rate variability and cognitive functions in young adults: A randomised controlled study'. *Cureus*, 14(2), e22187.
- Balban, MY, et al. (2023). 'Brief structured respiration practices enhance mood and reduce physiological arousal'. *Cell Rep Med*, 4(1), 100895.
- Kox, M, et al. (2014). 'Voluntary activation of the sympathetic nervous system and attenuation of the innate immune response in humans'. *Proc Natl Acad Sci USA*, 111(20), 7379–84.
- Carvalhas-Almeida, C, et al. (2023). 'The impact of insomnia on frailty and the hallmarks of aging'. *Aging Clin Exp Res*, 35(2), 253–269.
- Cedernaes, J, et al. (2015). 'Acute sleep loss induces tissue-specific epigenetic and transcriptional alterations to circadian clock genes in men'. *The Journal of Clinical Endocrinology & Metabolism*, 100, 9, E1255–E1261.

- Wang, X, et al. (2016). 'Short-term moderate sleep restriction decreases insulin sensitivity in young healthy adults'. *Sleep Health*, 2(1), 63–68.
- Richardson, RB, & Mailloux, RJ. (2023). 'Mitochondria need their sleep: Redox, bioenergetics, and temperature regulation of circadian rhythms and the role of cysteine-mediated redox signaling, uncoupling proteins, and substrate cycles'. *Antioxidants*, 12(3), 674.
- Elkhenany, H, et al. (2018). 'Tissue regeneration: Impact of sleep on stem cell regenerative capacity'. *Life Sci*, 214, 51–61.
- Chow, CM. (2022). 'Sleep hygiene practices: Where to now?' *Hygiene*, 2(3), 146–151.
- Wassing, R, et al. (2019). 'Restless REM sleep impedes overnight amygdala adaptation'. *Curr Biol*, 29(14), 2351–2358.e4.
- Chan, V, & Lo, K. (2022). 'Efficacy of dietary supplements on improving sleep quality: A systematic review and meta-analysis'. *Postgrad Med J*, 98(1158), 285–293.
- Esquivel, MK, & Ghosn, B. (2024). 'Current evidence on common dietary supplements for sleep quality'. *American Journal of Lifestyle Medicine*, 18(3), 323–327.
- Perlow, LA, & Porter, JL. (2009). 'Making time off predictable — and required'. *Harvard Business Review*, 87(10), 102–109.
- Lyubykh, Z, et al. (2022). 'Role of work breaks in well-being and performance: A systematic review and future research agenda'. *Journal of Occupational Health Psychology*, 27(5), 470–487.

Chapter 11

- Australian Bureau of Statistics (2022). *National Study of Mental Health and Wellbeing 2020–2022*.
- Basner, M. (2018). *Why Noise is Bad for Your Health*. TEDMED.

- World Health Organization (2011). 'Burden of disease from environmental noise'. WHO Regional Office for Europe.
- Freymueller, J, et al. (2024). 'Current methodologies of greenspace exposure and mental health research—A scoping review'. *Frontiers in Public Health*, 12, 1360134.
- Beyer, KM, et al (2014). 'Exposure to neighborhood green space and mental health: Evidence from the survey of the health of Wisconsin'. *International Journal of Environmental Research and Public Health*, 11(3), 3453–3472.
- Barton, J, & Rogerson, M. (2017). 'The importance of greenspace for mental health'. *BJPsych International*, 14(4), 79–81.
- Li, Q, et al. (2007). 'Forest bathing enhances human natural killer activity and expression of anti-cancer proteins'. *International Journal of Immunopathology and Pharmacology*, 20(2 Suppl 2), 3–8.
- Kaplan, R. (1995). 'The restorative benefits of nature: Toward an integrative framework'. *Journal of Environmental Psychology*, 15(3), 169–182.
- Ulrich, RS. (1991). 'Effects of interior design on wellness: Theory and recent scientific research'. *Journal of Health Care Interior Design*, 3(1), 97–109.
- Taylor, RP. (2006). 'Reduction of physiological stress using fractal art and architecture'. *Leonardo*, 39(3), 245–251.
- Ulrich, RS. (1984). 'View through a window may influence recovery from surgery'. *Science*, 224(4647), 420–421.
- Berman, MG, et al. (2008). 'The cognitive benefits of interacting with nature'. *Psychological Science*, 19(12), 1207–1212.
- Atchley, RA, et al. (2012). 'Creativity in the wild: Improving creative reasoning through immersion in natural settings'. *PLOS ONE*, 7(12), e51474.
- Li, Q, et al. (2022). 'Effects of forest bathing (shinrin-yoku) on serotonin in serum, depressive symptoms and subjective

sleep quality in middle-aged males', *Environmental Health and Preventive Medicine*, 27, 44.

- Li, Q. (2022). 'Effects of forest environment (shinrin-yoku/forest bathing) on health promotion and disease prevention – the establishment of 'forest medicine'. *Environmental Health and Preventive Medicine*, 27, 43.
- Perkin, MR, & Strachan, DP. (2022). 'The hygiene hypothesis for allergy — conception and evolution'. *Front. Allergy*, 3:1051368.
- Roslund, MI, et al. (2020). 'Biodiversity intervention enhances immune regulation and health-associated commensal microbiota among daycare children'. *Science Advances*, 6(42), eaba2578.
- Gould van Praag, CD, et al. (2017). 'Mind-wandering and alterations to default mode network connectivity when listening to naturalistic versus artificial sounds'. *Scientific Reports*, 7(1), 45273.
- Nguyen, PY, et al. (2023). 'Effect of nature prescriptions on cardiometabolic and mental health, and physical activity: A systematic review'. *The Lancet Planetary Health*, 7(4), e313–e328.
- Chevalier, G, et al. (2013). 'Earthing (grounding) the human body reduces blood viscosity — a major factor in cardiovascular disease'. *J Altern Complement Med*, 2013 Feb;19(2), 102–10.
- Chevalier, G, et al. (2015). 'One-hour contact with the earth's surface (grounding) improves inflammation and blood flow — a randomized, double-blind, pilot study'. *Health*, 07.
- Chevalier, G, et al. (2019). 'The effects of grounding (earthing) on bodyworkers' pain and overall quality of life: a randomized controlled trial'. *Explore (NY)*, 15(3), 181–190.
- Brown, D, et al. (2010). 'Pilot study on the effect of grounding on delayed-onset muscle soreness'. *J Altern Complement Med*, 16(3), 265–73.
- Chevalier, G. (2010). 'Changes in pulse rate, respiratory rate, blood oxygenation, perfusion index, skin conductance, and their

variability induced during and after grounding human subjects for 40 minutes'. *J Altern Complement Med*, 16(1), 81–7.

- Ghaly, M, & Teplitz, D. (2004). 'The biologic effects of grounding the human body during sleep as measured by cortisol levels and subjective reporting of sleep, pain, and stress'. *Journal of Alternative and Complementary Medicine*, 10(5), 767–76.
- Lin, CH, et al. (2022). 'Grounding the body improves sleep quality in patients with mild Alzheimer's disease: A pilot study'. *Healthcare (Basel)*, 10(3), 581.
- French, AN, et al. (2013). 'Time outdoors and the prevention of myopia'. *Exp Eye Res*, 114, 58–68.
- Ip, JM, et al. (2008). 'Myopia and the urban environment: Findings in a sample of 12-year-old Australian school children'. *Invest Ophthalmol Vis Sci*, 49(9), 3858–63.
- Ulset, V, et al. (2017). 'Time spent outdoors during preschool: Links with children's cognitive and behavioral development'. *Journal of Environmental Psychology*, 52, 69–80.
- Osman, B, et al (2025). 'Prevalence of noncommunicable diseases and developmental conditions in 5014 Australian adolescents, and their correlations with diet, other lifestyle behaviours and mental health'. *Australian and New Zealand Journal of Public Health*, 100225.
- Ulset, V, et al. (2017). 'Time spent outdoors during preschool: Links with children's cognitive and behavioral development'. *Journal of Environmental Psychology*, 52, 69–80.
- Wells, NM, & Evans, GW. (2003). 'Nearby nature: A buffer of life stress among rural children'. *Environment and Behavior*, 35(3), 311–330.
- Dadvand, P, et al. (2015). 'Green spaces and cognitive development in primary schoolchildren'. *Proc Natl Acad Sci USA*, 112(26), 7937–7942.
- Chawla, L. (2015). 'Benefits of nature contact for children'. *Journal of Planning Literature*, 30(4), 433–452.

- White, MP, et al. (2019). 'Spending at least 120 minutes a week in nature is associated with good health and wellbeing'. *Scientific Reports*, 9(1), 7730.
- Beatley, T. (2012). 'Exploring the nature pyramid'. The Nature of Cities.

Appendix A

- Read, J, et al. (2014). 'Adverse emotional and interpersonal effects reported by 1829 New Zealanders while taking antidepressants'. *Psychiatry Res*, 216(1), 67–73.
- Read, J. (2020). 'How common and severe are six withdrawal effects from, and addiction to, antidepressants? The experiences of a large international sample of patients'. *Addict Behav*, 102, 106157.
- Noetel, M, et al. (2024). 'Effect of exercise for depression: Systematic review and network meta-analysis of randomised controlled trials'. *BMJ*, 384, e075847.
- Ghaemi, S, et al. (2024). 'The effect of vitamin D supplementation on depression: A systematic review and dose–response meta-analysis of randomized controlled trials'. *Psychological Medicine*, 54(15), 3999–4008.
- O'Neill, S, et al. (2022). 'Depression, is it treatable in adults utilising dietary interventions? A systematic review of randomised controlled trials'. *Nutrients*, 14(7), 1398.
- Beyer, KM, et al. (2014). 'Exposure to neighborhood green space and mental health: Evidence from the survey of the health of Wisconsin'. *Int J Environ Res Public Health*, 11(3), 3453–3472.

Index

Printed and bound by CPI Group (UK) Ltd, Croydon, CR0 4YY

07/12/2025

14785976-0001

12 301